My Story

a love greater than any pain!

by

Esther Barbara Dennison

MY STORY   A LOVE GREATER THAN ANY PAIN!

Unless otherwise indicated, Scripture quotations taken from the
HOLY BIBLE, NEW INTERNATIONAL VERSION.
Copyright © 1973, 1978, 1984 by International Bible Society.
Used by permission of Hodder & Stoughton Ltd.
A member of the Hodder Headline Plc Group. All rights reserved.
"NIV" is a registered trademark of International Bible Society
UK trademark number 1448790.

Some Bible quotations (as stated in text) taken from:
KING JAMES VERSION (KJV)

THE NEW KING JAMES VERSION (NKJV)
Copyright 1982 by Thomas Nelson, Inc.

THE AMPLIFIED BIBLE (Amp.)
Copyright © 1954, 1958, 1962, 1964, 1965, 1987
By The Lockman Foundation.
All rights reserved. Used by permission.

NEW AMERICAN STANDARD BIBLE (NASB)
Copyright © 1960, 1962, 1963, 1968, 1971, 1972, 1973, 1975, 1977, 1995
by THE LOCKMAN FOUNDATION
A Corporation Not for Profit   LA HABRA, CA   All Rights Reserved
http://www.Lockman.org
"NASB" trademark is registered in the United States Patent and
Trademark Office by The Lockman Foundation.

Cover photograph by my son Leon, taken in 2013

All the Praise!

I give *ALL* the Praise and Honour,
Thanks and Glory to Jesus Christ,
the Lord of Lords and King of Kings,
the everlasting, living God.
HE gave me the instructions to write this book,
together with the inspiration, the courage and *HIS* words,
to testify to what *HE* has done in my life.
May this book bear much eternal fruit
and bring Glory to His Holy Name.
To Him alone
be ALL the Power, the Majesty and Glory,
forever and ever.
Amen

A Sincere "Thank You"

To everyone who befriended my sons and me
and helped us over so many years of toil and difficulty.
I am truly thankful and grateful
to each and every one of them for their love and kindness,
which will never be forgotten.
May they always know
the love and saving grace of
Jesus Christ in their lives.

A Special "Thank You"

To Dr. Helen Roseveare, my dear sister in Christ,
for being God's chosen vessel to lead me to Him.
And, for the invaluable encouragement and support
that she gave me, as I stepped out in obedience
to serve our dear Lord.
"Thank you Helen"

(21st September 1925 – 7th December 2016)

Dedication

I gladly dedicate this book to my two beloved sons, Leon and Ross.

I want to thank them, with *a mother's heart,* for always being such a joy to me and for giving me so many endearing memories; memories that I will cherish forever.

I want to thank them too, with *a loving heart,* for their constant love and support that gave me the courage to never give up and to carry on, even when under extreme hardship. It was their genuine willingness to help me and never complain, that was so exemplary. They were always ready to give me words of encouragement and even guidance, when I needed them most. It was just the three of us working together as a team. And we survived, thanks to our Heavenly Father who kept His hand upon us, even without our knowledge.

My two sons have both grown up now into fine young men, happily married to two beautiful girls and I'm so very thankful that they all know Jesus Christ as their Lord and Saviour. May our faithful Heavenly Father continue to bless and guide them, all of their days.

"Thank you!" Leon and Ross, for being such super sons.

I love you both!

Contents

PART TWO   My Life in Northern Ireland

PART THREE   Mission Moldova

EPILOGUE

Foreword

During my school years, the very thought of writing a *composition* for my English homework filled me with dread and marred every weekend until, at long last, it was completed and written. I hated doing it, for it seemed such an impossible task to me. So much so, that I remember all too often following my Daddy around our garden, whilst he busied himself tending the flowerbeds, and begging him to help me until eventually, he had nearly written the whole essay for me. Terrible I know, but I just *couldn't* do it.

You see, my Daddy was brilliant at inventing stories and creative ideas and words just flowed out of him. It was no problem to him at all. But for me, it was a real *nightmare.* So with this in mind, can you imagine how surprised I was when, over four decades later, during a time of bedtime prayer, I felt God leading me to write this book? I was *stunned,* to say the least.

However, since Jesus Christ became my Lord and Saviour back in April 1997, I have discovered that God has a real *sense of humour* and has a habit too, of asking you to do something that in the natural, you know you can't do. And this was one of them.

But the Lord didn't leave me to struggle alone in desperation. He helped me through every single page, leading and guiding me all the time. And as my dear Daddy, my earthly biological father kindly gave me the words to write when I was a young schoolgirl, my loving Heavenly Father faithfully gave me *His words* to write now, as a mother of two adult sons.

So how did the writing of this book *really* begin?

Well, let me tell you. It all began late one evening, on Friday, 14th October 2011 to be precise. I was quietly praying before going to bed when, quite suddenly, I was aware that God was speaking to me. And, as I listened, I soon realized that He had an unexpected surprise in store for me:

"*Write down your story.* And give it to anyone you meet who *doesn't* know ME."

Wow! What a command. I never expected this. I felt excited and anxious all at the same time. On one hand, I relished the idea and was eager to obey God and yet, on the other hand, I just didn't know how to begin and kept putting it off.

After several futile attempts, I decided to make an all-out effort. Only then, when I put my whole heart into it, did God begin helping me and giving me *His* direction and *His* words to write down.

God was waiting for me to take His instruction seriously and put my heart and soul into it. And that is what I have done. I have literally poured myself into writing this book.

G od knew I couldn't even write a school essay, let alone a *whole book.*   But, in His strength and with His help and guidance, I have achieved what I thought was totally *impossible.*

There was a *hidden* test for me too, in obeying His command. It forced me to search deep within myself and confront several issues and many circumstances which, I thought, I'd already overcome long ago. But I found I hadn't. And, as I began writing, God allowed me to suffer just a little bit more pain. Pain that has now surfaced and been removed. Pain that will never be hidden and buried again. It's all gone.

I trust that *My Story* will be *a blessing* to you and that you will find the love, inner peace and saving grace of Jesus Christ in your own life, and in the lives of your whole family circle, as you read about ...

a love greater than any pain!

Introduction

I t was such a beautiful, sunny afternoon. Just the sort of weather that beckons you to leave your chores till later and get outside. Gardening had always been a passion of mine, so happily I decided it was time to dig over our new front garden.

As I contentedly dug away, lifting and turning the heavy earth, my senses were enjoying the warm sunshine and the carefree sounds of my two young sons playing joyfully with our Sheltie dog "Bluey" in the back garden. My gaze lifted occasionally to admire the lovely views over the surrounding farmland and the rise of the Sperrin Mountains beyond.

It was early September 1991 and we hadn't long moved into our new home and, as yet, didn't know many people. But I became aware of two young men pausing in their Sunday afternoon stroll to talk to me and welcome me to their village. They were smiling and looked so friendly.

As we chatted together about village life and, in particular the local churches, they began to ask me some very *peculiar* questions ... ***"Are you saved?"***

I wondered, *"Whatever do they mean?"* I thought about it and quickly decided they were asking me, *"Do I know about Jesus?"* Of course I did, didn't everyone? So I boldly replied, ***"Yes!"***

They then looked even more pleased and their smiles broadened. Feeling encouraged, they continued to ask me another very confusing question, **"For how long?"**

I thought, *"What? That's a really funny question."* I'd known about Jesus all my life and I'd learnt many Bible stories at school, so I confidently answered, **"Always!"**

This answer seemed to surprise them somewhat and they looked at each other a little bewildered. They continued chatting for a bit longer, before very politely saying their *goodbyes* and leaving me to carry on with my digging.

Pensively, I began wondering, *"What was all that about?"* I'd been to church a few times back in England but I'd never ever heard anything about being **saved** or **born again**. What was that? This was a *new* language to me. It wasn't until a few days later, when I shared this peculiar experience with a friendly neighbour, that I learnt the error of my ways and, for the very first time, learnt the *true* meaning of, *"Are you saved? Are you born again?"*

However, it took me another six years before I could honestly say, *"Yes! I am saved. Yes! I am born again"* and for it to be really *true*. But I've gone ahead of myself, so please, let me explain. Let me tell you ...

My Story

Part One

My Life

In

England

Chapter 1

My Loved Ones

M y Grandad was Belgian and wore a *toupee.* And as a small child, this always fascinated me. However much I pressed Grandad to admit it, he wouldn't. And the more he denied it, the more I wanted to know *the truth!*

My Granny was kind, but very strict too, and could be quite stern at times. There was certainly *no messing around* with Granny. But we were good friends and when we went for walks together, she would teach me difficult spellings, such as the difference between *to, too and two* and *it, its and it's.* Quite confusing for a six-year-old.

I especially looked forward to seeing them every summer when they accompanied us on our family holiday. We spent two glorious weeks together in a rented beachside chalet at Elmer Sands in West Sussex. I can still remember how early every morning I loved jumping out of bed before anyone else was up and climbing down the garden ladder to the shingle beach below. Ecstatic freedom greeted me, as I ran off to enjoy the massive expanse of sandy deserted beach that appeared to reach to the horizon. This was my paradise.

One of these summer holidays will particularly remain in my memory. It was the summer when Granny introduced me to *Peter's Dark Chocolate.* As I walked excitedly by her side on our way to the local shop, she told me about this delicious chocolate and I could hardly wait to taste it. Well, I wasn't disappointed. That fine summer morning, Granny bought me my very first bar of Peter's Dark Chocolate and it was delicious. Rich and dark and velvety, and so wonderfully *chocolaty.*

This was the beginning of my passion for chocolate and yes, I blame Granny for that. However, whilst reminiscing about this delight, I discovered that Peter's Chocolate was created by Daniel Peter in his home town of Vevey in Switzerland during the 1870's and, amazingly, it is still available today.

Granny also taught me how to *dead head* flowers. Even now, when I pass a flower border, I automatically bend down to pick off the dead flower heads to release new blooms; an action that still reminds me of one who was so dear to me.

But Granny could be frustrating too. She and Grandad were the oldest people I knew and I wanted to know just how *old* they really were. Surely, they were *ancient?* Well, I hassled poor Granny at every opportunity, *"How old are you Granny? Please tell me."*

However, Granny had been brought up with the adage that, *"A lady never reveals her true age"* and she wasn't about to change that now. So, every time I pleaded my hopeful question, I always received, without the slightest hesitation, the same frustrating answer, *"I'm as old as my tongue and a little older than my teeth!"*

I missed my Grandparents and would have liked to have seen them more often, but they lived far away from us in northern England and we lived in southern England in Surrey. They had a modest semi-detached house in Birmingham where my Mum and her three brothers were born and brought up, and I can only remember going there once.

Life couldn't have been very easy for my Grandparents in the 1920's, because my Mum never forgot how one day, when she returned home from school, her mother had sold her beloved violin. This upset Mum so very much and I don't think she ever got over it.

As well as her musical talents, my Mum was sporty, being a competent ice skater and a champion *long-distance* swimmer. She regularly swam in galas, often winning bronze, silver and even gold medals.   She used to tell me how she would swim, *"one mile without stopping in a freezing cold reservoir every morning before breakfast."* Wow! I can't even start to imagine how she did it.   To me, such a thing is absolutely unthinkable.

But my Mum took pleasure in recounting this outstanding feat and told me that she had just one rival in these long-distance swimming races.   She explained that if a mile-long race was held in a swimming pool, thus requiring *turns* at every length, her competitor always won.   But if the race was held in a reservoir with *no* turns, she always won. This made me admire her even more.

M y Mum brought my sister and I up with three very *wise sayings,* that are worthy of remembering.

Firstly, she would sometimes reprimand us in a stern, but loving voice, *"There is no such word as **can't!**"* This usually had the effect of silencing every objection or protest that we came up with.

Secondly, she taught us this great truth: *"If you can't say anything **good** about someone, don't say anything at all."*

Lastly, she always advised us: *"When you give a present to someone, give them something **you would like to receive yourself.**"* These were great words of wisdom. Words that I have never forgotten and can still hear her saying.

In comparison to my mother's family, my father's parents were affluent and lived in a large house in the seaside town of Bognor Regis in West Sussex, not far from my beloved Elmer Sands. He had one older sister and they were brought up in the strict atmosphere of, *"children should be seen, but not heard."*

To my surprise, my father told me that he had a Governess to teach him before being sent away to boarding school in Oxford. I was fascinated too, to learn that his parents had servants in their home and, at mealtimes, they used elegant, heavy silver cutlery bearing the family crest. Even their crisply starched bed linen was heavily embroidered with the family initials.

This affluence was in stark contrast to my Mum's humble upbringing. She was brought up during the period when *"only sons mattered"* and she didn't even have a bedroom to sleep in, just a large cubbyhole on the landing. Hence, she didn't want to bear any sons, *only daughters.* Thankfully, she had two of them ... my sister and me.

B efore World War II, my father was a keen golfer and told me that one day he had the privilege of meeting King George VI whilst playing golf.   He was also an accomplished fly fisherman, possessed a magnificent collection of birds' eggs and butterflies, and was an avid stamp collector. Daddy was good at nearly anything he tried, from whistling like a song bird, blowing amazing smoke rings, skimming flat stones over a lake or beating us hands down at Scrabble. But one thing in particular he was expert at, and that was Shove Ha'penny. No matter how much I practiced, he could spin those Ha'pennies up our board and place them perfectly between the grooved lines, beating me every time.

Before my parents ever had a car, my father had a prized possession. His powerful, gleaming black *motorbike.* He really loved this huge machine and proudly rode it with Mum and me squeezed into the sidecar.   I was only one and a half but I loved it too. Happily, I would sit upon it all day long if I could, dressed up in my Daddy's helmet, goggles and heavy leather gloves that reached right up to my armpits.

My father was also blessed with a keen musical ear. Often, after hearing a tune he liked, he would sit intently at our piano tinkling the keys for a bit, before playing the melody perfectly.

He could also compose the most wonderful and exciting children's adventure stories. Every Saturday, when my sister and I were very young, we would sit with him in our car waiting for Mum to do the weekly shopping. But instead of

19

being bored stiff, Dad did a splendid job in keeping us entertained and totally enthralled with another one of his gripping tales. How we loved these stories and I only wish we'd thought of writing them down.

Unfortunately, I never knew my Daddy's father, as he had already died before I was born. Sadly, his mother died while I was still very young and I don't remember her at all. But my parents told me that she was resolutely hoping for a *grandson.* Thankfully, she immediately softened her severe stance when she saw me as a baby. Lovingly, she gently cradled me in her arms, adoring her new granddaughter.

During World War II, my parents were separated without a break for over three years. The Army posted my father out to Kumasi in the Gold Coast, now modern-day Ghana, in West Africa. Meanwhile my mother, a highly skilled shorthand typist, also served in the Army during the war. She told me how she was regularly locked alone in an office, sometimes all night, to type top secret documents that demanded 100% accuracy. Not one single typing error was allowed or it had to be *retyped.*

But poor Daddy, he must have looked a strange sight when he finally returned home from the Gold Coast. My mother told me that he was literally *yellow* from all the quinine he'd taken to protect himself against malaria.

My parents were always totally *in love* with each other and throughout their long wartime separation, they wrote to each other every single day. Daddy wasn't very tall but he was a fine, handsome man with lovely dark, warm eyes. No wonder my mother loved him so much.

Chapter 2

Where my life began

After the end of World War II, my parents managed to buy their first home. A nice semi-detached house in Ambleside Avenue, a pleasant quiet road in Walton-on-Thames, Surrey in southern England.

Many years later, I was delighted to find out that Julie Andrews, the actress famed for her starring roles in *The Sound of Music* and *Mary Poppins,* was born in the same town.

It was here, one early February morning in my parents' first home, that I was born. But it was not an easy birth and my poor, dear Mummy endured two days and two nights of labour, under the kind and efficient care of Nurse Nash and Dr. Roxbrough.

During my struggle to enter this world, my Daddy made himself useful by making endless cups of tea and good humouredly singing the very apt song, *"Slow boat to China!"* Then two years later, after six long months of strict bed rest and loving care from Nurse Nash, my younger sister Linda was born.

My earliest memories

I believe one of my very earliest memories was watching my Mummy sitting comfortably in the wicker nursing chair in our bedroom, cradling and breastfeeding my newborn sister. I was just two and had never seen anything like this before. I can remember standing watching them, carefully studying the situation, before coming to the conclusion that if my sister could do it, so could I. I wanted a try at it too. Mummy agreed, but I was hugely disappointed and squirmed away in disgust, *"Ugh! Horrible. It tastes awful!"* I never did understand how my sister liked it so much.

My best friend Geoffrey

After I was born, my Mummy proudly pushed me in my Royal Cross pram down Ambleside Avenue to the local park every day. It was here that she met Gwen, or Aunty Gwen to me, who became her faithful and true, and life-long friend. But it was her son Geoffrey who caught my eye. He was only one month younger than me and I thought he was wonderful.

As our mothers became best friends, so did we. Geoffrey became like a *brother* to me and was my closest friend for the next seven or so years. We longed for our mothers to meet so we could play together and, when we were about five years old, there was one visit that I will always remember.

I'd been waiting all morning for Geoffrey to arrive and when, at last, I heard car tyres crunching over our gravel driveway, I raced out to meet him. Geoffrey could hardly wait either as he wriggled to get out of his parent's car. He was bursting with excitement as he ran towards me and then, very nervously, he held out his prized gift to me. A gift that he had painstakingly made all by himself, by patiently threading lots of coloured tiny glass beads onto some thread, to make me a pretty necklace. As I held his masterpiece in my outstretched hands, I looked up adoringly at my childhood sweetheart, whose *love gift* had touched my tender young heart.

Back to when I was a baby

M any people are aware that babies, especially by the time they can sit up by themselves, can get into all sorts of mischief if they are left alone and my Mummy was about to learn this lesson.

After our daily visit to the park, where we often met Aunty Gwen pushing Geoffrey in his pram, we would stop at the shops before returning home. On this particular day, our routine was the same, but it was going to be a day that my Mummy would *never forget*.

It was sunny and warm, and the gentle rocking sensation of the big pram had sent me to sleep, so Mummy left me in our front garden while she went to prepare some lunch. Before long, she heard me awake and happily playing with the toys in my pram. Being used to listening to my baby banter, she continued with her chores until suddenly, she became aware that I was silent, no more chattering and laughing, and decided she'd better investigate.

But oh! What a shock she got when she walked into the front garden ... it was *white.* No, I don't mean covered in

23

snow, but with toilet paper. There I was, sitting up in my pram, as content as can be, with a toilet roll in my lap.

Somehow, but my mother never did work out how, I had managed to reach down to the shopping shelf and found the toilet paper. Beaming with delight, I was having a tremendous time, as I happily plucked the toilet paper into fine shreds, while poor Mummy had a mild panic attack.

My first words

Most parents look forward with some anticipation to their baby's first words and my parents were no exception. I was their first-born and they were really longing to hear me say, "Mum, mum, mum!" or "Dad, dad, dad!" However, things didn't work out quite the way they expected.

What my parents didn't realize, is that babies not only *look at us* and *watch* what we do, but they also *listen* to what we say. It is by listening to *our* speech that they themselves learn how to begin speaking simple words. Had my father understood this, he might have been more careful how he spoke in front of me. Just because I hadn't begun speaking, did *not* mean I didn't understand what was being said in my presence, as they were soon to find out.

It was Saturday, shopping day and, as usual, my parents took me with them. Like most Saturdays, my mother loved visiting her favourite dress shop and looking through the rails of new clothes. Whilst she did this, Daddy sat patiently waiting and I was allowed to totter off around the shop on my own. Very soon, my attention was drawn to an interesting looking manikin displaying some fashionable clothes. But it was not the clothes that interested me. I wanted to find out was what was *under* the clothes.

So I began to investigate further. Without much ado, I grabbed the hem of the dress in my tiny hand and, holding it high above my head, pointed with my other hand to the bared bottom of the dummy. Delighted with my discovery, I hailed across the shop at the top of my lungs, *"Bum!"* And just in case no-one heard me, I shouted it again. My parents literally *froze* on the spot. Embarrassed and in total shock at my unexpected outburst, they turned in unison towards me as I continued to gleefully inspect the anatomy of the shop's dummy.

This was certainly an experience they never forgot and my Daddy soon stopped saying, *"Stick her bum on the pot!"* and watched his words very carefully after that.

'Greens' for dinner

On another occasion, when my mother was busy in the kitchen, I was quietly busy too, this time in our back garden.   I liked our back garden, it was pretty with lots of colourful flowers and shrubs and I particularly admired a clump of iris in the far corner. My Daddy enjoyed gardening and in the evenings, after he returned home from work, he'd relax by tending the flowerbeds or mowing the front and rear lawns. At weekends, I can remember visiting a local nursery with them, to choose new plants and shrubs to enhance their very pretty garden.

However, on this specific day, when I was about two and a half years old, I'd made a decision. It seemed to me we always ate *greens* for dinner and I decided to get some more for my Mummy to help her and to give her a surprise present. So without any hesitation, I set to work to achieve my goal.

After a lot of effort and with my little arms barely able to cope with the huge pile of *greens* I was carrying, I stepped inside our kitchen and cheerily announced, *"Here you are Mummy. I've brought you some greens to cook for our dinner!"*

Me with Santa

My mother momentarily paused from her chores to look down at me. A look of complete surprise, followed by horror flashed across her face and then, composing herself, she turned to peer through the window into the back garden, her worst fears confirmed. The garden was *bare.* Every single plant and flower was stripped of its foliage. Not a single leaf in sight. This was a well-intentioned present that my mother never forgot.

The young Princess

There is one childhood memory that I have no problem accurately dating and that was when my parents bought their very first black and white television set. This certainly was a memorable occasion, but not as memorable as the reason *why* they bought it.

The previous year, just six days after Princess Elizabeth and her husband, Prince Philip had left for a tour of Australia via Kenya, her father King George VI sadly died. The nation was immediately plunged into deep grief and mourning and, quite suddenly, the young Princess became a Queen.

Now, more than a year after her father's death, Queen Elizabeth was to be crowned Queen Elizabeth II on Tuesday, 2nd June 1953. As the date of this auspicious occasion drew nearer, the level of anticipation and excitement in the nation increased to such a fever pitch, that more than half a million black and white television sets were sold, including one to my parents. But up until this point, owning a television was a rarity and fewer than two million homes in the UK possessed one. A fact that's hard to believe nowadays.

Of course, my parents were thrilled with the novelty of their new television with its tiny nine inch screen and portable aerial, and it took pride of place in their living room. Immediately, an invitation went out to their neighbours and it seemed everyone in Ambleside Avenue responded by cramming into our home, each wanting a glimpse of this historic occasion.

On the morning of the Coronation, the Queen looked radiant and so very beautiful, seated beside Prince Philip as they waved to the adoring crowds from the magnificent Gold State Coach drawn by eight superb white horses. This ornate and lavishly decorated golden carriage, built way back in 1762 and weighing an enormous four tons, transported the glowing couple through London's decorated streets, brimming over with three million or more jubilant spectators. As the Golden Carriage arrived at the entrance to Westminster Abbey, an exuberant fanfare of trumpets heralded the beginning of this majestic and solemn Coronation ceremony.

The nation was celebrating and so were we, as everyone crowded round our miniscule *nine inch screen* to watch the royal pageantry in all its finery. It was a splendid occasion and everyone was rejoicing and in high spirits. But, as a four-year-old child, I can still remember being totally puzzled as to *why* there were so many people, most of whom I didn't know, squeezing into our small living room. Standing in our hall-way, avoiding the crush and feeling rather dejected, I simply couldn't understand what all the fuss was about.

Yet only a couple of years later, when I was six years old, the pomp and majesty of the Coronation ceremony seemed like a wonderful fairytale to me. *A real princess becoming a Queen.* I was spellbound by it all and when my parents gave me a beautiful book on the Coronation, it became one of my most treasured childhood possessions. One that I still have to this day.

I adored this book and loved spending hours looking at all the lovely pictures. I greatly admired the Queen's magnificent white satin embroidered dress covered with golden crystals, diamonds and pearls. I marvelled at the immense Coronation Crown with its ermine border and over four hundred precious jewels, and simply loved her eighteen-foot-long silky velvet cloak, lined with Canadian ermine that flowed out behind her.   How I dreamt of wearing a cloak like this, one that would fly out behind me as I ran round our garden. As I fingered through the pages of my precious Coronation book, my childlike imagination wondered, *"What must it be like, to be a Queen?"*

In due respect for our new Queen, throughout my entire childhood and youth, my Daddy always taught us to *stand up and stand still* whenever we heard the National Anthem being played.   My father was very strict about this, even when the BBC played it at the close of their nightly television broadcasts, around 11 p.m.   In those early days of television, there was no chance of late-night viewing.

Chapter 3

When I was Four

S hortly after the Queen's Coronation ceremony, we left Ambleside Avenue and moved into our second home in Stoke Road, Cobham, Surrey. This was a beautiful house with six large bedrooms and my sister and I were so excited to have a bedroom each *and* a playroom. Another wonderful surprise for us, was the exceptionally large and wooded garden. How we adored our new home with its *magical* garden.

Large mature oak trees and tall pine trees surrounded the central lawn in the back garden and, from the branch of a mighty beech tree, hung our favourite rope swing where we played happily for hours. When our cousin Derek came to visit us during his bachelor days, we excitedly urged him to push us extra hard until we could swing so high, that we could see right over the tall hedge into next door's garden. This was something our Daddy would *never* let us do.

Skirting the lawn, were many towering rhododendron bushes which we loved walking around inside. They provided the most wonderful hiding places and, on one occasion, I enjoyed making my very own private den inside one of them by painstakingly weaving high walls of fine sticks and twigs. It took me quite a while to complete, but when it was finished, I was so proud of my handiwork. Yes, I loved being outside and if I wasn't in my den, you could often find me digging earnestly for flints in the steep earthen bank hidden behind the trees, at the far end of the garden.   Or, I would be busy searching for tiny tree and plant seedlings and interesting pebbles to create a mini-garden in one of my Daddy's wooden seed boxes. I could while away many happy hours doing this.

The Springtime in our garden was particularly beautiful, when there were carpets of white snowdrops and pretty blue scilla. The luminous shades of purple, ochre and white crocus made a colourful picture too, followed by magnificent golden daffodils and crisp white narcissus with flame red centres.

Then in late Spring, came an impressive sweep of bluebells, bowing their delicate heads and filling the air with their fragrant perfume. All this beauty was perfectly complimented by the backdrop of mature trees bursting into fresh new leaf and the prolific purple blooms of the mighty rhododendron bushes.

My sister Linda and I were indeed very fortunate to grow up in these truly beautiful surroundings and it was amidst this magical garden that my fantasy world flourished. I desperately wanted to *fly*. In my dreams and wildest imagination, all I had to do was *jump up and down three times* and off I went. What freedom! At other times, I would run around our lawn as fast as I could whilst gripping a strip of cloth to my shoulders, so it flew up in the air behind me. Oh, how I longed to have the Queen's long Coronation train. As I raced around our garden, I imagined I was flying and soaring high above the tree tops. This was my childhood dream and my *endless joy.*

Miscarriages

My parents had always wanted more children but tragically, my mother suffered three miscarriages which was devastating for them. Even though Nurse Nash, who very kindly came to live with us and admirably cared for and looked after my mother during lengthy periods of bed rest, she was unable to prevent my mother from losing these three precious unborn babies.

It was hard on us all having Mummy lying in bed for so many months, but we all loved Nurse Nash and missed her when she finally left us. Regrettably, my parents had more sorrow to bear when my sister Linda became increasingly ill with asthma and faced death many times.

All too often, I would come home from kindergarten school and burst into tears when I learnt that my baby sister had been rushed by ambulance, with sirens blazing, back into Kingston Hospital. She was ill so frequently and I sorely missed her, especially as I was never allowed into the hospital ward. Instead, I spent long lonely hours sitting by myself on the deep, highly varnished wooden benches in the quiet hospital hallways, with my crayons and colouring books as company. My sister was critically ill and rushed into hospital so often, that I began missing school and getting behind with my lessons. For a while, a kind and willing teacher came to our home each afternoon to help me catch up. But even this proved difficult. Eventually, my parents kept me away from school for a whole year and I was taught by a live-in Governess. She stayed in one of our two spare bedrooms and the other made an excellent classroom.

This seemed to be a perfect arrangement and helped my parents immensely. But I'm afraid to say, *I hated having a Governess.* She was incredibly strict and wouldn't give me any freedom to express my lively imagination. I particularly adored painting, but even this pleasure was robbed from me by her controlling influence. I was only allowed to paint what *she* dictated. Very soon, a battle of wills emerged and regrettably, we never did warm to each other. It couldn't have been an easy time for her either, but for me, it was a most miserable year.

Unfortunately, my sister remained very ill for quite a while. But whenever she wasn't in hospital, she needed an oxygen tent over her bed, together with a long-necked steam kettle to ease her laboured breathing. It was a very exhausting and anxious time for my parents and thankfully our friendly milkman's wife, Mrs. Bonner, came every day to give Mummy a hand in the kitchen. At weekends, her husband helped us too, by caring for our large garden. *The Bonners* soon became our faithful family friends and were a real help and support to my parents for very many years.

Linda became stronger

My sister and I didn't have many friends to play with and living beside a busy main road, we weren't allowed to go out by ourselves. But we were never bored. As Linda became stronger and was able to play with me, one of our favourite pastimes was to chase each other at breakneck speed in our sturdy, metal pedal cars on the rear patio that ran the length of our house.

At one end of this patio, was a square rose border surrounded by a narrow paved path, which served as an excellent race track. My sister pedalled a fire engine and I had a car and it took great skill and much practice to get around this narrow track *without reducing any speed,* and *not* fall into the prickly rose bushes. The faster we went, the louder the fire engine bell rang until, in complete exasperation, Mummy would confiscate it into silence. Our fun was over, *until the next time.*

However, even on rainy days, we were never bored and happily amused ourselves by playing with our large collection of glass marbles or challenged each other to a game of Ludo or Snakes & Ladders, and often enjoyed playing children's card games of Happy Families or Snap. At other times, I would pretend I was skiing in Switzerland, the country I dreamed of visiting. My parents had given me a pair of short metal skis set on wheels, together with ski sticks and, in my imagination, I would be speeding down snowy slopes as I raced around our house.

Yet one of my favourite pastimes was stamp collecting. Every Saturday morning, I would spend most of my pocket money buying packets of foreign stamps and then, after researching them in my Daddy's huge Stanley Gibbons stamp encyclopedia, I would carefully stick them into my very own loose-leaf stamp album. My father had always been a keen philatelist and just occasionally he would show me his most wonderful stamp collection. I admired it immensely.

My parents brought us up to love animals and before long we had a mini zoo to look after. Two black miniature poodles, two long-eared white rabbits, some guinea pigs, hamsters, tortoises, budgies and even a fish tank. There was always something to do around our house!

My sister Linda (left) and me

Children's television

Of course, our special treat every day was to watch television. Provided Linda and I had behaved ourselves, we were allowed to watch *one hour* of special Children's Television at teatime each day. Excitedly, we would sit glued to the tiny nine inch screen laughing at the antics of Sooty & Sweep, Noddy, Mr. Pastry, Billy Bunter and, of course, Popeye. Throughout our childhood, *westerns* were very popular. Indeed, I loved them so much, that I had my own cowboy outfit and dressed up in all the gear from a fringed waistcoat, large cowboy hat, sheriff's badge, twin holsters and a pair of revolvers loaded with rolls of caps. *I was ready for anything.*

Whenever I could, I watched the masked Lone Ranger riding his white stallion *Silver* beside his faithful friend Tonto. Then there was the handsome cowboy Bronco Layne in *Bronco,* played by Ty Hardin.   But never, could I have imagined that one day, when I grew up, I would meet Ty Hardin face-to-face.

Best of all though, I loved riding the huge rocking horse in our playroom. Dressed in my cowboy outfit, with my hat firmly tied on and two toy pistols in my holster, I was prepared to ride away into the sunset, singing along to my favourite Roy Rogers' cowboy song. But first, I had to set the scene and have some music playing. Lifting the lid of our portable gramophone, I would place my precious Roy Rogers' LP on the turntable and then, taking a firm hold of the side protruding handle, *wind up* the gramophone as far as it would go. Next, slowly and very carefully, I lowered the arm with its heavy diamond-tipped needle head onto the opening grooves of the revolving LP, without scratching it. As the needle point reached the soundtrack, it was time to leap up into the saddle and get ready for action.

Enthusiastically, I began rocking as fast as I could, while singing heartily along with Roy Rogers, the popular 1950's cowboy, who cheerily sang about *Trigger,* his famous Palomino horse ...

"A four legged friend, a four legged friend,
He'll never let you down.
He's honest and faithful right up to the end,
That wonderful, one-two-three-four legged friend."

Oh! How I loved that huge rocking horse and, at a squeeze, three of us could fit on to it, singing and laughing, and having great fun.

Childhood sweetheart

Geoffrey and I were still the closest of friends and had such fun and exciting times together. We played and explored in each others' gardens, climbed trees, even wrestled together. Yes, it's true. When Aunty Gwen brought Geoffrey to visit me, we loved wrestling. I mean, this was serious business. We were no longer friends but opponents, in for the attack, both wanting to defeat the other. It was all-out war with arm twists, bear hugs, the lot. And yet our mothers just let us get on with it and never once interfered, however loud the howls for *mercy.*

Geoffrey and I adored each other and didn't ever want to be parted. So when *going home time approached*, we'd try to hide in the garden or run upstairs to one of our spare bedrooms, climb up into a double bed and lie there motionless, pretending to be asleep. But the trick was not to laugh or blink when our mothers, heads together, peered down at us, whispering to each other in case they woke us. When they finally crept out of the bedroom, we knew we'd won. Geoffrey could stay the night. Hooray!

And so we spent the next few years enjoying each other's company until one fine summer's day, when we were happily playing cricket in my back garden, our innocent childhood romance became sorely tested. I suppose we must have been around seven years old, when Geoffrey dropped the bomb-shell that shattered my entire world. While he prepared to bowl the next ball to me, he suddenly became very serious and announced, *"When we get married, you'll have to go out to work!"*

I could hardly believe my ears and my heart missed a beat. I dropped my bat and ran broken hearted into the kitchen, crying my eyes out as I clung to my Mummy wailing, *"How can I go out to work when we get married? Who's going to look after all the babies?"*

It was not long after this life-changing trauma, that our childhood love affair took another severe blow. We were again playing cricket when Geoffrey exclaimed in total exasperation, *"Can't you throw the ball any harder?"*

And so, very sadly, I lost my childhood sweetheart over a game of *cricket.*

Blissful days ahead

Every summer, my sister and I looked forward to spending two wonderful weeks at Elmer Sands. And, like most children, we were always eager and impatient to reach our destination. So, once Daddy's car was packed and everyone was ready to go, we set off full of anticipation for the south coast of England.

With a journey of just over an hour and a half, my sister and I sat quietly on the back seat for as long as we could, until the expectancy within us rose to such a pitch, that we couldn't sit still any longer. We didn't have seat belts or child seats in those days and every few miles, we stood behind Daddy's seat tormenting him by asking, *"Can we see the sea yet?"*

The journey seemed to go on forever until finally, high upon a crest of the South Downs, we caught our first glimpse of the English Channel, glistening so invitingly in the distance.

Linda and I always got overexcited and could hardly contain ourselves as we imagined spending nearly every waking moment on the wide open beach and paddling in the safe, shallow waters. *It was such fun.*

These were blissful days indeed but first, my sister and I had something *very* important on our minds, a visit to the local seaside gift shop with all its tantalizing wares spilling out onto the pavement. It was every child's dream with buckets and spades of every shape and shade, colourful kites with pretty tails, bouncy beach balls, whirling windmills on hand-held sticks, sand shoes, rubber rings and the all important prawn and shrimping nets. No holiday was complete without a visit here first.

Our holiday was exciting for another reason too. It was when we annually saw our Granny and Grandad, my Mum's parents who always came with us. They looked forward to spending a relaxing fortnight sitting on deck chairs on the lawn, watching us playing on the beach until, of course, I began taunting Grandad about his toupee.

As far as I can remember, we always had hot, beautiful sunny weather and I loved the exhilaration of spending our whole time outdoors. From our garden, there was a detachable ladder reaching down the sea wall to a stretch of deep crunchy shingle, interspersed by long arms of wooden groynes, before opening out onto a beautiful wide sandy beach which, when the tide was out, seemed to disappear into the horizon. It was in these safe, calm, shallow waters that I first learnt how to swim.

However, occasionally we experienced exceptionally high tides, but even these we found exciting. Daddy would haul our beach ladder up to safety as enormous, powerful waves battered our sea wall and spilled over into the garden. To my sister and I, it was great fun as we dared each other to dart between the foaming spray of these giant waves.

Unfortunately, Daddy was never able to take time off his work and commuted the long distance to London every day by train. But at least he was back with us for the evenings, when we happily paddled together in the clear shallow sea, as it gently lapped the warm beach.

My dear Daddy

These were very special times for me and I still fondly remember how Daddy took me shrimping with him almost every evening. He taught me how to carefully push the flat wooden bottom of my shrimping net over the ridged sand while dragging one of Mummy's old stockings behind me, which held our prized catch.

If the tide went out far enough, a bed of small rocks was exposed and we then changed our nets for strong triangular ones, to prize out large prawns hiding in the rock pool crevices. It was such fun and so rewarding to catch these delicious shrimps and prawns for our tea every day.

But more than that, I still treasure the memories of these precious times spent with my dear Daddy.

Chapter 4

I was Eight now

My childhood hero had always been the famous cowboy Roy Rogers, riding his beautiful Palomino horse *Trigger,* with his lovely German Shepherd dog *Bullet* at his side. I adored this TV programme and always dreamt of having a Palomino horse and a German Shepherd of my own. And I'm still hoping.

However, Roy Rogers who appeared in the TV series with his wife Dale Evans, were both Christians and Roy encouraged all children to go to Sunday School. Consequently, I begged my parents to let me attend the Sunday School held in my primary school and, when they agreed, I was eager to go.

I'm not quite sure what I expected, but I was surprised to find my school Assembly Hall full of people, formally sitting in semicircular rows. I didn't know a soul and I just sat there amongst all these strangers, with no-one speaking to me. Then someone stood up and spoke to us for *ages and ages.* It was all so serious and solemn and I didn't know what they were talking about. In fact, it seemed far worse than ordinary school and I just couldn't understand it. I reasoned that if Roy Rogers said all children should go to Sunday School and learn about Jesus, then it should be fun and friendly and interesting.

But to me, this Sunday School was awful, unfriendly and totally boring and after trying it a second time, I'd had enough. Unfortunately, I was really disillusioned and never ever did go back to Sunday School. Through this sad experience and the fact that my parents *never* took us to church, except to my cousin Youla's wedding when I was fourteen, I grew up with no meaningful Christian teaching.

However, my Mum unsuccessfully tried to persuade me to attend after-school Confirmation classes, but I totally refused. I felt it was ridiculous to be Confirmed when I'd never attended church or intended to do so. Sadly, my heart grew hardened towards God.

I had a passion for horse riding

My weekly lesson at Heather Taylor's riding stables was the highlight of my week.

Every Saturday, I joined a group of other young enthusiastic children as we rode through the beautiful Oxshott Woods. For me, this was the greatest fun and I was thrilled when Mummy and Daddy kitted me out in jodhpurs and yellow string gloves, to ride my favourite horse *Shelley*.

For my eighth birthday, all my friends came to our house for a party and we played the usual games of Pass the Parcel, Blind Man's Buff, Musical Chairs and Pin the Tail on a Donkey. But there was a *fishing game* that I particularly liked. It involved Mummy spending hours patiently cutting out hundreds of gold paper fish, threading a sewing pin into each and placing them in the bottom of a very large, tall box. She then secured small magnets to lengths of string tied on to short bamboo canes and each child, being blindfolded, tried to *catch* as many fish as they could. I had always loved going fishing in our local river, so this game held a special fascination for me, especially as I was assured of a catch.

My eighth birthday party was in full swing and everyone was having great fun. Some of my friends were playing indoor games, some playing out in the garden on our two swings, some happily pushing dolls' prams around, two others racing up and down the patio in our pedal cars, while another two brave souls catapulted themselves around on our two-seater, lever-propelled roundabout that revolved at such an amazing speed, that every child became hopelessly giddy.

However, without our knowledge, my parents had something very special in store for all the children. Quite unexpectedly, my favourite horse *Shelley* was led into our back garden and my eyes nearly popped out of my head. *Wow!* It was such an incredible surprise and one that I shall never forget.

Shelley was so gentle and calm amongst all the shrieks and laughter, and patiently trotted round and round our garden until every excited child got a ride. *"Thank you Mummy and Daddy for this wonderful birthday present!"*

Orange squash was such a *treat*

I t was my own fault. *"Why did I have that glass of orange squash?"* Watching Mummy pour out those delicious looking glasses of squash this afternoon was just too tempting and, as I watched my friends enjoying their tasty drinks, I just couldn't resist having one too. I reasoned, *"I'm sure I won't be ill this time, it's only one glass."*

But a few hours later, I was doubled up in pain, gripping my stomach in pure agony. Poor Mummy, all she could ever do was comfort me, as I lay curled up crying in my personal misery. This had happened before, loads of times, so why didn't I learn my lesson? But I was only nine years old and drinking orange squash was such a *treat.*

However, I wasn't to bear this suffering for much longer because Dr. Myers, our friendly family doctor, had other plans for me and before I knew it, I was sitting up in bed, in hospital, waiting to have my appendix removed.

This was to be my very first operation and I was given a room to myself at the rear of the small Cobham Cottage Hospital, where I stayed for two long weeks. Not only was this my first experience of suffering severe pain, but the first time too, that I'd ever been away from my parents and I was feeling dreadfully homesick.   But horrors, there was something else *even worse* than this, it was *breakfast.*

Every morning, a nurse tried to force me to eat *salty porridge.* My Dad made porridge for us every morning and it was absolutely *delicious,* especially with demerara sugar sprinkled on top and some cream from the top of a bottle of gold top milk. But this porridge was *awful* and the more I pushed it around my bowl or tried squashing it to make it disappear, the fiercer I got scolded. To this day, I still hate *salty* porridge.

"So did removing my appendix make a difference?" you may wonder. *"Yes it did!"* Happily, I was able to drink all the fruit squash I wanted after that, with no ill effects at all.

No more riding lessons

Although I recovered well after my appendix operation, there was one big negative I hadn't planned on. Dr Myers refused to allow me to go horse riding for six whole months and I was so disappointed.

Tragically, during those six months, Heather Taylor who owned the riding stables had a fatal accident. She wasn't wearing a riding hat when she was thrown from her horse and, hitting her head, she died. It was such terrible news and I was really upset. Shortly afterwards, her stables were closed down and very sadly, I never ever saw *Shelley* again. In fact, I never once went horse riding during the rest of my childhood and it was nearly thirty years later, before I sat on a horse again.

Oh No! Not another operation

Just one year later, I found myself in Cobham Cottage Hospital *again.* This time, it was to have my tonsils out. But now, my room was at the *front* of this single storey hospital and, at visiting times, I eagerly watched for my parents' car to make its way up the winding driveway. But when it was time for them to leave, it tore at my heart as I watched them drive away, leaving me behind. I cried and cried. In fact, I became so desperately homesick and distraught that, instead of recovering after my operation, I actually became more ill. Even a bowl of delicious ice cream couldn't pacify me. My heart was breaking, my throat was on fire and I was in absolute agony. All I wanted to do was to go home to my Mummy and Daddy. Thankfully, that's exactly what Dr. Myers advised and soon I was happily recovering back in my own bed.

I was growing up

Like it or not, my cowboy outfit just wouldn't fit me any more and I was outgrowing our beloved rocking horse too. So with no more riding lessons to look forward to, I had a dilemma on my hands and a big decision to make. *"What could I do now?"*

To my parent's great surprise, I turned my energies into building Airfix model airplanes. But to their dismay, every Saturday, I commandeered the dining room table as my official workshop. This new hobby was quite a challenge at first, because *I didn't even know what the cockpit was.* But I persevered and successfully built bigger and more complicated planes until eventually, I had a whole fleet hanging up in my bedroom.

Going to the cinema

I shall never forget the very first time I ever went to the cinema. *It was so wonderful!*

I was only nine years old and my school friend Veronica very kindly invited me to go with her family to see the 1958 Rogers & Hammerstein's hit musical film, *'South Pacific'* showing at the very grand Dominion Theatre in Tottenham

Court Road, one of London's very first wide-screen cinemas. And what an amazing time we had.

Going up to London was always a real treat, but entering this superb theatre was something else. I looked around me in awe as my eyes ran over the plush foyer with its high ceilings and elegant decor. Yes, this was certainly a new world and a new opulence that I'd never seen before. *Oh my, it was so impressive.*

I stuck close to my friend as we surveyed these unfamiliar surroundings, before tiptoeing as gracefully as we could up the deeply carpeted steps to where we were ushered to our comfortable seats. Here, we sat admiringly, while waiting patiently for the film to begin.

At last the lights dimmed and I instinctively gripped the arms of my seat in eager anticipation. I didn't really know what to expect but I was sure it was going to be great. Then suddenly, the huge widescreen came *alive* as my expectations exploded within me and I could hardly take it all in. *Wow*! This was far more sensational than I'd ever imagined.

The massive screen seemed to literally engulf me as the wonderful music and singing filled my senses. The expansive screen seemed to suck me right into the picture and I blissfully drifted off into another world, a beautiful world, far away on a tropical island in the South Pacific. I was *in* the film, I was living it, becoming totally immersed in it, unaware of anyone or anything around me.

I adored the wonderful music, especially the songs *Some Enchanted Evening, Bali Ha'i* and *Happy Talk.* But near the end of the film, when the handsome young Lieutenant died in

47

the arms of a pretty little Polynesian girl, it was just too sad and I cried, utterly broken-hearted.

For me, seeing this film was such an unforgettable experience and I kept the wonder and magic alive by playing the *South Pacific* LP over and over again, joyfully singing every song until I knew them all by heart.

Little did I know that fifty years later, I would visit and make dear friends with some present-day Polynesian people, in far away Papua New Guinea.

Chapter 5

Manor House School

B oth my sister and I from the age of nine years old, attended Manor House School for Girls, aptly named after the beautiful Georgian manor house which formed the main school building. It was a small private school set in extensive grounds with only one hundred and fifty pupils in total, approximately fifty being boarders, and we were divided up into two houses, which competed against each other.

One of the houses was named after Capt. Cook's most famous ship *Endeavour,* in which he sailed on his first voyage around the world. The second house was named after his consort ship *Discovery,* commanded by Lt. Charles Clerke, that accompanied Capt. Cook on his third great Pacific voyage. I was in *Endeavour,* whilst my sister was in *Discovery.*

The Obstacle Race

I was never very sporty, unlike my Mum. In fact, I was totally hopeless at all athletics but, on my *last* school

Sports Day when I was sixteen, I was entered into just one race ... *the Obstacle Race.*

I actually enjoyed this race and even thought I had a good chance of winning it. At the start line, I stood alert, full of anticipation and set off at a great pace, leaving all my competitors way behind me. Encouraged, there was now a good chance of winning if I could just maintain this speed.

I was still way ahead by the time I reached the final obstacle that proved to be a *real* challenge to me. Sitting on a chair, I had to throw a tennis ball into a distant metal bucket and once I'd achieved that, I only had to run to the finish line and *win.* I'd never ever won *any* race before in my whole life, but today I might, for the very first time.

However, this feat turned out to be more of *an obstacle* than I realized. *"Could I get the ball into the bucket?"* I threw and threw, retrieving my ball over and over again. I tried with all my might, but it went everywhere, except into the bucket.

Before long, the other girls had caught up and began to easily overtake me and reach the finish line. The crowd of eager parents were cheering us all on, but suddenly, they turned their attention to my obvious plight and became silent, gasping at every failed throw. In fact, although other races had commenced all around, the crowd seemed more interested in watching me making a complete fool of myself.

But finally, I did it. And to my surprise, a roar went up from the crowd. Suddenly, my miserable failure turned out to be a joyful and humorous episode amongst such serious competitiveness. As it turned out, I crossed the finish line

with *more* applause than if I'd won. So my joyful perseverance became a *victory* after all.

I loved playing hockey

T hankfully, I was reasonably good at one sport and
that was hockey. So when I was chosen to play the
position of *right inner* in our school team, I was delighted.
Anyone who has ever played hockey will know that it's quite
a rough game and even wearing protective shin pads, didn't
prevent me from being laid up for many days at a time with
battered legs. Once, in an aggressive tackle, my opponent's
stick shot up mine and took my right thumb nail off.

During the winter season, we often played hockey
matches at other schools and, as we didn't have a school bus,
my parents volunteered to help out. Before we knew it, there
was nearly half a team piled into the back of our Cortina
estate car. A terrible squeeze, *but great fun.* That was, of
course, before any seat belt rules and regulations.

My very real fear

T hroughout my school years, I had one very real *fear*.
And that was standing up alone in front of my class
to recite some poetry or Scripture verses. I could manage
nearly anything else, except this. And yet, so often Miss
Green, our elderly Head Mistress and Scripture teacher, gave
us verses to learn by heart for homework, with the inevitable
consequence that each of us, in turn, had to stand up to repeat
the passages. A simple and easy task for many children
perhaps, but a constant stab of abject *fear* for me.

This same *fear* engulfed me during our French lessons when Miss White, the Assistant Head Mistress and French teacher, fired random questions at us. I spent each lesson fearful that she would suddenly pounce on me and ask me something in French that I couldn't understand, let alone answer.

Then, when I reached the lower and upper sixth forms, the most senior classes in our school, I had another nightmare to face. This time, it was at *lunchtime*.

School lunchtimes

At our school, there was no such thing as an automatic electric dinner bell. Morning breaktime, lunchtime and end of school was marked by a chosen senior girl vigorously ringing a brass handbell outside the school's front door. This was a duty we all wanted, as it meant getting out of class early.   When at last I was chosen to perform this responsibility, I was delighted, as it was also considered a great honour.

Thus, every day when we heard the welcome sound of the lunchtime bell being rung, each class queued up in an orderly manner in the main hallway. Above the din of the noisy chattering and rumbling tummies, one hundred and fifty ravenous girls were waiting for the *gong* to be sounded. Only then, was the dining room door opened and we were allowed to enter.

But we weren't permitted to sit just anywhere we liked, because at the beginning of each new term, every girl was allocated to a specific dinner table. Nine girls sat randomly on benches at an oblong table, with a teacher at the head, who dutifully dished out the food *Oliver Twist* style, as plates of food were passed down the table. There was no choice of food either, and we had to eat whatever came out of that pot, like it or not.

So, upon the sounding of the gong, there was a minor stampede into the dining room as everyone made a dash to claim a seat at their table, preferably as far away from the teacher as possible.   Once seated, *Grace* was given and we could all get on with eating.

This was the general procedure throughout our school until you reached the two most senior classes, when the teachers at the heads of each table included Miss Green and Miss White. And the strict rule here was, *we had to speak in French throughout lunch. No English could be spoken at all.*

Also, instead of being able to randomly grab a seat anywhere at the table, every day we had to move round the table *one place,* until it was our turn to sit beside the teacher for two lunch periods, *speaking French.*

There was no getting out of it and however hard I tried to think of what to say in French, my mouth either dried up or I nearly choked on my food in fright. On one occasion, I can still remember Miss Green asking me, in French, *"Aren't you going to speak to me?"*

Somehow, I managed to survive two years of these dreaded lunchtimes but, unfortunately, I never overcame my *fear* of stage fright.

Stage fright

E very morning began with School Assembly, when a chosen pupil stood up on the stage to read a Bible passage, followed by hymns and a prayer. All pupils sat cross-legged on the floor, except for the two upper classes who squeezed on to narrow benches. The form teachers sat on chairs at the end of their row of girls and Miss Green sat up on the stage, alongside Miss Miles at the grand piano.

This was all fine and I always loved singing the hymns. It only became a dire problem when *I was the one chosen for the Bible reading.* Instead of being a privilege and an honour, it was my very greatest *fear* and my heart would literally leap out of my chest as I slowly mounted the steps up to the stage and stood alone, *shaking in absolute fright,* in front of the whole school.

I was given this 'honour' on several occasions, but each time the very thought of it simply petrified me and filled me with an unquenchable fear, that gripped me completely. A paralyzing fear, that caused me many a sleepless night. A fear, unfortunately, that I never managed to conquer throughout my school days.

We all loved 'The Beatles!'

I f there was *one thing* that every girl in my class agreed upon, it had to be ... "We all *loved* The Beatles!"

In the early Sixties, we were all mad about pop groups with their catchy tunes and simple lyrics that we knew by heart. Mum must have despaired with me, as every inch of wall space in my bedroom was smothered with pictures of

The Beatles and heart-throbs like Elvis Presley, Cliff Richard, Ricky Nelson and Billy Fury. Then one day, our teenage dreams came true.

It was 1963, the year The Beatles began their journey to superstardom, after the release of their first single hit record, *"Love Me Do!"* They were *new* and very different with their 'pudding basin' haircuts and unusual collarless, round necked jackets. They soon took the pop scene by storm with their hugely popular Lennon/McCartney compositions. Their song, *"I want to hold your hand!"* became their fourth consecutive No. 1 hit record in one year. It seemed the whole world loved The Beatles and there was no stopping them. Wherever they went, huge crowds of adoring fans amassed, and airports were overrun with tens of thousands of fans all hoping for a mere glimpse of them.

So, when the girls in my class learnt they were coming to perform at the Odeon Cinema in Guildford, our home town, we could hardly believe it.   There was absolutely no way we were going to miss this opportunity of seeing The Beatles *live.* With heartbeats racing, we booked a whole row of seats in the downstairs stalls, which held over one thousand seats *and every girl in my class went.*

At last, the big night arrived and at 8 p.m. on 21st June 1963, our group of excited fourteen year olds took our seats, ready to enjoy a night that we would *always* remember.

The cinema was packed to capacity and everyone was waiting for The Beatles, the stars of the show. But first, we had to patiently endure the supporting acts which tended to be lewd and totally awful. But when the clean-cut foursome came onto the stage, the audience went absolutely *wild.* Fans

55

were screaming and shouting and cheering hysterically. It was *crazy. And quite unashamedly, so was I!* I was shouting and shrieking too, along with every other teenager in the place.

The atmosphere was electric as the deafening rhythmic sound of guitars and pounding drums filled the auditorium. Paul McCartney and John Lennon, beaming from ear to ear, sung out with all their might above the incredible roar, backed up by George Harrison playing his electric guitar and Ringo Starr on the drums.

Although this was the first and only time I've ever been to a live pop concert, it was certainly one Friday night that I'll never forget. And do you know something? *I guess I'll always be a Beatles' fan at heart.*

Chapter 6

My parents new Business

W hen I was eleven years old, my parents bravely ventured to set up their own business, *Adrian Essential Oils* in the docklands region of London which, back then, was a dismal and run-down area. Their company was the UK branch of the parent company, run by Mr. Adrian and his family, which was based in the warm and sunny Mediterranean port of Marseille, in southern France.

Mum organized all the administration side of their new business from our dining room at home. Dad on the other hand, spent his days in a grim old warehouse in Cable Street, deep in London's East End, as it was necessary for him to be near the docks to import the huge metal drums of concentrated essential oils. These oils are incredibly pungent natural essences, mostly derived from flowers, herbs and trees.

At that time, Cable Street was not the most attractive place to work and had been notorious from Victorian times through to the 1950's, for cheap lodgings, brothels, drinking inns and opium dens. But it was in these austere surroundings that my father spent his day mixing and blending the heady essential oils ready for use in perfumes, cosmetics and toiletries, and as flavourings in confectionery and food products. Sometimes, during the school holidays, Dad would take me with him to his warehouse and often the air was so heavy with the aroma of a particular oil, I could hardly breath and felt certain I would surely suffocate. And yet my Dad hardly noticed these overpowering and often highly obnoxious smells.

Each evening when he arrived home, his suit always smelt of the oils he'd been blending that day and the strongest was usually garlic and eucalyptus. I'm sure it must have been an overwhelming experience for some of the unfortunate passengers who had to sit next to him on the train home every evening.

This new business venture was a major decision and a huge financial step for my parents, which sadly meant leaving our childhood dream house in Cobham with its magical garden. We now had to dramatically downsize, which included losing our beloved rocking horse, pets and many of our toys, as we moved into our compact new bungalow, set at the head of a quiet private road in the picturesque village of East Horsley, Surrey.

Happily though, we soon found out that our new home had many great advantages, including the *luxury* of solid fuel central heating with a radiator in every room and even a heated towel rail in the bathroom! My sister and I were also pleased to discover that almost every house in our road had children around our own ages, so it didn't take us long to make new friends. We especially enjoyed the welcome *freedom* of being able to walk and bike with our new friends around the myriad of quiet roads around us.

To our added joy, within a short walking distance, were some lovely recreation grounds and a pretty lake surrounded by pine woods. It was in these beautiful surroundings that we spent much of our time playing tennis in the summer and, whenever possible, skating on the frozen lake in winter.

Sunday was always a family day

Although I can never remember my parents taking us to church, not even at Christmas or Easter, my Dad had been brought up to respect Sundays as *a day of rest.* He was very strict about this and flatly refused to even take us to a nearby ice skating rink on a Sunday.

Consequently, throughout my childhood, we enjoyed long family walks every Sunday afternoon to local beauty spots such as Wisley Lake, surrounded by sweet smelling pine woods; Newlands Corner, set high on the chalky ridge of the North Downs with incredible views over the valley below; and Frensham Ponds where, in the summer, we enjoyed leisurely picnics and sometimes fishing with Dad.

Both my parents were always so loving and kind, caring and very generous. I can honestly say that I *never, ever* heard a single cross word between them. And that's not an exaggeration. I am forever thankful to them both for giving my sister and I such a privileged and happy childhood, with so many wonderful memories.

My first real boyfriend

Once a week, my new group of friends converged on the local Village Hall for ballroom dancing lessons. One kindly lady played the piano, while another very patiently did her best to transform us into a future Fred Astaire or Ginger Rogers. I don't think many of us ever lived up to her expectations, but we certainly had fun and enjoyed our weekly episode of stumbling around trying to imitate the Waltz or Cha Cha Cha.

But it didn't take much to please youngsters in those days and, to us, it was not only fun but a way of meeting new friends too. At the end of each season, these two brave ladies very kindly held a dance for us and I can still remember the first one I went to. Mum bought me a new white dress covered in tiny crimson rosebuds, caught in at the waist, and flaring out over my new layered stiff petticoat. I can still remember being so proud of this beautiful party dress.

It was at this dance, when I was only twelve years old, that I met my first *real* boyfriend. He was thirteen, blond and very handsome, a keen golfer and his name was Stephen. He was also extremely clever and, to my amazement, he had already passed seven O'Levels including Greek and Latin and begun studying for his A'Levels. *Oh my goodness.* I hadn't even begun the syllabus for my O'Levels.

And yet, we got on really well and soon became inseparable. I enjoyed accompanying him while he played a round of golf at the nearby golf club and loved going on long bike rides with him through the beautiful hilly countryside all around us. He was kind and generous too, often having a small present for me in his saddle bag, like a bar of chocolate.

60

I believe we briefly fell in love even at that tender age but after a year or so of being best friends, he started talking of marriage. Of course, it was all too much for me, too soon and I became frightened and ran away, leaving him totally heartbroken. But I shall always remember him as my dear friend and a fine young man, who really cared for me.

My thirteenth birthday

I was just coming to the age when I was beginning to enjoy pop music and loved listening to the latest songs on my Dad's huge old radiogram in our living room. Even when my school homework was over, instead of watching television, I preferred to relax by listening to the radio or playing some of my single records by artists like Neil Sedaka, Marty Wilde and the Everly Brothers.

Then for my first *teenage* birthday, my parents had a really wonderful surprise gift for me. A neat, lightweight, pocket-sized transistor radio in a smart red leather case and *I was over the moon.* This tiny radio was the latest invention and so small, that I could take it with me anywhere, even to bed. And many a night I had it tucked under my bed sheets, secretly listening to Radio Luxembourg.

Nowadays, with so much technology at our fingertips, it's hard for the younger generation to imagine what it was like back in my youth when laptops, computer games, camcorders, iphones, ipads, Kindles, digital cameras and even digital and quartz watches, just didn't exist. Nor did we have internet, satellite and cable TV, fax machines, photocopiers, DVD's, CD's, videos or even cassettes. Just old-fashioned records.

So how on earth did we ever survive?   Without even a mobile phone?   And yet we did, perfectly well and quite happily too.

Robin

A little later, when I was fifteen, I had another special boyfriend. His name was Robin. He was a fine, good looking, gentle boy who lived just around the corner from me and we became close friends. As often as possible, when our heavy load of homework and studying for exams was over, he would visit me and we'd contentedly listen to records ranging from The Beatles to the folk legends of Bob Dylan and Joan Baez.

Robin was a keen cricketer and during the summer months, I spent every Saturday watching him and his school friend Bob Willis playing in their school matches. Little did any of us realize at the time, that Bob Willis would later become famous as an England Cricket Team Captain.

Chapter 7

What to do Now?

A t the age of sixteen, my schooling appeared to have come to a welcome end, after successfully passing eight O'Level exams. I now reckoned, with this hurdle over, that the end of my happy childhood was drawing to a close. I questioned, *"What to do now?"* My school didn't teach A'Levels, so moving to a new school in a different area was a daunting prospect to me. I'd been happy enough with my pass marks, although I didn't really excel in anything. So what subjects should I take if I studied for A'Levels, and for what purpose?

As I tossed these thoughts around, I reasoned that as I didn't want to go to university, why would I need A'Levels? There was, after all, only one thing I was crazy about and that was *dressmaking.* This was my real passion and what I dearly wanted to study as a profession.

But my Mum and I had a difference of opinion. In fact, she gave me just two options. First, to attend the acclaimed Tante Marie Cookery School or, second, to enroll for a one year course at The London College of Secretaries.

I didn't mean to be ungrateful or want to upset Mum, but I didn't want to do either. I realized the Tante Marie Cookery School was a fantastic opportunity, if you liked cooking. *But I hated it.* I also understood the logic of taking a secretarial course, but I wanted to learn *dressmaking.* It was, after all, the only thing I really enjoyed. But Mum was unmoved and I was soon given the stern ultimatum, *"Which is it to be?"*

A few months later, I begrudgingly succumbed to Mum's wishes and became a reluctant commuter. Now, every day, I made the tedious forty-five minute mainline train journey up to London, to begin my one year course at the eminent London College of Secretaries. This College was situated in one of the grand terraced properties in Park Crescent, overlooking Regents Park. Every morning, as I arrived to start a new day, I would pause a moment to admire this stunning and very beautiful semi-circle of impressive buildings fronted by tall, graceful white columns, designed by the famous architect John Nash.

It was within the walls of one of these splendid buildings, that I was pledged to become a fully qualified secretary. My goal was to study Pitman's shorthand and typing which, to my surprise, was actually interesting and became a real challenge.

I particularly enjoyed the typing lessons and soon learnt how to help other students change and disentangle the messy, inky ribbons on their heavy manual typewriters. Our teacher was strict, but kind too and often walked around the classroom telling us to, *"Sit up straight. Shoulders back!"* and *"Wrists up!"* as we pounded away on our heavy, steeply tiered *manual* typewriters. The noise was *deafening.*

The syllabus also included several other subjects that I found more difficult and also incredibly boring. All too often, I struggled to stay awake during these classes. But I was aware that my parents were making a huge financial sacrifice to send me to this grand College and I didn't want to let them down.

To qualify for a First Class Diploma, I had to get a pass mark of over 120 w.p.m. (words per minute) in shorthand and over 60 w.p.m. accurate error-free typing, plus over 80% in all the other subjects. I knew this was going to be a serious hurdle to overcome, but after a great deal of perseverance plus dedicated and determined hard work, I managed to achieve this goal and was totally delighted. I was now ready and eager to start work and earn a living. I could hardly wait.

My dear Dad

So my Dad and I continued to travel up to London together on the 7.50 a.m. train. And every morning it was the same race. The race to grab one of the last remaining free seats, preferably in a carriage *without* a pipe smoker. Back then, there were no restrictions on smoking and to make a misjudgement meant breathing clouds of pipe smoke within your confined carriage for the next forty-five minutes or so.

Very soon, each of the twelve-seater individual carriages were filled to capacity with hardened commuters, many standing unsteadily holding a newspaper in one hand, whilst hanging onto the luggage rack with the other, as the train noisily rocked and jostled its way up to Waterloo, London's busiest railway station. Today, it is estimated that ninety-one million passengers pass through Waterloo every year. That's more than the population of the whole of Britain.

However, we never had to face this daily ordeal without a tasty, cooked breakfast inside us. This was Dad's job. Diligently, he got up early every morning to cook us a feast fit for a king, including fried potatoes, fried bread, bacon, sausage, eggs, tomatoes and even mushrooms. He loved his food and for him, to start the day without breakfast, was unthinkable.

My dear Dad, always thoughtful, considerate and kind, was a real *gentleman* too. Every morning, after we arrived at Waterloo, we continued our journey together on the underground tube trains. When it was time for me to get off and leave him, he always lovingly and respectfully lifted his trilby hat to me. *Old fashioned?* Maybe ... *but so nice.*

New shoes

W orking in an office was very different to attending secretarial college and I soon realized that I had a great deal to learn before I could really call myself a *Secretary*. I was growing up rapidly now, from a young schoolgirl into a budding career woman, and it took me quite a while to adjust to this transformation.

I also realized that I had hardly any suitable *office* clothes to wear. In fact, I only possessed one smart skirt from when I was thirteen, plus a pretty red wool suit and a pair of low-heeled shoes that I'd worn to my cousin Youla's wedding when I was fourteen. Thankfully, they all still fitted me perfectly, nearly five years later, including the shoes.

My first salary was the princely sum of £13 per week which, after paying tax, buying daily snacks and train fares up to London, plus a donation to Mum, left me with just a few pounds. This definitely wasn't enough to buy myself any new clothes or shoes, even though a brand new *mini* dress only cost £3 from *Biba,* Kensington's most fashionable boutique.

So I decided to save what I could and then every three months, have a grand spending spree. In the meantime, with the help of my Mum's electric sewing machine, I enjoyed making my own clothes from fabric remnants bought cheaply from Harvey's, our local department store in Guildford. I even managed to make a lovely matching skirt and waistcoat, with pretty tortoiseshell coloured buttons, from some old brown velvet curtains we found in our attic.

I have to admit, even as a teenager, I have always loved *shoes. And handbags too.* They were definitely my weakness and I adored pausing to look longingly in the most expensive shoe shop windows and then admiringly at their wonderful handbag selections. Yes, now that I was working and earning some money, I wanted some for myself. My mind was made up and I was certain they were worth waiting for.

With this goal in mind, I kept on saving until at last, I had enough to buy myself a beautiful pair of fine leather shoes and a little later on, an exquisite matching leather handbag. This to me, as a newly-fledged and fashion-conscious young lady, was the height of sophistication and the ultimate in luxury.

At last, after three months, when I'd saved as much as I could, I headed straight for the enormous Drapery Department in John Lewis, my favourite department store in

London's famous Oxford Street. Here, I could easily spend all day pouring over endless rolls of beautiful dress fabrics of every texture, hue and shade. I was in my element and would slowly and carefully make my way around the countless rows of fabrics, affectionately examining each roll, whilst imagining how best to turn it into a beautiful garment.

I studied dress patterns too and particularly loved the challenge of using Vogue Original Designs which, although very difficult and intricate, taught me a great deal and many useful techniques. This may seem very boring to some, but to me, it was pure joy as I carefully picked fabrics, zips, buttons and buckles to suit my dress patterns, which I had so lovingly chosen.

My next stop was just around the corner into Bond Street. Here, I treasured every single footstep, as my eyes danced from one enticing shop window to another. The profusion of fashionable clothes and incredible shoes took my breath away and many of the shops were so exclusive, that I hardly even dared look into their windows ... the prices were unbelievably exorbitant.

One of these shops was Elliot's Shoes, with its stunning twin display windows wrapping around a stylish carpeted entrance. I hovered at the open doorway, not sure whether to enter. I felt rather intimidated wearing my old and badly scuffed shoes, but I knew exactly what I wanted. I wanted a lovely new pair of *red leather shoes* with chisel toes, curved Louis heels and a bow across the toe, to match the pretty red suit I wore to my cousin's wedding.

It took all my courage to cross that threshold and, as I did so, I gasped in awe at the array of splendid footwear. *Oh, what to choose?* Each individual shoe was a work of art, beautifully made from the finest leather and in gorgeous shades. Surely, this must be where Cinderella's slipper came from.

Standing wide-eyed, looking around me, I noticed that everyone else appeared so confident and at ease in these plush surroundings, amongst the Christian Dior and other haute couture shoes. Nervously, I tried to become inconspicuous, as I tiptoed around on the deep soft carpet in my shabby shoes until finally, I was sympathetically ushered upstairs, to where the *cheaper shoes* were on display.

As I mounted the curved staircase to the upper floor, I felt like a fly in a spider's web. I wanted to see upstairs, but I was acutely aware too, that it would be far harder to just disappear back to the safety of the street below.

Cautiously, I sat down on a spare seat and anxiously waited for an assistant, all of whom were really busy serving the other customers. As I looked around me, I was amazed at the number of people who appeared to be quite at ease buying these very expensive shoes. It obviously wasn't a special occasion for them, as it was for me. Then suddenly, it was my turn and I whispered, *"I want a pair of **red** shoes please."*

Apparently red wasn't the *'in'* colour and it caused a bit of a dilemma for the young female assistant. But I was determined ... *they just had to be **red**.*

Finally, the harassed assistant passed me over to another who, hopefully, could manage to find me a pair of size 4, *red* shoes amongst the thousands of boxes of different shoes in their large stockroom. It was like looking for a needle in a haystack. But I wasn't in a hurry. I'd been waiting a long time for these shoes and I wasn't about to give up hope. And my determination paid off. *Success!*

My new assistant approached me smiling confidently. In his outstretched hands, he held the most beautiful, the most exquisite, the most incredible pair of *red leather shoes.*

Bending down, he took one red shoe and gently placed it on my raised foot ... *it fitted perfectly.* I felt just like Cinderella. Was this dashing young salesman, who I'd just met so unexpectedly, destined to be my Prince Charming?

Chapter 8

Last echo of Youth

For the last few years, my boyfriend Robin and I had become very close, enjoying each other's company immensely and we went everywhere together. However, when I left secretarial college and took my first job, our friendship became tested. I had plenty of free time now, but he was still at school, studying long and hard for his A'Levels. I also knew that he planned to go to university and would, very soon, be going away from home for the next three years which, to me, *seemed an absolute eternity.*

As the time drew nearer for him to leave for university, far away in northern England, we both became very upset. It was as if we knew our childhood was ending and everything was about to change. But we wanted to cling onto it, to the very last moment, until it inevitably slipped away, forever. My dearest friend was gone, far away from me and how I missed him.

Simultaneously, our whole childhood group of friends broke up, each going their own way, whether to university or

71

college, or beginning a first job or apprenticeship. Not one was left. Suddenly, everyone had gone.

I was so very alone and during these unwelcome times of quiet solitude, I reminisced over our happy and carefree but all too short teenage years. Light-hearted fun and laughter, long energetic bike rides, friendly tennis matches and Sunday afternoons huddled around a friend's radio, eagerly listening to the week's Top 40 pop hits.

I fondly remembered the many hours spent visiting each other's homes when we chatted, listened to records and tried out the latest dances ... the Shake, the Twist and the Loco-Motion. Then, on warm summer evenings, we often gathered to play French Cricket. And the excited cries of a fielder could be heard whilst rescuing the ball from a neighbour's garden.

Yes, such happy, innocent young laughter. What joy we'd shared together. What fun we'd had. But alas, it was time for us all to grow up and move on. Nothing stands still. It seemed *the last echo of our youth* had sounded and faded away, never to be relived except in our memories. And yet, what wonderful memories they were.

But for now, there was only silence. All my friends had wordlessly disappeared. Gone away. A great gulf of emptiness swept over me, as I experienced my first ever taste of loneliness, and even a glimpse of despair.

Me at 19

It was during this contemplative period, that my Mum decided it was time for me to learn something new. *Learn how to drive a car.*

72

Driving lessons

My younger sister had already passed her driving test long before I even started taking my lessons, but I'd never had any desire to learn. In fact, I had no interest at all. The real truth be known, I was terrified.   Mum had to literally drag me to my Saturday morning driving lessons, while turning a blind ear to my woeful pleading and protesting against taking them.

As we neared the test centre in Guildford, my hands broke out into a sweat, my heart pounded and I dreaded the very thought of it. My driving instructor must have been exceptionally patient and kind, because he never got cross with me and finally, *after loads and loads of lessons*, he delightedly exclaimed, *"You've got it!"*

Believe it or not, my parents paid for my driving lessons with their *Embassy cigarette coupons.* They must have continued smoking just to pay for them!

However, after much perseverance, in varying degrees from *all* of us, I finally overcame my fear and passed my driving test first time. As you can imagine, my parents were exceptionally relieved. And me? I was totally overjoyed.

Over the years, I have been repeatedly grateful to my mother for her dogged determination in helping me to overcome my fear and for literally forcing me to learn how to drive. It's hard to imagine now, how I would ever have managed without this skill. So I will forever say, *"Thank you Mum, for not giving up on me."*

Some super jobs

After spending a few years working in Westminster, and then back home in Guildford, I decided it was time to return to London. It certainly wasn't the long train journey I missed, but I did miss the buzz of a vibrant city and being amongst so many different people, interesting places and fashionable shops.

I missed seeing imposing and historic architecture, monuments and fountains, and the famous red double-decker buses from which you soon learnt to nimbly jump on and off the staging platform, as they slowed down through the busy London streets. I'm referring, of course, to the now iconic buses, with their BIG steering wheels and noisy engines.

Thankfully, with my good qualifications and after several years of valuable office experience, I became at last, a competent Secretary/PA and enjoyed some really super jobs. I would like to tell you about *two of my favourites*.

The first, was as Secretary/PA to Jean Toogood, the Chief Editor of the prestigious *Brides and Setting Up Home* glossy bridal magazine at Vogue House, in Hanover Square. This is where the famous magazines of *Vogue* and *House & Garden* were also produced. I learnt a great deal working for Jean and every day was exciting and fun, but extremely hard work too, and I often voluntarily worked overtime to keep on top of the workload.

But for me, a particular joy was seeing glamorous top models like Maudie James and famous photographers like Lord Snowdon and Norman Parkinson, walking around the offices preparing for a photo-shoot.

Then one day, Jean invited *me* to do some modelling and I jumped at it. It was for an article promoting '*The best wedding gifts*' and I was photographed seated beside my groom (a male model) surrounded by household items and electrical gadgets. Then another time, I was photographed in a luxury beauty salon for an article recommending different facial treatments for a bride before her wedding day. *This was such a special treat.* And how I enjoyed myself.

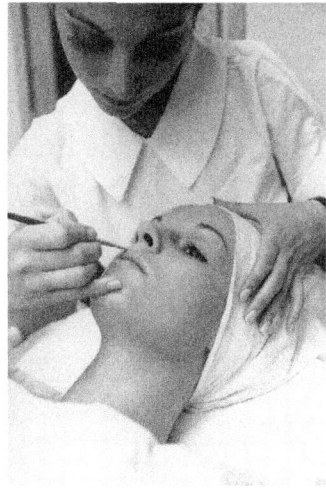

Modelling   Facial treatment

However, because jobs at *Vogue House* were like gold dust and it was considered such a *privilege* to work for these magazines, the salaries tended to be on the low side, including mine, at just £17 per week. So eventually, when Jean, whom I really liked and respected decided to retire, I felt it was time for me to move on too.

This led to my second favourite job as Secretary/PA to Doreen Cooper, the Public Relations Officer for *Estee Lauder Cosmetics,* in their elegant and very swish offices in

Grosvenor Street. In *my* day, there were less than twenty staff working in these luxurious offices and I felt so fortunate to be one of them.   Plus, to my added amazement, my salary increased by almost *fifty* per cent.

Within these fashionable offices and under Estee Lauder's umbrella, was the now famous *'Clinique'* skin care and cosmetic range of products which, at the time, was in its infancy.   Gaining rapid success too, was the gentlemen's *'Aramis After Shave'* range of products.   But what really excited me, was the in-house *Training School* for Estee Lauder's beauty consultants.   When Doreen offered me the chance to be trained too, I was really thrilled.   Without any doubt, this was *the icing on the cake.*   So during the week, I worked for Doreen as her Secretary/PA and then on Saturdays, as often as I could, I worked as an Estee Lauder beauty consultant in all the large West End stores.   It was fantastic and I loved every single minute of it.

I was also delighted and very privileged to meet Estee Lauder *herself,* together with members of her family, when they arrived from America to visit their London headquarters. I was quietly in awe too, when I accompanied Doreen on several visits to Estee Lauder's personal and most prestigious London home. I was only twenty-two years old at the time and was mesmerized by it all. I thought it was so exciting.

When I look back on those days, I am so thankful that I really did experience *Estee Lauder Cosmetics* in their early stages when they first came to London because, during a visit to their Grosvenor Street premises in 2011 with my husband, they told me there were about *three hundred staff* in their offices now.

Chapter 9

Courting

I hadn't long been working in London before I met Michael. He was a dashing, handsome young man who worked in Elliot's Shoe Shop, in Bond Street. *Yes, you guessed correctly.* He was the smiling young man who placed the beautiful red shoe on my outstretched foot ... my very own Prince Charming.

You see, at the time of purchasing these shoes, I naively agreed to complete an official Customer Request form. When Michael saw my home address, he cheerily commented that he too lived near Guildford and, from our brief conversation, realized that we both knew some of the same friends. Elated at his unexpected friendliness, I went on my way, carefully carrying my prized new pair of red shoes.

When my next shopping spree came around, I returned to Elliot's. But on this occasion, I was a little less timid. After all, *I was nearly a regular customer.* Again, I knew what I was looking for. I wanted a pair of *cream* shoes this time, with the same chisel toes and Louis heels that were so fashionable at the time. With excitement and anticipation rising up inside me, I mounted the staircase and *there he was.* Beaming and radiant as he ably served his discerning customers.

Feeling suddenly very shy, I sat calming myself, waiting to be served. And yet, I couldn't help wondering, *"Will he remember me?"* To my pleasure, he recognized me immediately and I left Elliot's that day with a beautiful new pair of *cream* fine leather shoes ... *and a luncheon date.*

A new friendship

S o our friendship began. And over the following weeks, we met many times during our lunch breaks, which was always exciting and great fun. But I was feeling just a little guilty as I was still seeing my dear friend Robin, who was studying hard for his A'Level exams and Michael had a girlfriend too. Although we weren't doing anything 'wrong,' it was difficult for both of us and, after receiving a kind but sensible letter from Michael, we ended our untimely friendship.

"So was this the end of your friendship?" you may wonder. *"No it wasn't. It began again, quite unexpectedly."* Let me tell you how.

It was Saturday and a lovely mild Autumn day. Robin had already left for university to begin a fresh phase in his life and make new friends. Now, in my loneliness, my sister accompanied me for a few hours of shopping in Guildford. We were leisurely strolling along, chatting happily, when we paused to cross a street. A van drove towards us and the driver looked familiar. Yes, I'd seen that smile before. Then I realized it was Michael. To my sister's alarm, he pulled over, opened the passenger door and shouted *"Get in!"* So we did.

With hearts racing, we greeted each other and he kindly offered to take us into *Boxers,* Guildford's first *real coffee shop.* Flushed with excitement, my sister and I climbed the narrow stairs up to the popular first floor café, off Tunsgate. This was the place where fashionable young folk and students met, but had always been strictly *out of bounds* to me and my group of friends, as younger teenagers.   Now here I was, all grown up, and finally being taken to the place I'd always hoped to visit. This was fun and, before I knew it, we were sitting enjoying a bottle of Coke and an iced ring donut.

Sounds silly nowadays perhaps, but to go to *Boxers* back then and mix with the *trendy set,* was a real treat.   In fact, even a bottle of Coke was special in those days and eating a delicious donut was just bliss!

Of course, I was eagerly waiting to hear the 'all-important' news as to whether Michael was free from his girlfriend. And he was. But I wasn't expecting to learn that he had left Elliot's too, and was now working locally for a carpet and soft furnishings company. Then, as a further surprise, he invited me out that *same* evening to his friend's twenty-first birthday party. I gladly accepted.

Quite suddenly, my days of loneliness ended as Michael literally *exploded* into my dull, humdrum life. He was so different and I was easily wooed by his lively and fun-loving nature.

Very soon, he took me back to his home to meet his parents and grandmother, who lived together in a nice bungalow, only twelve miles away. And, as our relationship developed, I knew I had the difficult task of breaking this news to Robin, my dear friend.

It was a hard letter to write and I hated upsetting Robin, but in my youthful impatience for fun and pastures new, I just couldn't imagine waiting for three long years until he qualified and tried to get a job. I could only think of *now*. I was lonely and foolhardy and Michael was exciting, witty and made me laugh. And so began our courtship, in earnest.

Michael

My new boyfriend was tall, dark and handsome. Athletic and full of life, always laughing and cheerful. He was a strong swimmer and a keen cyclist and early on Sunday mornings, he loved competing in time-trials around Guildford, on his specialist racing bike.

Fishing was another one of his passions, even in the rain and sometimes all night. In the years to follow, I enjoyed going sea fishing with him too. He was also an excellent dancer, full of rhythm and proudly boasted that he had been a dancer on the popular TV pop programme, *Ready, Steady, Go!*

Michael was always very generous and amazingly romantic too. He loved having surprise presents for me, especially on Valentine's Day, when a beautiful arrangement of flowers would unexpectedly arrive on my office desk. Then one Valentine's Day, he stood waiting for me at Waterloo Station, totally unabashed amongst the rush hour crowds, holding a huge bouquet of flowers.

Michael proposed

To my delight, Michael proposed to me after only a few months together. But as the age of consent was still twenty-one, we felt it wiser to wait awhile before asking my parents for their permission to get officially engaged.

Then one evening, much later, we decided to approach my parents. As usual, they were both in the kitchen, where they routinely sat up high, *on top of the kitchen work surfaces,* taking a corner each, with their legs dangling. Unusual? Yes, but this was their nightly habit, sitting totally engrossed in their evening newspapers, doing the crossword puzzles.

Tentatively we entered, clasping the little jewel box containing the pretty sapphire and diamond engagement ring, a generous and kind gift from Michael's Grandmother. He took a deep breath, then courageously, but carefully and respectfully, delivered his request to my parents. But in our youthful excitement, we hadn't anticipated the ferocity of the sharp reply we received. Before my Dad could even respond or lower his newspaper, my Mum voiced her fiery protest, *"No! Certainly not! Wait a year."*

Mum's severity was quite a shock to us and we retreated hastily to the living room to recover. We were stunned and deeply hurt at her hostile rebuke, but we made a decision between us that we would obey my mother's wish and indeed wait another year. And that is what we did.

Sadly, my father didn't have a say in the matter. He never spoke to me about it or offered any advice as to whether he thought I was planning to marry the right person or whether he thought I was making the right decision to marry so young.

Instead, I faced the beginning of a very tense and difficult relationship with my mother as, unfortunately, a barrier had now formed between us. Sadly, this was a lengthy phase that caused us both much heartache and pain.

Unrest at home

For the next year or so, the relationship between my mother and I was often very strained, as she was really strict with me. I was now over eighteen years of age, working in London and yet had to be in at night by 9.30 p.m. and, if Michael and I went to a party at weekends, it was extended to only 11 p.m. Regrettably, I must have been a real handful, because I was often stubborn, argumentative and rebellious and didn't want to listen to my mother who, to me, felt like my enemy. It was a really difficult time for both of us.

I have often wondered if I would have calmed down and listened to my Dad, had he kindly taken me aside and had a good, sensible chat with me. But he never did. In fact, Dad never spoke to me or ever gave me any guidance about growing up, boyfriends or moral issues on how to behave. He left all of that to Mum and, moreover, never interfered or ever offered a word of advice, even during our long hours of travelling together. In hindsight, how I wish he had. I'm sure I would have listened to his gentle approach and loving fatherly concern, care *and wisdom*, had he offered it.

Although Dad and I had a deep loving respect for each other and travelled together each morning, we had never built up a close father-daughter relationship, where I felt I could confide in him or ask him for personal advice. Sadly, I never heard his words of wisdom. Words that I, as an inexperienced and vulnerable teenager, so dearly needed to hear. *Words that all young women need to hear.*

But to make matters worse ...

Like many young men, Michael enjoyed driving fast cars and his pride and joy was a white Sunbeam Alpine, a two-seater sports car with protruding tail fins. One evening, after having been to the cinema in Guildford, we were happily driving back to my home in East Horsley, feeling quite relaxed and carefree.

The cold, frosty wintery weather didn't concern us at all, as we sped along chatting. And anyway, we knew the road home like the back of our hands. However, in those days, there was a treacherous Black Spot hairpin bend along the route, responsible for many serious accidents.

Perhaps our chattering distracted Michael's attention from the road? Perhaps he was driving too fast? Perhaps he was just not taking enough care as we approached the deadly hairpin? Or did we hit black ice? All I know is that suddenly, we felt the car go out of control and *time seemed to stand still.* I felt no fear, just the certainty that we were going to crash. The tail end violently switched and swerved, as the little sports car skidded uncontrollably across the road and headed straight into an earthen bank, masking a very solid stone wall beneath.

The impact was so sharp, so ferocious, that the car's detachable hardtop roof was opened by the impact of our foreheads. I was knocked unconscious and didn't wake up until several hours later in Guildford Hospital. My face was a mess. My eyes were mere slits and I could barely see. Michael was acutely distressed, anxiously waiting at my bed-side for me to regain consciousness. He had been diagnosed with a fractured skull and some broken fingers in his left hand. Just before impact, he instinctively stretched out his left arm across me to prevent me from being catapulted through the windscreen, causing his fingers to be broken.

Amazingly, we had both survived. Besides considerable bruising, a few deep cuts and being stitched up here and there, we had no major injuries. A miracle indeed.

Thankfully, that Black Spot hairpin bend doesn't exist anymore and the road has long since been straightened out. But for our parents that night, it must have been a terrible shock and a dreadful worry. A worry that did little to improve the tension between us.

Another brush with death

Unfortunately, this wasn't to be my last visit to Guildford Hospital, for just a year later, I was back there again. But this time, it was definitely *my fault*. My own carelessness.

I had taken a new job to be nearer home and was working in an office beside Guildford's busy outer ring-road. In those days, there were no *'green man'* signals at traffic lights and where I had to cross, it was just a matter of weaving your way as carefully as possible through the *four* lanes of traffic.

Each morning, my bus dropped me off at the T-junction, leading on to the ring road, which meant crossing *two* sets of four lanes of traffic to get to my office. The first two lanes

84

were for cars slowing down as they approached the T-junction. The opposite two lanes were for cars speedily leaving the ring road, heading towards the town centre. In the morning rush hour, the lanes were full of people intent on getting to work on time and so it was a truly hazardous exercise crossing over.

Every morning, I faced this daily torment and although I was very careful, keeping watch on all four lanes, one morning I just wasn't careful enough. As I entered the first lane of waiting cars, I didn't notice a car creeping up on my right, in the second lane. Checking that the oncoming two lanes were clear, I stepped out to run across the road, *but alas, I was hit.*

I was thrown off my feet and landed on my back before rolling over in the road. I never saw the car coming and when I regained consciousness, I was lying with my warm cheek pressed against the cold, wet road.   Opening my eyes, all I could see was wet black asphalt, barely an inch away.

I felt confused, *"Whatever had happened?"* Pain was searing through my body. I couldn't move. Then I heard voices, as ambulance men gently picked me up and carried me to safety.

I spent a whole week in Guildford Hospital before Dr. Myers would allow me home to recuperate. My right hip had been severely bruised and my back badly wrenched but quite amazingly, *for the second time*, no bones were broken. Again, I was on the road to recovery. Miraculously, I had survived yet another accident without any serious injuries.

"And my guardian angels?" Oh, I seemed to be in the habit of keeping them busy, protecting me.

Thankfully, when I returned to work, my considerate and caring elderly boss, who had been deeply distressed over my accident, insisted on meeting me off the train at Guildford Station each morning and driving me safely and comfortably to our office. I was very grateful for his kindness.

Was it the stress?

Was it the underlying shock and stress from my two accidents? Was it the stress between my mother and I? Was it my fear and anxiety over Michael's fast and sometimes reckless driving? Or, perhaps, was what happened next, the combination of all three?

About six months after my accident, I decided to leave my job in Guildford and return to work in London. I had been offered the opportunity of a super new job as Secretary/PA to Jean Toogood, the Chief Editor of *Brides and Setting Up Home* glossy magazine, and I was excited about starting.

To my surprise, Jean and I shared the same office together and, at first, it seemed a little unnerving working side by side with my new boss, but I soon got used to it. Her desk was beside the upper floor window, with fine views down over Hanover Square, and I sat near the doorway. In front of us, was a half glazed wall, giving us both full view of the main editorial office, where the other magazine staff worked.

It was my very first day at this new job and I was feeling nervous. One by one, I was introduced to the other editors and staff responsible for creating different articles for the magazine, all under the leadership of Jean Toogood. The office, as always, was a hive of activity, with telephones ringing, photographers and models coming in and out, arrangements being made for photo-shoots, photographs being chosen for the next issue, articles to be written, as well as constant deadlines to be met.

I quickly warmed to this exciting atmosphere and enjoyed the busy pace of my new surroundings. Settling down at my desk, I began trying out my new typewriter while, at the same time, keeping an eye on the hustle and bustle going on around me. I instinctively knew it was going to be fun working here, but I also became increasingly aware that I was not feeling my best. For some annoying reason, I had a nagging tummy ache that just wouldn't go away. Something was amiss.

The next day, my tummy ache was even more severe. By the end of the third day, I left my desk and literally dragged myself along the streets. I was almost reduced to crawling along the pavement to the tube station. I was in absolute *agony*. Before leaving work, I had telephoned Michael to ask him to meet me off the train at Cobham and take me straight to Dr. Myer's surgery. To my great relief, he was waiting for me on the platform and, as I stepped off the train, I collapsed into his arms, in unbearable pain.

Without hesitating, Dr. Myers sent me straight away to Guildford Hospital. *Here we go again. I was becoming quite a regular visitor.*

All the following week, the doctors thought I had inflammation of the ovaries because my pain was so intense, and so low in my body. They put me through lots of different tests and gave me pain killers to ease my suffering. But the agony persisted, baffling all the doctors. They just couldn't seem to diagnose what was wrong with me.

In total exasperation, Dr. Myers suddenly had an inspiration and confidently announced, *"Test for a gastric ulcer!"* And he was right. Immediately, I was taken off all painkillers and given boiled fish to eat. He was so pleased with his correct diagnosis and delighted that he could now accurately help me, to ease my crippling pain. As I look back on this incident, I can't help wondering whether it was *'Divine inspiration'* that Dr. Myers received that day.

I was off work for a whole month and yet, incredibly, Jean Toogood kept my job open for me. This was a great blessing and, to my surprise, my period of illness proved to be an unexpected blessing too. For, during those first three days working for *Brides & Setting Up Home* magazine, everything had seemed so new to me and the work totally different. To be honest, I quickly began to feel overwhelmed, under-qualified and unable to cope. This was, after all, the first time I'd really been treated as a *Personal Assistant*, with corresponding responsibilities. Jean had daily stretched my capabilities to the limit, by passing over from her desk to mine work that I had never ever handled before.

However, during my month-long convalescence, I was able to mentally prepare myself for this unfamiliar and challenging workload. With the result that when I returned, I slid back into my new role with no problems at all. As the Bible very encouragingly tells us, **"All things work together for good."** (Romans Chapter 8 : verse 28 KJV).

Meanwhile, Dr. Myers continued to keep a close eye on me, making sure I kept to my strict diet. I was very careful what I ate and just one year later, when I returned for medical tests, there was barely any sign remaining of my ulcer. Brilliant news indeed.

Night-time Prayers

I t was during this difficult period with my Mum and challenging time at my new job, that I began talking to God before sleeping each night. As I lay in bed, I chatted away to Him and even asked Him questions. But I can't ever remember asking Him the one vital question that I needed to ask at that stage in my life ... *"Should I marry Michael?"*

Of course, God knew the answer to this question and what was best for me ... *if I had asked it.* But regrettably, I didn't. I never did ask God for His opinion.   You see, I have found out since then, that in His graciousness, He will never force us to do anything against our will. God has given each one of us *a free will* to make decisions and choices and He knew full well that my heart was firmly set on marrying Michael. Even if He had spoken to me, would I have had the ears to hear, or the heart to obey? I somehow doubt it, as my mind was made up.

Now, in hindsight, I have learnt through my own failings and weaknesses that God is, after all, our loving Heavenly Father who cares about each one of us and knows *everything* about us. We can hide *nothing* from Him, however hard we may try.

Hence, I would sincerely recommend that if you, dear Reader, are on the threshold of marriage, that you **pray first** and genuinely ask God this vitally important question, *"Should I marry ... him or her?"* If you are in any doubt at all or even the slightest bit uncertain, then STOP. Please don't marry that person while there is any shred of concern in your mind and heart.

Marriage is a BIG decision and you must be 100% certain and totally at peace about it. It is so important to make sure you are planning to marry the right person ... the lifetime partner that Almighty God has chosen for you.

And yet, I can honestly say that throughout our two and a half year courtship, Michael was always loving and kind, very romantic and always fun to be with. But as I look back now, I can clearly see the warning signs which were there at the time. Signs I either chose to ignore or chose to forgive. As the saying goes, *"Love is blind"* and that's so true.

Never did I ever suspect though, just how much Michael would change the minute we were married. But sadly, I changed too. I stopped praying each night to my Heavenly Father.

Chapter 10

The Ultimatum

L ife at home was difficult for both Michael and me. For me, it was my rebellion and antagonism with my mother and for Michael, it was *nowhere to sleep.* When we first met, his Grandmother was living with his parents in their two bedroomed bungalow, but after she died, his parents slept in separate bedrooms which still left no room for Michael.

Remarkably, he'd persevered by sleeping in a small, slatted wooden tool shed down in their garden, but with another summer drawing to a close, he understandably flatly refused to spend a third winter in this damp and cold *hut.* His clothes were now becoming musty and mildewy and walking up and down through the garden to the bathroom in all weathers was no fun.

It was obvious he needed somewhere else to live *and soon,* but I hadn't expected the serious ultimatum he presented to me ... *"Either we get married in three months' time, or I won't marry you at all!"*

This ultimatum was certainly a great shock to both my parents and me, especially as Michael and I hadn't any savings between us. Neither of us earned very much money and even if we did manage to have a few spare pounds after paying for necessities, it was usually spent on going out and having fun. What was I to do?

I'd always had one great desire, one ambition throughout my childhood and that was to be an Air Hostess. I'd always dreamt of flying from an early age and even spent my pocket money on buying model airplane kits. But all the Airlines had very strict rules in those days and you had to be over twenty-one and *unmarried* to apply. I knew that if I married Michael now, as he wanted, I would lose my one chance of becoming an Air Hostess.

But I loved Michael and didn't want to lose him. With no-one to sit me down and bring me to my senses, a wedding date was arranged, just a few months before my twenty-first birthday. What I was unable to see, was that this was not a mutually discussed and planned decision but was, in fact, a threat and I was stupidly allowing myself to be bullied. Yes, I was so foolish. I actually kidded myself that Michael was being *romantic.* We'd never talked about *when* we would marry and, as I'd already waited two years for this moment, how could I refuse? I even thought it was exciting and fun. How very blind I was.

A church wedding?

I know this may sound somewhat hypocritical, but I had always dreamt of having a beautiful church wedding, in a picturesque olde worlde village church, to the wonderful sound of church bells. In England, whenever you heard church bells, you knew a bride was due to arrive for her wedding and, to this day, I still love listening to the peal of bells. However, there was only one question that could hinder this dream, *"Was I Christened?"* I didn't know the answer.

I began asking my parents this important question, but they kept avoiding me. Then one day, whilst standing opposite my Dad on the tube train, I plucked up the courage to ask him point blank, *"Dad, am I Christened, or not?"* As his soft, kind brown eyes met mine, he paused as he noticed the searching and hopeful expression in mine. Then honestly, and very gently, he replied, *"No, you're not."* My huge disappointment must have shown in my face, because Dad looked so sad. It was as though he felt he'd let me down.

My disappointment was so great, that I even considered attending our village church, even if it meant going by myself, with the sole intention of being Christened. I so wanted a church wedding.

Sadly, I was soon forced to accept that any efforts on my part would be pointless because, one evening, Michael told me that he wasn't Christened either. And worse still, that he was *an atheist.* In my foolishness, this didn't concern me at all when, in truth, it should have set off even more alarm bells. It should have caused me to stop and think carefully, *"What sort of man is this, that I am planning to marry and expecting to spend the rest of my life with?"*

At this point, however, his confession seemed a minor detail. I was too upset to care and it didn't really matter to me at all. All I knew was that my romantic vision of a church wedding, pealing bells and wearing a lovely long flowing

93

wedding dress had been crushed. If I was to marry Michael, there was no other choice but to accept a Register Office wedding, where it was customary to wear a short dress, with no chance at all of hearing the joyful peal of bells. This was so far removed from my hopes, dreams and expectations.

So, at only twenty years of age, my ambitions of becoming an Air Hostess and having a beautiful church wedding vanished. My dreams of these things just disappeared.

Wedding preparations

With only three months to go to the Big Day, our household was in a constant buzz of activity. And like any other bride-to-be, I was happy and exuberant about my forthcoming wedding and thought of little else.

Thankfully, my Mum and I had at last overcome all our differences and were getting on really well now. She was enthusiastic too and lovingly helped me plan my wedding outfits, from my stunning knee-length white crepe wedding dress adorned with a beautiful *Paris House* crystal and white china bead necklace and matching earrings, to a beautiful black, calf-length coat with a deep furry collar and matching hat, for my going-away outfit. My parents really did spoil me and I was so excited and eager to wear my lovely wedding outfits, hoping that my new husband would be impressed and delighted too.

Our Wedding Day

Our wedding day finally arrived and Michael and I were married in Guildford Register Office one bright, crisp, late November morning in 1969. The weather was sunny and glorious, but freezing cold. Then, to everyone's amazement, it began to snow. By the time we reached our reception, the sparkling white snowflakes lay more than two inches deep.

My parents had planned a brilliant reception for us, held in a warm and cosy olde worlde restaurant, with lovely oak beams and leaded light windows. It looked even more perfect and picturesque against the winter wonderland outside.

I was really thrilled to greet all my aunts, uncles and cousins who had made the very long journey from northern England to come to our wedding and it was such a marvellous family reunion. Everyone was so happy and enjoying themselves and the wedding buffet that my Dad had personally planned, was absolutely splendid.

Later in the evening, my parents generously hosted an excellent gourmet dinner for everyone at *Thatchers,* a renowned local restaurant and we all had a grand time. In fact, we were enjoying ourselves so much, I hardly wanted to leave them. But finally, the time came to change into my going-away outfit and say a very fond farewell to our parents, friends and relations.

I was so very thankful to my parents for all they'd done for us and for their devotion, extreme effort and loving care. I was aware too, that they'd made a huge financial sacrifice to give us such a perfect and joyful wedding day and in my heart, I never stopped praising them ... *"Thank you Mum and Dad, for your loving kindness and immense generosity. I really appreciate it. And I love you both."*

Husband and Wife

So, with our Wedding Day celebrations drawing to a close, Michael and I drove slowly away, with the romantic, snow covered countryside shimmering in our headlights. We left behind us our beloved family and now set off together for our short honeymoon in London, as *husband and wife.*

It had been such a wonderful day and everything had gone so smoothly. I couldn't feel any happier, sitting beside my new husband, wearing my brand new going-away outfit with its lovely soft warm collar and matching hat, together with my smart new boots *and* matching handbag. *I felt like a million dollars.* In my euphoric state of blissful happiness, we made our way carefully along the quiet, snowy roads towards London. We were a pair of newly-weds, off on our honeymoon and I was bubbling over with joy. Everything just seemed so perfect.

But oh, how unprepared I was for what my ears were about to hear. How totally unprepared I was for my deliriously happy world to suddenly come to an abrupt standstill. How unsuspecting I was, when I received the *first* shock from my new husband. Very coldly, he turned to me, and in a contemptuous tone of voice, breathed, *"I hate that outfit. Don't ever wear it again."*

His callous words hung in the air, before shooting like savage arrows into my heart, piercing deeper and deeper, shattering my joy. *How could he be* so *cruel? This was our wedding night.* Where was his love for me? Where was his kindness and compassion? How could he be so brutal and unfeeling?   His words hurt me more than I can possibly express.   Inwardly, I silently wept.

Married life

E ven though I forgave Michael for his cruel words on our wedding evening, I have to admit that I found the reality of married life far tougher than I imagined. It was not a bit like the romantic fantasy I had thought it would be, with my new husband giving me big hugs and whispering sweet nothings in my ear. I suppose I had no idea just how spoilt and molly coddled I'd been all my life, until I found ourselves shivering in front of a tiny gas fire in a dingy bedsit, with a shared bathroom and a damp kitchen with water running down the walls. *"A bargain,"* we were assured, *"at only £6 per week."*

It was a poor start to married life and we found ourselves arguing and disagreeing almost every evening when we came home from work. Our kitchen was dismal and freezing cold and when we did try cooking, we had to keep our coats on. Finally, we decided to eat out in a cheap local café where we could get a big plateful of spaghetti bolognese for just fifty pence.

However, within three weeks, we both had bad colds from our icy, damp living conditions and gladly welcomed my parents' kind invitation to stay with them over Christmas. We really did appreciate being in warm, dry rooms and having good food to eat again.

Thankfully, we soon left our damp, first lodgings behind us. But still, all we could afford near London were bedsits, often living out of just one room. This new lifestyle took a lot of adjusting to, and even though Mum and I hadn't always seen eye to eye in the past, I missed my parents very much. I missed not having a nice, clean warm home to come back to and hot wholesome meals waiting for me when I got home from a long day at work. Instead, there were just bills and chores. I had no choice now, *I just had to learn how to cook.*

During our first two years of marriage, we must have moved about a dozen times. In those days, there were no deposits required and we just gave one week's notice, and off we went again. This was really unsettling though and I longed to find a place that we could call 'home', where we could stay a while. But just as we settled into one place, Michael would move us on again. He was constantly restless and wouldn't stay anywhere for long.

Michael was the same with our cars, always changing them for one reason or another. He also had the habit of constantly getting speeding fines which we couldn't pay and my parents often bailed us out. He just didn't learn and even after being charged with dangerous and reckless driving, which cost him his licence for a year, he still didn't calm down.

Fines, debts and bills accrued and before long we were struggling to survive. Michael took out one loan after another, each time for a greater amount, with the express purpose of repaying the previous one. And so it went on and on. He became increasingly highly strung and temperamental and, in the end, his doctor put him on valium. In reality, *I think it was I myself who needed the valium most,* to calm my tattered nerves.

Chapter 11

A new Job prospect

We'd been married for just over two years when, one evening, Michael arrived home brimming over with excitement. He could hardly wait to tell me about a *new* job prospect he'd read about in the London Evening Standard newspaper. *So what's NEW about that?* I thought casually, as I busied myself making our dinner. He was always looking for something *new.* Anything from a home to a job, a car to a racing bicycle, or even a new fishing rod. So what could be so *special* this time?

Michael's extrovert personality and the gift of the gab suited his varied sales career perfectly. His lively mind, together with his sense of fun, was always looking for new challenges, and I quickly perceived he was preparing me for another. But nothing could have prepared me for what he was about to tell me. Something that literally shook the boots off me and left me dumbfounded.

He proceeded to tell me about this advert for a new job as a *Trainee Croupier.* I immediately quipped, *"Whatever's that?"* And when he told me more, I gasped, *"Surely, you can't be serious!"* I can tell you, this caught my full attention and dinner just had to wait. I didn't even know what a *Croupier* was, but I felt sure I was about to find out.

It was *Casino* work.   Roulette tables and the like.   As Michael continued to unravel his startling news to me, I became more and more stunned.   For, without saying a word to me, he had *already* applied for this job, *already* been for an interview and was *already* due to begin his training course in just two days' time. I was nearly paralyzed with shock. *"Whatever was he thinking of?"* For this was *night-time* work and it meant he would be working throughout the night and I would be working throughout the day. I couldn't think of anything more terrible and I could barely take it in.

I was currently working for Estee Lauder Cosmetics in their Grosvenor Street office and I adored my job. I was so happy there, enjoying every day and I didn't want to move. This news threw me into complete and utter turmoil. I could hardly think straight and didn't know if I was coming or going. My poor parents were alarmed. Doreen, my kind boss was alarmed. *Everyone was alarmed.* Except Michael.

Michael loved this new job

However, six weeks later, when my husband finished his daytime training course, he began working as a *Trainee Croupier* in Ladbrokes' Golden Nugget Casino in Shaftesbury Avenue, off Piccadilly Circus, in London's busy West End.

Like all trainees, he spent the first few weeks working the afternoon shift to help acclimatize to his new job and surroundings, before moving to the night-time shift which began around 7.30 p.m. and finished around 5.30 a.m., with his two days off usually being mid-week.

From the very start, Michael loved this new job with its challenging lifestyle. He simply thrived on the vibrant buzz, tension, noise and atmosphere of *chance* all around him. He adored the constant fast pace, working amongst so many other young people and the socializing after work. The thrill of gambling was soon in his blood. In fact, there was nothing he *didn't* like about it.

On the other hand, I felt my life had crashed all around me. Our lives were now poles apart and we barely ever saw each other. Michael had already begun making a new life for himself and enthusiastically socialized with the other croupiers. *"So how on earth could our marriage survive?"* It looked an impossible situation to me.

As time passed, I saw that Michael became even more addicted to his new job and had never been happier. I loved my job too, so what was I to do? I knew a decision had to be made, and quickly too, as our lives were getting out of control. But there were only two choices. My job or my marriage. Which was it to be? It seemed I couldn't have both.

After what felt like weeks of agonizing, I finally made the painful decision to leave Estee Lauder Cosmetics, the job I adored so much, and join my husband in the *casino business.*

What on earth?

I t was only when my six-week course began in the training centre at the Golden Nugget Casino, that it

101

dawned on me just how difficult this was going to be. I had never been very mathematically minded and this job was going to test me to my utter limits. As part of the course, I had to learn lots of difficult multiplication tables such as the 17 and 35 times tables, but up to 20 times each and all at the *snap* of a finger. *Snap! Snap! Snap!* What is 17 x 19? And what is 35 x 13? Quick now!

I had to learn by heart lots of other multiplication combinations too, or what we called *picture bets* and then be able to mentally add them all up together. *Snap, snap, snap!* No pen and paper or calculators were allowed. It was OK for Michael. He had a sharp, calculator-type brain and it was easy for him. But for me, it was a living nightmare.

But the mental torment didn't let up. In fact, it increased. To my horror, I found out that it was possible for just *one customer* to place such a high quantity of chips (small round, coloured plastic discs) on a number that, if it won, their winning payout often totalled around 500 or 1,000 chips, or even more.

"How could I begin to add up all of this in my head?" But worse still, there could be two or three additional people on the *same* winning number ... all at the same time. Oh help! This was far too much for me. *"What on earth had I got myself into?"*

When one of these nightmare situations confronted me, with winning bets so huge that I could barely add them up, it didn't take rocket science to quickly realize that this was definitely *not my idea of fun.*

Ambidextrous

I had to learn to become ambidextrous too. *Why?* Because there are *two* types of Roulette tables. Right-handed and left-handed tables, and you have to learn to work on both. I had to become ambidextrous in order to spin the ball and handle the chips with both my hands.

I had to learn how to hold a stack of 20 chips in *each* hand, *cut down* a stack into smaller quantities by *feel,* and then be able to push the full stacks, or combinations of full and part stacks, across the green baize covered tables with *either* hand, without the stacks collapsing on the way to the customer.

Another real problem

In my early days, I suffered with another *real* dilemma. I had a problem spinning the ball with either hand. No, I'm not kidding. The more I tried, the more difficult it seemed. The harder I concentrated, the more I failed. The ball just wouldn't go where it was supposed to go and it either fell into the centre of the revolving wheel or worse still, *it shot out like a cannonball across the room!* Strange isn't it, how this absurd situation resembled the embarrassing memories I had of my school days' Obstacle Race.

But my bosses didn't see the funny side and nearly gave up on me. They warned me several times that if I couldn't spin the ball properly, I may lose my job. So, although this incident appeared humorous and gave some light relief, I was under pressure to succeed.

Inside a casino

I had never been inside a casino before and I had never wanted to be. But now, I didn't really know what to expect, except I got a huge shock when I first saw how *massive* the place was. It was hard to believe that here I was, standing on the floor of the famous Golden Nugget Casino. Not to be entertained, but to work.

Apprehensively, I looked around me at the new and foreign world that I was about to enter. A world that concealed a hive of humanity all hell-bent on gambling. All waiting and hoping for that one *big* winning bet that they believed would change their lives and their fortunes. A bet that seldom ever came.

As I gazed through the cloud of cigarette smoke hovering over hundreds of bent heads, all intent on chancing their luck, I could see across the floor of the casino. There were more than twenty Roulette tables, a long row of Blackjack tables and, coming from the far side of the floor, I could hear excited shouts rising from the two Craps tables.

To me, it was not at all exciting or stimulating. It was nothing more than a horrible gambling *factory. And worse still, I was now a part of it.* It didn't seem to matter which day of the week it was, or whether it was 2 p.m. at opening time or 4 a.m. at closing time, there were always customers crowding around each Roulette table. Often, they were two or three deep, crazily pushing and shoving with their arms outstretched, anxious to place their bets. But now, the time had come at last, to put my training into practice and face this demanding and unrelenting public, whose sole aim was to win as much money as possible.

But first, let me explain

T he customers, or *punters* as we called them, didn't play with real money but with coloured chips. These chips were small round plastic discs and the minimum value for one chip was only 12.5p in those days. At the head of the table, where the croupier stood, the coloured chips were all lined up in neat stacks of 20's, beside the Roulette wheel. There were ten stacks of each colour, which amounted to a total of 2,000 chips. And, to avoid confusion between the customers, they were each given a different colour.

So, if you can possibly imagine, it was possible to have well over one thousand different coloured chips circulating on just *one* Roulette table, at any time. But only one croupier to pick them all up and put them back into *straight* and *neat* columns of 20's. That croupier was now *me.*

Mistakes were sure to happen

I t was certainly a daunting prospect being a novice croupier, facing a mass of experienced gamblers who knew the ropes. They were fully aware that a trainee was more likely to make mistakes, and every mistake gave them the opportunity to claim for bets they had never placed. In their eyes, it was *justifiable winnings.* But in the trainee's eyes, it was *unjust winnings,* gained by outright lying. There was nothing you could do about it, except to learn quickly and make fewer and fewer mistakes.

Often, when punters noticed a new trainee, they would crowd around that table like vultures, almost *willing* the nervous new employee to make a mistake. It was very

intimidating to say the least. But however hard a trainee concentrated, mistakes were sure to happen.

Let the action begin

A s a novice, I often felt totally lost and even desperate
at times, as I stood behind my Roulette table, waiting
to spin the ball. I would look down the long table before me,
and watch the punters placing their bets on the numbers
printed on the felt baize surface.

Then, as soon as I'd successfully spun the ball, *the action
began.* They all clamoured to put down their chips and often
totally smothered the numbers to such an extent, that not
even a scrap of the lines separating each number was visible.
Meanwhile, my hands went into overdrive, working like crazy
picking up and stacking hundreds and hundreds of chips from
the last spin, ready to pay out again as winnings.

Thankfully, there were usually one or two relief croupiers
dashing from table to table, frantically helping where they
could to clear the massive backload. It was such an encouragement to see one of them rush to your table and rapidly
reduce the mountain of chips, which often threatened to
overspill onto the floor. Should there ever be a shortage of
staff due to sickness or holidays, no-one could be spared to
help in this way, and we all suffered as we struggled to keep
up with the ever increasing demand.

With experience, I learnt that the harder and faster I could
spin that ball, the more time it gave me to catch up. But it also
gave the punters more time to place their bets and, in the

blink of an eye, my table resembled the Manhattan skyline. It was a never ending battle.

One huge hazard

You might ask, *"Could BIG mistakes ever happen?"* Oh *yes* they could, and they *did!*

There was *one huge hazard.* In fact, it was the worst possible mistake of all. A mistake that every inexperienced croupier faced, including myself. You see, a number that is *near* you on a right-handed table, is *away* from you on a left-handed table, so you always needed to be fully alert and keep your wits about you. But this was particularly hazardous for the inexperienced who, after working on a *right*-handed table, returned from a short tea break to work on a *left*-handed table where the numbers were printed in *reverse.*

I was always *listening*. Listening to the hum of the ball spinning around the wheel and listening for punters' requests to place an out-of-reach bet for them, whilst still trying to pick up and stack as many chips as I could. Then, all too soon, the humming sound softened as the ball slowed down, and it was time to call out, *"No more bets!"*

Rapidly, the ball would drop down from the rim of the wheel and rattle around the base before settling into zero or one of the thirty-six alternately coloured red and black slots. Fleetingly, there was a moment's hush as looks of hopeful anticipation came upon the punters' faces, while they waited for me to announce the winning number.

Then, very carefully, I would begin to push away all the losing bets from around the winning number. With my hands arched to form a scoop, I would firmly sweep the huge quantity of losing bets away to the rear of the table, to join the hundreds of other chips still needing to be sorted and stacked. This was certainly good physical exercise, as it meant stretching and leaning down the long table countless times every night.

But alas, with just one quick momentary lapse of concentration, usually caused by exhaustion, when the losing chips were finally cleared away, the *wrong winning number was revealed. What a disaster!*

Oh, you can't imagine what utter desperation fills your heart when this happens and I assure you it does, because I did it *more* than once. Horror upon horrors overwhelms you as *every* punter within an arm's reach of your table, claims to have had a winning bet. And they know you can't prove otherwise. How easy it was for a weary and nervous novice to clear away the losing chips from around the *wrong* winning number.

Michael was in his element again

Ladbrokes never allowed husbands and wives to work together in the same casino. So when my training ended, Michael was transferred to the Hertford Club. This was a much smaller, quieter casino situated in Hertford Street, beside the Hilton Hotel in Park Lane and often frequented by aristocracy. It was plush by comparison to the Golden Nugget and, to Michael's delight, he was chosen to be a trainee Punto Banco dealer, handling large amounts of money from wealthy customers. He was in his element again and, after work, he excitedly told me about the famous people he'd met that night, including the mysterious Lord Lucan. It was certainly a world apart from the masses I faced every evening.

There was no getting away from it, I just wasn't enjoying the *casino experience* the way Michael was. I didn't have his enthusiasm and every single night was an ordeal, like facing a dreaded exam. It was both mentally horrific and physically exhausting and I honestly thought I'd never make it. But gradually, my brain started to respond and I became faster, stronger and more experienced.

Yes, I persevered and eventually became quite confident as a croupier, *but I hated it.* I lost a lot of weight and went down to only seven and a half stone. I was so thin, that my ribs were sticking out of my back. I also suffered with dreadful nightmares. I had horrible dreams of hundreds of outstretched arms and hands closing in all around me and I'd wake up in a fearful panic. I had, afterall, only agreed to become a croupier to keep our marriage together. Never had I realized it was going to be so difficult and so very tough. I went through nine long months of mental torture, until I knew emphatically, that I just had to get out of that place.

I'd had enough

I was never sorry when 4 a.m. came round and the casino doors were closed to the public. But, unfortunately, that wasn't the end of my night. The cash deposited in the safes beneath every Roulette table during the previous fourteen hours of gambling, had to be counted by each croupier. That meant I had to wait *on guard* by my table for nearly one and a half hours until the Floor Managers systematically worked their way round every table.

It was during one of these marathon waiting sessions that I began chatting to a friendly casino waitress. She'd been serving light refreshments all evening to the punters, and now she was busy cleaning up their mess. You see, there weren't any *no smoking* restrictions in those days and nearly all of the customers smoked. The tables needed cleaning from overflowing ash trays, and dirty cups and saucers had to be collected. The place could be in quite a mess by the end of the night.

But it was now after 4 a.m. and the frantic frenzy of gamblers had all left, many only to return at 2 p.m. the next day when the doors reopened. But for me, it was another night over, and I could begin to unwind.

As I prepared for the customary long wait to *close* my table, knowing I still had another hour or more to go, I suddenly felt envious of this waitress, who would soon be going off home. I watched her as she deftly cleaned the spilled ash off the baize on my table, and in a moment of spontaneity, I dared to ask her how much she earned. With a big smile and without pausing, she quipped, *"Twice as much as you luv!"* Well, you could have knocked me down with a feather. Her bold words kept ringing in my ears and wouldn't go away. Yes, it was definitely time to get out of this awful place. *I'd had more than enough.*

Chapter 12

Time to try something New

S urprisingly, it wasn't working nights I found hard to adjust to, just *gambling.* The trick was not to sleep too late, so there was time to go out in the afternoons. Then, after our two days off, we didn't return until the evening of the third day, which was great. Very gradually, I found myself settling into this new lifestyle, except for one thing. I *hated* being a croupier in the Golden Nugget Casino. It was definitely time to try something *new.*

However, it was several months later before I stepped through the doors of the elite Casanova Club in Grosvenor Street. A Club that apparently Princess Margaret had once adored visiting in her younger days. As I was shown around, it was hard not to be impressed by the beautifully decorated interior, the plush furnishings and the deep soft carpeting.

I had been mistaken to think all casinos were like the Golden Nugget, with Roulette tables stretching as far as the eye could see. Because here, in these elegant surroundings, there were only a few Roulette and Blackjack tables, plus one Craps and one Punto Banco table. But more wonderfully,

111

there were no pushing crowds, no overflowing ashtrays and clouds of smoke, no shouting and jostling, just *quietness* and a welcoming calm. It was like stepping into a different world. A world I was liking better by the minute.

Unexpected surprise

As my interview progressed, I learnt that female croupiers *only worked in the afternoons* and male croupiers worked at night. I momentarily felt a tinge of disappointment when I heard this. But my concerns were short-lived, when I was offered two choices.

First, if I wanted to remain a croupier, I would have to work in the afternoons. But secondly, if I accepted a *waitressing* position, I could work at night. This certainly was an unexpected surprise and remembering my conversation with the friendly waitress at the Golden Nugget, it was not a difficult choice to make.

So, just one week later, I found myself wearing a very elegant full-length, halter-neck, navy evening dress and enjoying the quiet, salubrious atmosphere of the Casanova Club. I can't express what a relief it was to leave the hectic pace of the Golden Nugget behind me. It was an even greater relief to say, *"good-bye"* to my nightmare croupier days. It had certainly been an experience, but one I didn't miss even a tiny little bit.

Now each evening, I could arrive for work with no more fears of mental worries, no more torment, no more intimidation, no more heaving crowds pushing and shoving around me, no more late nights. It was like being on holiday and surprise, surprise ... *I enjoyed being a waitress!*

Don't spill the tea

B eing a waitress was not as easy as I thought and serving the well-to-do was quite nerve-wracking at first. Cups and saucers would rattle in my hands as I nervously bent down to place them on low tables beside each customer, while being overly conscious *not* to tip over the remaining items on my tray. As I gained more confidence, I learnt how to carry trays heavily laden with cups, saucers and refreshments and, at the same time, deftly carry and place down a coffee table *without spilling a drop of tea.* Good! I was definitely improving.

Having achieved this basic skill, I then learnt how to memorize more than one order at a time, which made me quicker. I soon found out that the quicker I could serve a customer, the better the tip. But I also learnt from watching the other waitresses the art of *timing.* A customer could get very agitated if you interrupted him while he was placing his bets. I had to learn to watch for the *gap* between the bets to have any hope of getting a good tip, and *that* was important.

My heart missed a beat

S ome evenings were more exciting and memorable than others, notably when famous people arrived. One evening, I spotted Roger Moore (007 James Bond) chatting to the Casino Manager. They were sitting a distance away from the gambling tables and relaxing in soft comfortable chairs. I was delighted when they asked me to bring

113

them some light refreshments, but I had difficulty controlling my nervous and trembling hands.

Count Basie, the great jazz pianist and band leader, became quite a regular visitor and I looked forward to seeing him. He was always cheerful and friendly, and to me, he seemed a nice man. He usually arrived very late, in the small hours of the morning when the casino was very quiet. He was then able to relax and play Blackjack in peace, with no-one bothering him.

But it was when Ty Hardin arrived one evening that my heart flipped and missed a beat. (Remember *Bronco Lane* from my childhood days?) I went all weak at the knees and felt like a young girl again, gazing adoringly up into his incredibly handsome face. To my great joy, he visited several times and even once came into our kitchen for a chat. I can tell you, trying to carry my tray without spilling the tea for the rest of that evening was nearly impossible! But I'm delighted to have had the privilege and pleasure of serving them all.

Poker

However, there was one thing at the Casanova Club that was not so pleasurable. In fact, I hated it. It was when it was my turn to patiently sit on duty in the private 'high stakes' *Poker Room.*

The atmosphere in this room was so tense, that you hardly dared breath, and often I would have to sit silently for hours. Usually, it was only when the men had finished playing poker for the night, that they would request some refreshments.

I didn't have any interest in the game but to me, playing poker seemed like *real gambling,* so reminiscent of the old-time western movies. And believe it or not, one of the poker players was called *Maverick.*

Small change

M ost young people were attracted to the casino business solely for the money they could earn, and *greed for money* was always nipping at our heels.

In the early 1970's, Arab princes were frequent visitors to London and some of them loved gambling. Often, a group of Arab men and their friends would come into the Casanova Club, and I had to learn how to respectfully serve these wealthy visitors.

But alas, I also began looking forward to receiving fabulous tips after serving them soft drinks and sandwiches and there was one evening in particular, that I shall always remember. It was when an Arab gentleman took a handful of his *small change* and put it on my tray as a tip. This *small change* was a mixture of £1, £5 and £25 chips, totalling *over* £300. *Wow!* This was a small fortune in the early 70's.

The evil of greed

B ut receiving tips like this could become intoxicating and lead to *greed, horrible greed.* And I humbly admit that I became prey to this entirely selfish and wrong mentality. Always wanting *more.* Sadly, without even realizing it, I was becoming seduced by this lust for money. I found myself wanting to work longer hours *just in case* the Arabs came in and I could make some extra bucks. You see, all the waitresses kept their *own* tips at the Casanova Club which, unfortunately, only encouraged greediness and selfishness. So instead of working *with* the other waitresses, I worked *in competition* to them. Bit by bit, I fell under this evil, creating disharmony with the other girls.

Thankfully, my female boss was both astute and kind, and pointed out my shortfall. I was truly sorry and repentant to the other waitresses over my selfish behaviour and wonderfully, they were all very understanding and forgiving.

I was deeply ashamed and horrified how easily I had fallen into this 'sin.' This *same sinful greed* that I had seen and so despised in many of the punters at the Golden Nugget Casino. Yes, this was definitely a humiliating experience to go through, but it proved to be a very valuable lesson. Afterwards, peace reigned again and the other waitresses and I all worked happily together, as true friends and in unity with one another.

Humbling experience

T hrough this humbling experience, I learnt that *greed of any kind,* whether for success, power or fame, but especially for money, is always detestable. Now that I had encountered this ugliness in my own life, I never wanted to get caught in it again. My eyes had been opened and I was thankful that I'd learnt a very big and important lesson in life. A lesson I hoped, I would never have to repeat.

Nevertheless, I still hated seeing so many customers caught in this vice of avarice and the story of one of them comes to mind. He was a dignified, polite and well-groomed gentleman when I first met him and he owned a successful chain of shoe shops. But over several months, as his gambling success dwindled, he became a sad and lost man. I don't know what happened to him in the end, but it really upset me to see this once cheery, happy and bright man reduced to a broken, hapless figure, slouched despondently over a Blackjack table. Sadly, I saw many others like him. Some of them lost everything.

Time to move on

A fter working in the Casanova Club for nearly a year, I felt it was time to move on and gladly accepted a rare vacancy for a casino waitress in the Hertford Club, where Michael worked. This presented the opportunity for him to move on too, as we weren't allowed to work together.

To his delight, he was promoted to Cyril Stein's premier casino, The Ladbroke Club.   Here, he completed his training and became an experienced and adept Punto Banco 'baccarat' croupier, perfecting his exuberant flair of handling the long wooden palette, when dealing to incredibly wealthy customers. If you have ever been an avid fan of the 007 films, as I was, this was James Bond's favourite casino game.

The Hertford Club

I found the Hertford Club quite a different kettle of fish to the Casanova Club.   It was busy most of the time and I had to work *really* hard and know what I was doing. How very grateful I was that I had gained my basic waitressing experience in the quiet and peaceful surroundings of the

Casanova Club. The Hertford Club was no place for trainees. It was back to serious hard graft, but then I was working for Ladbrokes again. In all fairness though, Ladbrokes were good and generous employers under the Chairmanship of Cyril Stein, and neither Michael or I ever had any complaints.

"So what was so different?"

Well, primarily, there was no-one in our small kitchen to help us make the masses of sandwiches we served each evening or do the mountain of washing-up. First, I had to learn how to competently make and attractively present sandwiches at *breakneck speed* in our small kitchen. Then, confidently use the *hissing* and steaming boiling water taps to make tea and coffee. I was shown how to correctly snip the ends off cigars and display an opened packet of cigarettes. And, as well as this, help with the washing-up.

But that wasn't all. I also had to be incredibly fit and not get out of breath running up and down the *straight flight of twenty-five steps* from the casino floor up to our kitchen, *whilst carrying a heavy tray, laden to the ceiling.* One night, it was so hectic, I lost over 2 lb. in weight running up and down those stairs. And yet, even though it was so physically and mentally demanding, *anything seemed easy after the Golden Nugget.*

But it would have been impossible to work this hard and climb all those stairs in an elegant long evening dress and instead, I was given a sexy coral red, skin tight, halter-neck top and trousers to wear. Oh my! If Mum had seen me, I don't think she would have approved.

A great team

There were only five of us. Three waitresses and two valets and yet we all managed to take our two days off each week. But should one of us be ill or on holiday, the rest of us had to stand in, by working double shifts from 2 p.m. till 4 a.m. which was unbelievably exhausting. Several times, I had to work up to two weeks like this, without a day off. Yes, it was incredibly hard work, but enjoyable too. We made a great team, always willing to help and support each other. And at the end of each week, we *shared* our tips.

Who ordered what

Thanks to my intense croupier training, my memory was now like a computer. While I whisked around the casino floor emptying ashtrays and collecting dirty cups and saucers, customers would stop me and give me their orders for tea, coffee, juice, sandwiches, cigarettes and cigars. More often than not, I held up to seven or eight different and complicated orders in my mind, *without writing anything down.* Amazingly, I never ever made a mistake or forgot anything and always managed to remember *who* ordered *what.*

Crazy days indeed

The Arab visitors continued to cause quite a stir in all the London casinos, spending fabulous amounts of money. One of these visitors was the Saudi arms dealer Adnan Kashougi, who played French Roulette at the Hertford Club. He often arrived with an entourage of pretty girls.

Similar to the private Poker Room at the Casanova Club, I would patiently wait in attendance while Kashougi and his friends enjoyed playing French Roulette in *their private room.* Often, I would have to wait many hours for their requests for refreshments, which could range from freshly squeezed orange juice, bowls of fresh fruit salad, to hot steak toasted sandwiches and often, even a whole crispy salted duck.

These special orders meant racing down many flights of back stairs to the large main kitchens in the basement to get the food as fast as I could. But it was definitely worth the effort because quite amazingly, I always received a £100 chip for looking after him and his party of friends.

However, it soon appeared that I was his favourite waitress, because if one of the others served him, they never got a tip.   So even on my day off, if Kashougi was due in, a member of our team would frantically ring me and tell me that *I must hurry into work.* Once, when a button fell off his suit jacket, he gave me a £100 chip for sewing it back on. *These were crazy days indeed!*

So just how much was £100 worth back in 1974? Well, according to 'Measuringworth,' it is equivalent to £1,300 today. So you can understand *why* my team was so anxious for me to come back to work, even if it was my day off.

Nightly bombings

During this period, in the early to mid-1970's, the IRA was very active in London, causing widespread fear. As a nightly precaution, Michael and I always checked under our car before getting into it, just in case a bomb had been planted underneath. Sometimes, as we drove home through the quiet London streets, we would pass another building that had been a bomb victim.

Then one evening, there was a car bomb placed in the street *right outside the Hertford Club* where I was working. I can still remember walking across the casino floor when it went off. There was a mighty blast that seemed to shake the whole building. Immediately, intense shock waves vibrated upwards into the first floor. Everyone stood paralysed in fear. These jarring waves continued right up through the soles of my feet and into my body. The explosion was so loud and so sudden, that it took all my strength not to burst into tears.

Fortunately, and thank God, we were later informed that the true impact of the blast had been thwarted, due to the fact that *the detonator had been put in upside down.* If not, I feel sure that everyone in the building that night would not have survived and I wouldn't be writing this book now.

Only later that evening, when everyone had calmed down, did we all realize what a narrow escape we'd had. The busy first-floor casino had huge floor-to-ceiling windows extending the full width of the building, facing right out on to Hertford Street. If that bomb had exploded the way the perpetrators expected, those windows would have shattered into millions of daggers and surely killed and maimed most of us, including customers. It was too horrible to imagine.

Very sadly, a little later, two of Ladbrokes' croupiers did lose their lives in the Hilton Hotel bombing on 5th September 1975, while waiting to meet a friend in the hotel lobby.

But thankfully, the bombing has stopped altogether now, even in Northern Ireland. Truly, thank God, those days are over.

Chapter 13

Samoyed puppies

A fter moving from home to home countless times, Michael and I finally managed to rent a large and comfortable mansion flat in Maida Vale, north London. It was really enjoyable choosing some stylish and ultra modern new furniture and, at last, we had a lovely home. This flat was such a blessing, especially as it was only a stone's throw away from the West End and Park Lane, where we both worked. This meant that after a long and tiring night, we could be home quickly and easily.

Now that we had a secure and spacious home, we decided to get ourselves two adorable fluffy white Samoyed puppies. A male we called *Neige* (French for *snow)* and his sister we named *Blanche* (French for *white*). They were the cutest little pups ever and we had such fun watching them playfully scampering about, rolling and tussling with each other and then turning their adorable smiling faces up at us. We both loved animals and these little pups brought us such joy.

Although we had a third floor flat, we thankfully had a spacious metal balcony off our large kitchen-diner, which

123

proved invaluable when house-training them. As they grew, Michael began the habit of throwing them our potato peelings and cabbage stalks and, to our amazement, they loved them all. And so this became a permanent habit, that always met with their approval.

It was a real delight having these puppies and I would daily walk them in the park right behind our block of flats, which was so convenient. But there was a little boy who loved our puppies too. He had seen me walking them and almost every day after school, he would come up to our flat and ask permission to walk them. He was such a lovely, polite little boy and as I got to know him better, I became quite fond of him. His name was Leon.

Many fun times together

Michael and I enjoyed many fun times together during these hectic *casino* years, when we earned plenty of money. But there's a saying, *"Easy come, easy go!"* and in our case, it was true. All our cash literally flowed through our fingers as we enjoyed eating out at good restaurants and buying lovely new clothes. Also, as often as possible, we loved escaping the rat race by spending a few days walking the quiet Blakeney and Cley peninsula beaches in Norfolk, or staying with my dear cousin Derek and his lovely wife Maggie and five lively children, at their home in Huntingdonshire.

At other times, we would visit our parents in Surrey, or stay a night with my dearest friend Yolanda and her husband in their beautiful period cottage in Hertfordshire. We always enjoyed going for wonderful country walks with them and their two gigantic Irish Wolfhounds, who dwarfed our pair of Samoyeds.

E-type Jaguar

Michael had a relentless passion for fast cars and now, at last, he could afford to buy one. I mean a *good* one. But the trouble was, he was restless and kept changing them. Over the years, we'd owned an Alfa Romeo Giulia Spider convertible, a Triumph Herald and the more powerful 6-cylinder Vitesse convertible, a throaty V8 Sunbeam Tiger, a Rover TC 2000 and a highly tuned Jaguar 340 that, at one point, was stolen from us and used as a *getaway car* for a robbery.

We'd also had an original Mini Cooper S, an MGB and a red Midget sports car that had belonged to the wife of the popular radio DJ Tony Blackburn, plus a stunning Jensen Interceptor that my Mum enjoyed taking for a test drive.

In truth, it was not unknown for Michael to leave home in one car and arrive back in another. But there was only one car that I really loved and it was *a pristine navy blue, 2+2 E-type Jaguar with cream leather interior.* Yes, it was *awesome.* Fantastic. Fabulous. So *very* beautiful and *I loved it.*

But one day, to my absolute horror, *without saying a word to me,* he traded it in for an American speed machine. *A Shelby Cobra Jet Mach 1.* My heart broke as he proudly showed me this beast of a machine and my mourning for the loss of our beautiful E-type went totally unnoticed. This throaty, gurgling, powerful *cobra* monster may have been *a man's dream car* (and probably still is) but it was certainly not mine. I felt hurt and disappointed, even angry.

A maternal plight

During our engagement, Michael had told me he didn't want any children. But neither did I at the time, as I was petrified of childbirth, so this didn't present a problem. But now, when we'd been married for nearly five years, I was surprised when my feelings unexpectedly changed. Suddenly, and with strong emotions, I really wanted to start a family.

Even though I'd never been very maternal as a child, usually preferring to climb trees or dig for flints rather than play with dolls and prams, I suddenly found myself acutely *wanting a baby.* It was as if my whole being was crying out for a child. It was an all-consuming desire that overwhelmed my emotions and I couldn't walk past a woman with a young child without yearning for a baby of my own.

My feelings and longings had changed but alas, Michael's hadn't. He totally refused to understand my maternal feelings and became really angry, threatening to leave me if I ever became pregnant. To press his point, he took a job away from home for three months until, as he put it, *"I got over it."*

This whole heartbreaking experience was extremely painful and I was left with little choice but to control my natural instincts and indeed, *get over it.* Nevertheless, it both saddened and shocked me seeing the dramatic and anta-gonistic way Michael had reacted. So much so, that I made a firm decision to never let myself get obsessed like this again and buried all thoughts and desires of starting a family.

Socializing

I only ever made *one good friend* while working in the casinos and she was Ladbrokes' very capable Casino Personnel Manageress. Her name was *Fran* and we got on really great together. Perhaps it was because I'd been a secretary, like her, and was more used to running an office than working in a casino. Her husband was a creative jewellery designer in London's famous Hatton Garden and they both became our dear friends. Sadly though, they later separated and divorced, but Fran and I remained close friends for many years.

Michael on the other hand, enjoyed every aspect of casino life, especially the socializing after work when he visited various clubs and restaurants. But unfortunately, this *fun* only encouraged his drinking habit more and more.

Our flat in Maida Vale was so convenient for our work, but now, it was proving almost too convenient. Every single working night, and I mean *every* night, Michael would collect me from my casino and then drive me back home. He'd drop me off at the entrance to our block of flats and then drive away to go socializing and drinking, returning home many hours later.

While he insisted on his nightly freedom, my enjoyment came from our lively Samoyed puppies, who always gave me a rapturous welcome when I arrived home. In return for their adoring affection, I loved walking them around our local streets that were blissfully quiet and peaceful in those early hours, just before dawn. And as the world was stirring to face a new day, I was going to bed.

So the *casino business* may sound exciting and fun, but the glam and glitz was only surface deep. While Michael thrived and revelled in his world, I just barely survived in mine.

And yet, bit by bit, almost without realizing it, I succumbed to the tantalizing temptations of the *casino lifestyle* with its deceptive glamour, heady pace and endless money. It was like quicksand that grabbed us both and drew us deeper and deeper, until we felt we couldn't get out.

Eaton Socon

At one point, however, we actually made an effort to escape this addiction and both returned to daytime jobs. We even moved away from London and bought a small modern, inner terraced house in Eaton Socon, a pretty village on the western boundary of Cambridgeshire. This was convenient for the A1 motorway whenever we travelled south to visit our family and friends, and yet was only half an hour or so away from my cousin Derek and his family.

I became a secretary again, working for the Chief Engineer of W.R. Grace & Co., but I found it difficult to enjoy working in a mechanical, noisy, factory atmosphere.

In addition, I hated the machine right outside our offices that tested the strength of massive plastic bags, the size of parachutes. This machine would noisily blow air into a *huge* plastic bag and as it grew bigger and bigger, expanding in size until it nearly reached the factory roof, I could feel myself tensing in anticipation, waiting for the alarming explosion as it finally burst. The noise was deafening and the sensation went right through you. It was really *horrible.*

I persevered for two months under this *daily* nervous assault but in the end, it was too much for me and I began looking for another office job. Yet there were not many options available and I ended up working for the Financial Manager of HRC (Huntingdon Research Centre) that carried out controversial tests and experiments on animals. Tests that really appalled me.

Although this job was quiet and peaceful and I had a nice office, it proved to be very monotonous. *All* day and *every* day, I typed up endless sheets of hand-written accounts figures onto huge, blank sheets of paper, using a long-carriage electric typewriter. This required a lot of patience and skill, to compose the numerous headings, with centred columns of figures beneath, stretching right across the page. It also necessitated complete concentration and 100% accuracy. But I didn't find this difficult, just tedious.

Little did I know at the time, that this job was giving me excellent experience and practice for a future job, in the coming years.

One of the joys of working *days* again, was that we loved entertaining and having friends round for a meal. This was definitely a challenge that put my cooking skills, or lack of them, to the test.

But to avoid a competition forming between us as to who could provide the best meal, I came up with the idea that each host should spend a maximum of £5 on the total meal, including refreshments. Everyone thought this was a good idea and it meant we could all meet more often.

Blanche

As our Samoyed puppies grew larger, we decided to keep just one of them. Neige was becoming too strong and boisterous and we thankfully found him a nice new home. But we kept Blanche, his adorable and very gentle sister. I suppose, if I'm really honest, she became my *baby substitute* and I really loved her.

She came to Eaton Socon with us and adored the freedom of running in the fields instead of walking around London streets. Children loved her too and often, when I arrived home from work, there was a group of eight or more children sitting on the grass verge outside our home, waiting to play with her. Very politely, they would file through our house into the small rear yard, eager to greet their enthusiastic friend. When a little later, I looked through our kitchen window to check up on all the children, they were gone. Not a child in sight. Then I looked again and realized *they had all squeezed inside Blanche's large kennel.* Oh! how she adored this attention.

But Blanche had some amusing habits too. She loved water, *any* water. She would think nothing of rolling her spotless, fluffy white coat in a deep muddy puddle or, while out walking along the river bank, exuberantly leap from the footpath into the nearby River Ouse, confidently swimming off midstream.

Then on one occasion, while we were visiting my cousin Derek and his wife Maggie, we left Blanche behind with them while we took some of their children out for a drive. When we arrived back several hours later, they told us Blanche kept barking and barking and, although they had tried giving her everything they could think of, they just couldn't understand what she wanted.

I guessed immediately and asked them, *"Did you peel any potatoes today?"* *"Yes we did,"* they replied.

To their amazement, I told them, *"Well, she was asking you for the peelings!"* Poor Blanche, if only she could have made them understand her.

Blanche had a passion for blackberries too. When I took her into the local fields to go blackberry picking with me, I had to be really quick, because she would dart forwards and bite the largest blackberries off the bushes before I could even get near them.

Blanche with me and a
Pyrenean Mountain Dog

She was more than a dog to me. She was my faithful companion who slept on the floor beside my bed every night, curled up on my dressing gown. She was totally trustworthy and would never turn on me, even if I took a bone out of her mouth. *She was the most beautiful dog I have ever had the privilege to love and look after.* And she brought so much happiness and joy into so many lives, including mine.

Chapter 14

The pain of Infidelity

And so I thought our rural life in Eaton Socon had settled down into a better and happier routine, far away from the noise and bustle of London. Sadly though, Michael didn't adjust so well. He continued his nightly habit of drinking and his endless love of fast cars, which soon stretched our reduced income to the limit. Before very long, we were faced with the reality of being in serious debt again.

Then came the news that every wife simply dreads. Michael arrived home from work one day and unashamedly confessed to having been unfaithful to me. Never having suspected anything amiss, I was totally unprepared for what he was telling me. Something every woman hopes she will never have to hear.

But, as he went into more detail about his affair, his words cruelly attacked my consciousness and I felt my insides crumple. I passed through recurrent emotions of shock, devastation, rejection and then hurt. Followed by deep pain. Yet, through all this agony, I can still remember trying to think clearly and not make any rash decisions. I still loved

132

him and didn't want our marriage to end. So I *chose* to forgive him. But it never occurred to me that he would do it again and again until eventually, I became accustomed to the tell-tale signs and knew even without him saying a word that once again, he was being unfaithful. And once again, I experienced the pain of infidelity.

Hook, line and sinker

I wanted to save our marriage and reached deep within myself to forgive Michael. I did all I could to make him happy and give our marriage another chance. But, with his unfaithfulness, flamboyant lifestyle and the fact that we were quickly falling into debt again, it was difficult to have hope.

You may wonder, *"How did Michael deal with this debt? Did he stop drinking, driving fast cars or get an extra job?"* No. Of course not.   He simply put an advert in The Times newspaper, under the 'Furniture for Sale' section and, before I knew what was happening, *he'd sold every scrap of our beautiful and expensive furniture.* He sold the lot for a song. We didn't even have a chair to sit on or a table to eat at. Nothing. It was all gone. *Crazy!*

My life was in shatters. I had an unfaithful husband. No furniture, a boring job and a mortgage to meet every month. However, I did have one joy left. *Blanche.* She was my faithful and loving friend and walking her for miles every day helped keep my sanity.

Then one day, out of the blue, our friend *Fran* rang and offered us our jobs back in the casinos in London. Well, the temptation to leave our dull and poorly paid jobs was too much. The lure of the casinos and receiving high incomes again succeeded in recapturing our hearts ... *hook, line and sinker!*

Michael enthusiastically returned to The Ladbroke Club as a Punto Banco dealer and I returned to The Hertford Club, as a waitress. And do you know what? Just one week later, I had earned enough money in tips to buy ourselves an old, but excellent E-type Jaguar. *What an amazing turn around.* We could now travel the one hundred and forty mile return journey from our home in Eaton Socon to the West End of London effortlessly and in comfort.

I had company

Yes, I had to admit it, I really enjoyed being back in the casino business as a waitress and being behind the wheel of an E-type again. Even the long drive to work each night didn't seem so bad. Michael drove into London and I drove out. Then one morning around 5 a.m., whilst driving back home on the motorway to Eaton Socon, I got a shock. Michael was fast asleep in the passenger seat by this time and I was enjoying a leisurely drive in our old E-type, keeping to a comfortable and steady 90 m.p.h.

At this time in the morning, in the mid-1970's, the motorway was quiet and peaceful with not another car in sight. Wonderful. Just the way I liked it. Then all of a sudden, *I had company.* A quick sideways glance revealed an unmarked police *sports* car, driving right alongside me. *"Oh help! Where on earth did that come from? I never saw it approaching."*

As we sped along at 90 m.p.h., our car windows parallel to each other and *so very close,* the police stuck to me like glue. But they didn't pull me over, *so I held my nerve and kept going. I didn't flinch or reduce my speed at all.   I kept my eyes on the road, not turning once to look at them.*

Quickly, I realized these two uniformed police officers in their powerful, highly tuned MGB GT V12 were having some sport with me, and enjoying it! They were testing my courage by staying right beside me.   But I was game too.   I never wavered, slowed down or turned to look at them.   In fact, I did my best to totally ignore them.   Then several miles later, with their fun over, they put the foot down and went speeding off into the distance.   *Oh!*   That was really close, *but a great victory too.*

Verbal bombardment

P reviously, when I'd worked in the Golden Nugget and Casanova Club, there was a definite *pecking order. "What do I mean?"*   Well, the Managers didn't mix with the croupiers, and the croupiers didn't mix with the waitresses. Each group had their *own* rest rooms.

But in the Hertford Club where I now worked, it was different.   Only the Managers remained separate and the rest of us all mingled together in the same large room.   Sometimes, a kindly lady came to cook us the most delicious Spanish omelettes.   You see, once you stepped inside the casino to begin your shift, you weren't allowed to go outside to get something to eat, even if you had to work a double shift from 2 p.m. in the afternoon right round the clock to 4 a.m. the next morning.   So I can tell you, a slice of hot tasty omelette was a very welcome treat. Our rest room was always busy, as it was customary for croupiers to stay no longer than one hour without a break at their tables, due to the intense concentration of their work. But waitresses, on the other hand, were expected to just keep going and grab a few minutes when and if they could.

It was always nice having others to chat to during a short break but, unfortunately, the men didn't mind their language in front of the girls. Gradually, with this constant verbal bombardment, I'm ashamed to admit that I picked up several of these ugly words. But I was quite unaware that one of them had a particularly offensive meaning. Then, a while later, Michael asked me if I understood what this word meant and when he told me it's meaning, I was mortified and never spoke it again.

I have since learnt a Bible verse that sums this up pretty well, *"Bad company corrupts good character"* (1 Corinthians Chapter 15 : verse 33). And how true this is. All of us are influenced by what we hear and see around us, especially children.

Deep emptiness

In many respects, the casino business was great fun, but the fun was only temporary and didn't bring lasting happiness or contentment. Just when our life should have been so enjoyable, I felt a *void,* a loneliness and a deep emptiness inside me, that nothing seemed to fill. Everything seemed so fanciful and superficial. I can still remember one Saturday in particular, when this *empty* feeling became a real burden and I didn't know what to do about it or how to make it go away. Michael had already gone out for the day and I was left alone. It was a lovely fine summer's day and I thought getting outside and visiting the picturesque village of Hampstead in North London would make me feel better, especially if I found some nice new summer clothes to buy.

Hampstead was one of my favourite places to visit and I just loved walking through the narrow streets and alleyways or slowly browsing round the interesting antique market. There were so many exciting chic boutiques in those days and it was easy to pass a few hours wondering around admiring all the beautiful clothes. But I never visited Hampstead without stopping to drool over the display of exquisite handmade cakes in the Louis Patisserie shop window and *surprise, surprise,* it's still there today. I know, because I went there at Christmastime in 2012 and indulged in a strawberry and chocolate delight. A memorable treat indeed, as it was my first visit to Hampstead in over thirty-five years. But back to *My Story ...*

Yes, it certainly was fun having the money to buy new clothes whenever I wanted and on this specific afternoon, I bought some fabulous new French outfits. And yet, when I arrived back home, I still had that gnawing *emptiness* inside me. I just couldn't understand it and was really disappointed that my lovely new purchases had made no difference to me at all. I had really believed that treating myself to some new summer clothes would make me feel better, make me feel happy, but it didn't. I felt just the same ... *empty.*

"So what was wrong?" It didn't seem to make any difference how many new clothes I had. Or how exciting or fashionable they were. Or how expensive they were or even what label they boasted. I still felt *empty.* Clothes, cars, eating out in fancy restaurants or weekends away couldn't and didn't fill the gaping hole within me. *"But what could?"* I had absolutely no idea. I had come to believe that money solved every problem and fulfilled every need and, to a great extent, this is true. So *why* then, did I feel this *empty* void inside me when at last, we had more money than ever before? I didn't know the answer, because *there didn't seem to be one.*

But there was an answer, a simple answer. An answer that didn't cost any money, an answer that was *free.* A timeless, unchanging answer that was the same then, as it is today. But I was blinded and just couldn't see it. My ears were blocked and I just couldn't hear it. My heart was hardened and I couldn't receive it. I was lost and so very ignorant of the fact that all I needed ... *was the love of JESUS CHRIST in my life.*

Only knowing JESUS would have filled this *empty void* inside me. Oh, how I wish I'd understood this. How I wish I'd understood the hidden, but true message of the popular Beatles' song, *"Money can't buy you love!"*

Sadly, I was strong willed and rebellious. Even whenever I heard the famous evangelist Billy Graham's voice on the radio, I immediately switched channels. I just didn't want to know the truth ... the truth that could, and would, have set me

138

free. *The truth that is just as powerful today and ever will be,* for all who will humble their hearts and dare to believe it. Dare to believe in Jesus. *For He alone is the only answer.* The answer I needed so badly. The answer I refused to accept.

How I wish I'd humbled my proud heart. And Michael too. It would have saved us so much pain. But Jesus was a complete stranger to me. I was so far away from the *only One* who could fill my empty heart with lasting peace and true happiness. The *only One* who could fill the gaping hole inside me with the *deep love* I was yearning for. A perfect, pure love that is so amazing, so divine and yet so kind, so gentle and totally understanding of all our needs.

Yet how could I possibly know this? No-one had ever told me the life-changing words, *"Jesus loves you!"* that I so dearly needed to hear. Oh how I wish I'd known the truth. The truth that, *"Jesus loves me. He always has. And He always will."*

Regrettably, it would be twenty more years before I would discover this truth. Imagine, *two whole decades* before I found the perfect love and true happiness, the wonderful inner peace and joy that I was longing for. A LOVE that I could depend upon and trust in, knowing it would never ever let me down. A LOVE that would give me the strength, courage and wisdom to face up to life's many trials and unknown challenges that lay ahead ... *a love greater than any pain!*

And that's why I'm writing this book. So that *you* won't have to go through *your* life, NOT knowing the truth. The truth that ...

"JESUS LOVES YOU!"

Chapter 15

Many changes in Store

I shall always remember the scorching hot summer of 1976 when I was twenty-seven years old. We experienced a heat wave that broke every known record for the last three hundred and fifty years. Temperatures rose to above 27ºC every day for weeks on end, with many days reaching in excess of 32ºC. It was the summer when my crop of green pepper plants shrivelled and died within a few hours and poor Blanche dug a tunnel right under our garden shed to get some relief from the unrelenting heat.

The heat was so tremendous, that one day while I was waiting for a bus into town, I had to resist crying out in agony as the sun's fierce rays seared my fair skin. It was a summer of unexpected personal surprises too, with *many changes in store.*

Promotion

Michael continued to revel in the casino business and his personal aim to become a Floor Manager was finally fulfilled during this memorable summer, when he

140

received the promotion he so coveted. A Management position awaited him, not in London where he expected, but in Ladbrokes' brand new and very plush Adelphi Casino in *Liverpool.*

Neither of us had ever been there before but for me, it symbolized the city that birthed The Beatles, Billy Fury and Cilla Black. Yet little did we anticipate that this move would hold changes for both of us, that neither of us had ever contemplated.

The first of these changes came rapidly when Michael began living in Liverpool, coming home only at weekends. He was away nearly all that summer preparing for the opening of this luxurious new casino, set in the lower ground floor of the grand and majestic Adelphi Hotel, in Liverpool's city centre.

As Michael was whisked off into a new life full of excitement and adventure, it meant changes for me too. Suddenly, I found myself left alone with no car and an impossible journey home at the end of a tiring night working in The Hertford Club. There just weren't any trains or buses running at 4.30 a.m. in the morning.

For several weeks I persevered, waiting hours for the first train back to Harpenden, a pretty village where we were living at the time, in a small rented house with an enclosed garden for Blanche.

Eventually, the long journey from Eaton Socon had become too strenuous for us and we had moved nearer to London. Happily, we now lived not far from my best friend Yolanda and her husband.

But I was totally wrecked at the end of each hectic evening, especially if it had been a double shift. This long wait for a train, followed by a bus ride home, was just too exhausting. It was time to make a decision. Time for a change. Time to work my very last night ever, as a casino waitress.

At 3 p.m. every day

And what *a complete change* this made. It turned my life around and before I knew it, I was working *days* again as a *temp secretary* at Alginate Industries, a London based company dealing in *seaweed.*

Truly, I enjoyed being back in an office again, except for one big problem. Re-adjusting my body clock. At 3 p.m. on the dot every afternoon, *I fell asleep.* My boss, and all the other secretaries in my office did everything they could to keep me awake. They tried standing me outside on the office balcony to get some fresh air, they sent me down to the local shop to buy everyone an ice cream, but *nothing* worked. At 3 p.m. every day, *I was fast asleep.*

Amazingly, no-one ever got cross with me and, in fact, it became an amusing daily challenge trying to keep me awake. Thankfully, I didn't need to sleep for long, just ten minutes or so, and then I was as bright as a button again.

Grand Opening Night

At last, Ladbrokes' new Adelphi Casino was nearly ready and I had to say *"good-bye"* to my kind and friendly companions at Alginate Industries, and make my first visit to Liverpool. And what a *buzz of excitement* met me.   It was a hive of activity as instructions were issued, last projects completed and not a detail overlooked in the final countdown for the Grand Opening Night. As an ex-Ladbrokes' employee, I was thrilled to be part of it all, especially when I was asked to be a member of the Welcoming Team, to host the invited guests.

Wow! This really was a glamorous and fun evening with everyone looking resplendent in their best bib and tucker. And, all around us, newspaper cameras flashed enthusiastically as *James Hunt,* the current Formula 1 Champion Racing Driver, arrived as the star guest.

Desperately homesick

However, once all this excitement had calmed down and life resumed its normal pace, I found permanently leaving London and all that was familiar to me really hard. In fact, I missed London more than I could ever have imagined. It was truly an amazing city back in the mid-1970's and for me, it was very special, with many fond memories.

It was vibrant, fashionable and bursting with excitement. I missed the chic boutiques, wonderful shoe shops and, of course, John Lewis for the amazing range and choice of dress fabrics. I missed Paris House too, for their incredible buttons and buckles. Yes, these shops and boutiques were where my dreams were made. *London was in my blood and I missed it, like missing a person.* That may sound peculiar to you, but it was true. I missed London dreadfully.

143

Nowadays, whenever I return for a fleeting visit, it has changed almost past recognition. The boutiques have long gone, the individuality has disappeared, the fun and headiness has vanished, and the *Englishness* forgotten. It has naturally become more populated and changed with the times but sadly, in my opinion, not always necessarily for the better.

It was also the first time I'd ever lived such a long distance away from my parents, who were still in East Horsley, and from my friend Yolanda. I missed them all so very much, and I was quickly becoming *desperately homesick.*

Our new home

There was, however, one great advantage in living away from London. And that was being able to buy ourselves a small detached house, just inside the Welsh border, with an enclosed garden for Blanche. We found that houses were a little cheaper in Wales and yet still convenient for Michael driving to Liverpool every evening.

As we settled into our new home, we faced another unexpected problem. A problem we'd never ever considered. We found out that the Adelphi Casino was the *only* casino in the surrounding area and, according to Ladbrokes' rules, I wasn't allowed to work with Michael in the same one. *"So what was I to do now?"* We were suddenly confronted with a change we had not contemplated.

Starting a family was still out of the question for Michael and not even negotiable, but I had to do something. *"But what?"* Having a permanent daytime job wasn't a good option, presenting obvious risks for our marriage, yet there appeared to be little other choice open to me. In fact, the more engrossed Michael became in his new job, together with his after-work socializing, the more I became homesick, un-settled and alienated. I even considered the possibility of returning to London.

Eventually, feeling very lonely, needing a job and being without a car, I began looking for secretarial vacancies near our home. I'd been so used to working in London where it was easy to get a good, well paid *temp* job, but I quickly found out that this was not the case here.

It was also customary in London to dress in your smartest clothes and look as presentable as possible for an interview. But I soon discovered too, that this custom was inappropriate and even a deterrent to getting a job, as I passed through one dismal and shabby office, one after another. Before very long, my enthusiasm waned, as interview after interview I was always told the same thing, *"You're too experienced and I'm sorry, we can't offer you a job."*

My endurance was being sorely tested as I became increasingly frustrated and returning to London looked more and more tempting by the day. I was teetering on the verge of doing just this, when I received word of another vacancy. I was feeling so discouraged by now, that it took all my resolve to even attend the interview. I didn't even bother to dress up and went in my mac and woolly hat. I'd made up my mind that if this job wasn't any good, I was returning to London, and that was that!

Well, what a surprise was waiting for me. I could hardly believe my eyes when I was politely ushered into large, ultra-modern, light and airy, open-plan offices. They were bright and colourful and beautifully decorated with up-to-the-minute equipment and the best electric *memory* long-carriage typewriter on the market. I was really impressed. It was as good, *if not better*, than anything I'd ever seen in London.

"So why hadn't this fantastic job been snapped up by now?" Well, I soon found out the answer. There was a snag, a big snag to most people. I was duly informed, *"At the end of each quarter, the accounts need to be typed."* But to me, this wasn't a problem. I was used to typing accounts. *"Oh, but they have to be typed after work in the evenings, working till 10.30 - 11 p.m. every night, for three weeks."* That wasn't a problem to me either, and so I got the job.

With these obstacles settled, it didn't take me long to adjust to my super new position as Secretary/PA to the Chairman of this multi-million pound company. After a while, I was given two junior secretaries to nurture and train as my assistants, to help me with my busy and heavy workload. As an added company bonus, each employee was given the opportunity of a free swimming session *every* day in the local ultra-modern sports arena, plus a weekly session in the fitness room. So, with no-one to rush home to, this was a very welcome after-work social activity. *And I really enjoyed it.*

A car of my own

There was only one thing missing now, I really needed *a car of my own*. I loved my new job and didn't mind working late to keep up with the workload, but waiting for the bus home, followed by a lengthy walk was tiring, especially during the winter months. Plus, at every quarter's end, when I worked till very late, buses were non-existent and

I had to take a taxi home. There was no doubt in my mind, a car of my own was the answer. So the search began.

My dear friend Yolanda's skilled and very talented husband worked with cars and, one day, she rang to say they'd found me the perfect one ... *a tiny, bright yellow Honda N360. A little gem.* And better still, it only cost £400, which I could repay by monthly instalments. I was absolutely thrilled and said *"Yes!"* immediately, without even seeing it. To me, it was the most beautiful and perfect little car and I was so proud of it.

But this wasn't the end of my surprises. Shortly afterwards, I received *a huge annual pay rise.* A pay rise that *covered* my monthly car payments. How amazing was that? So at last, I had a car of my own and was enjoying life to the full again.

Michael was enjoying his life too as a Floor Manager in the Adelphi Casino, although it meant we hardly ever saw each other. When we did, we liked taking Blanche for long walks through the forests around Nannerch, high in the Welsh hills. I loved these forest walks, so reminescent of my childhood. And I loved the aroma too, of the magnificent tall fir trees which graced the steep hillsides, and never tired of the wonderful views of valleys beyond. It was here, in these wonderful peaceful surroundings, that gave us the time to relax together from the pace of our busy jobs.

As perfect as this all seemed, there was still a pervading menace which kept creeping between us. Michael continued his perpetual habit of going out drinking and never arriving home before I left for work in the morning. Then, by the time I got home in the evening, even if I didn't go swimming, he'd

147

already left. I had weekends off and he usually didn't. A serious rift was forming between us as he socialized with his casino friends. And so, naturally enough, after a while, I began to make some friends of my own. This was, of course, a potentially disastrous situation and indeed, our marriage was soon in serious trouble.

The more immune I became

N ow please remember, as you read on, that I'd already been through many years of silent suffering during our seven year marriage. Suffering caused by Michael's incessant drinking, infidelity, motoring offences with constant fines and loss of his licence, frivolous spending and endless debts. So now, living in these lonely conditions, so far from my family and friends, I humbly admit that I met someone else and unexpectedly fell in love. *I* was the one to be unfaithful now and commit adultery. *I* was the one to do wrong and sin.

I had never ever been unfaithful to Michael before. And I had never wanted to or intended to be at any time. So when this happened, it was totally unpremeditated and unplanned. It was the very last thing I imagined I would ever do or would happen. But it did. I had always loved Michael, even when he had hurt me so badly. I never wanted to hurt him or cause him any pain. But now, living in these prolonged difficult conditions, I found myself beginning to live a double life.

In the midst of this situation, I did my best to continue being a good wife to him and even enjoyed his company when we were together. And yet, I knew I was deceiving him behind his back, when he was away. I knew full well too, that my behaviour was dishonest and quite despicable. It's easy to look back now and feel disgusted at myself but, at the time, I was blinded *and welcomed the opportunity of receiving some love and friendship.*

Forbidden fruit may look tempting at the time, but it is forbidden because, in the long run, it only brings you even more pain. It doesn't bring you the happiness that you are longing and hoping for, *regardless of how your other half is behaving.* Wrong is wrong and the saying, *"Two wrongs DON'T make a right,"* is true.

Up to this point, I could honestly say that I'd never ever intentionally lied about anything in my whole life. But now, caught in this steely grip of deception and sin, and lying about my whereabouts to Michael when he was at work, became surprisingly easy. My conscience was hardly touched at all. In fact, I would even rationalize that some happiness and some love was my due. *"Why shouldn't I have some?"*

Yet the deeper involved I got, the more I lied and the more immune I became. How cunning Satan is. Before I knew it, the devil himself had me believing that what I was doing was OK, even justifiable. But I was being deceived and led astray by my own personal wrong desires and longings. I had become ensnared in a horrible web of deceit, lies and sin. *Yes sin.* That 'old fashioned' word so rarely used today, but still true, as I wilfully continued to commit adultery.

My own miserable failings

As I humbly recount my own miserable failings, I am reminded of how the Bible warns us ...

"Be self-controlled and alert.
Your enemy the devil (Satan) prowls around
like a roaring lion looking for someone to devour.
Resist him, standing firm in the faith."
(1 Peter 5:8)

You see, I didn't know *how* to resist the devil *or* stand firm in the faith, and anyway, *"What faith?"* I'd never knowingly heard the true gospel message of Jesus Christ. And Michael? Well, he was a confessed atheist. As I grew up, the subject of God, Jesus or faith was never mentioned in our home, and all our friends and family members seemed to be the same. If my parents possessed a Bible, I never saw it. I'd learnt some Bible stories and scripture verses at school and once had to learn the 23rd Psalm, but that was all. I suppose you could say we were a heathen lot.

So, having no firm Christian foundation to guide me and no firm faith to lean upon, I was very vulnerable and an easy prey for the devil to devour. And yet, when Michael and I first married, I firmly believed in the sanctity of marriage and that a wife should be submissive to her husband and obey him. I took this seriously, and I still do. I always made every effort to obey and give honour and respect to Michael even though very often, as you've read, he didn't deserve that respect. But these principles didn't help me or protect me when the devil came prowling around, knocking on my door with his cunning array of temptations. Nor did they prepare me for the rigours to come.

Finally, God must have been watching over me because my conscience began to kick in again. I knew what I was doing was very *wrong.* My irresponsible, egotistical and self-centred desire for *love, fun and happiness* ended in dis-illusionment and a deep conviction of guilt. Somewhere, from deep within me, I found I still had some love left for Michael and knew I wanted to save our marriage.

You may wonder, *"Was it really that easy to let go?"* and my answer was, *"No, it wasn't easy at all."* I left a man that I truly loved and there were times when I felt my heart would break. But knowing there could never have been a future for us, without causing even more pain, I knew I'd made the right decision. The right decision for *both* of us. Now, I needed to put my energies into strengthening and restoring my own marriage. A marriage that I felt was still worth fighting for. And my lover, in this affair, needed to do the same.

"Any regrets?" None, because it was the *right* thing to do. And when you do the *right* thing, you'll never regret it, however costly. Living a dishonest life of deceit and lies does *not* bring you the peace and happiness we all long for. I found this out. The Bible tells us, *"There is no peace for the wicked,"* (Isaiah 48:22 NASB). Inner peace and a clear conscience is what we all need and search for. *It is priceless.*

My parents came to visit us

I t was during this really difficult period that my parents made the long journey north to visit us. How wonder-ful it was to see them again.

Then one evening during their stay, Mum seemed very agitated and asked to speak to me alone. I took her upstairs to our bedroom and, as we sat together on the bed, Mum began to cry. I'd never seen her upset like this before and I became anxious. *"Whatever was the matter? Was she or Dad ill?"*

My dear Mum
and Dad

Mum began to speak, faltering between her tears, *"If you want to disown me and don't want anything more to do with me, and your Dad too ... we'll understand."* My thoughts were racing now, *"Goodness me, whatever's the matter?"* I couldn't start to imagine what was grieving her, and it was really awful to see Mum so desperately distressed. My heart went out to her. She was in a terrible state.

Weeping pitifully and full of despair, she continued to confess and deeply repent of the grief in her heart. A grief that had kept both my parents gripped in fear for years and years. A private, secret fear, that they had borne together for far too long. But now at last, they had made the brave decision to share their grief and their dreaded secret with me, and my sister too, even at the risk of losing the love and respect of both their daughters.

My Mum's heart was breaking as she sat close to me, telling me that for countless years, they'd carried a heavy burden of guilt and shame. A secret, they believed, that was too dreadful to share. But now, unable to bear their burning conviction of shame any longer, they wanted to do what was right. They wanted to tell me the truth. The truth that, *"They were not married!"*

Tearfully, as I nursed Mum's shaking hands in mine, she explained to me that years ago as a young man, my Dad had fathered a child out of wedlock which, if made public, would have been a huge family scandal and social disgrace. Consequently, he felt there was no choice open to him but to marry the girl. Sadly, the baby died at only six months old and their relationship ended, with plans to divorce.

My father offered her a very handsome divorce settlement, enough to buy a nice house in those days. But she kept asking for more and more money until, in the end, my father lost his temper. In a rage, he refused to meet her unreasonable demands and thus, refused to divorce her. Instead, he agreed to pay her a fixed, generous monthly sum and to my utter amazement, *he was still paying her.*

Incredibly, my father continued to do so for the rest of his life, until he died at over eighty years of age. It was honourable indeed that he kept his word to this woman but, for my Mum, it was heartbreaking. It meant she could never marry the man she loved so dearly. The nearest she came to marrying my father was to change her name by Deed Poll to *his* name, and they treated this as their unofficial wedding day.

My poor, dearest Mum had prepared herself for her greatest fear. Her fear that I would completely reject her, and my father too. But I could hardly bear to see her in such agony. Hardly bear to see her in such terrible pain. We clung to each other weeping, as I did my best to comfort her. I loved her, and I always would. She was my beloved Mum. I would never, ever reject her.

As gently as I could, I reassured Mum that I was certain Dad would be granted a divorce quite easily now, after all these years of separation. I pleaded with her to have the courage to go to a solicitor and make some enquiries. I begged her to do this as soon as possible, so that she and Dad could marry. I knew how much it would mean to her and the joy and peace it would bring to both of them. My sister and my parents' closest friends, with whom they had also confided, all urged them to do the same thing.

But the long years of *fear,* had taken too strong a hold over my parents. They were terrified of their secret reaching the local newspapers and what their neighbours, friends and business associates would say. Fear had paralysed them both and ruled their thoughts and actions. Tragically, it robbed them of their peace and joy. In the end, they never did anything about it and never did *legally* marry. I still feel tremendous sorrow and heartache, mixed with deep regret and sadness, that they carried their hidden secret of fear and shame to their graves.

Oh, if only ...

If only they'd known the loving kindness of Jesus. If only they'd known His goodness and let His love, grace and complete forgiveness *heal* their hurting hearts. If only they'd let His precious blood wash them clean of all their guilt and shame, and every sin they'd ever committed. If only they'd known how much Jesus loved them. And if only I'd known this too. *Oh, if only ...*

But sadly, we were ALL so ignorant. So ignorant there was a Saviour willing to forgive ALL of us and heal our deepest pain and sorrow. Regrettably, it was years and years later before I learned this truth. The truth about the one and *only* love that can save us from our sins, our fears and our shame. The precious, divine love of Jesus **.... *a love greater than any pain!***

154

Chapter 16

Life in North Yorkshire

Amazingly, Michael and I had now survived nearly nine years of turbulent married life, when we had the chance of *a fresh new start in Yorkshire*. Ladbrokes had offered Michael an even better Management position in their Leeds casino, another place we'd never been to. We gladly accepted this opportunity but, this time, we moved with fresh anticipation of a new beginning and I was ready to give it my best shot.

City of York

I can still remember the very first time we visited the City of York in North Yorkshire. We arrived by train and, as we walked from the station, we were suddenly confronted by the breathtaking view of the magnificent Rose window adorning York Minster, the City's splendid 13th Century Gothic Cathedral. It was such an awesome sight and immediately, I knew I wanted to live near York. Sadly, several years later on 9th July 1984, this beautiful Rose window was shattered into thousands of fragments when, it was

155

presumed, the Minster was struck by a bolt of lightning. Fire ravaged this splendid Cathedral to such an extent that it took four years to complete the renovations. Everyone was so upset at the enormity of the destruction, that even young children were donating some of their pocket money to the Minster's Restoration Fund.

York is a fascinating city and I always loved exploring the cobbled pedestrian streets or *Lanes,* with their heavily beamed buildings that look as if they're holding each other up. In the many Squares, between the myriad of Lanes, you can often find a group of minstrels dressed in period costumes playing their melodious tunes, and even a traditional Punch & Judy show.

The most famous of the Lanes, *The Shambles,* is an incredibly narrow cobbled street that makes you feel as if you have stepped back in time a century or two. Here, every tall and heavily beamed building has crooked, leaning walls, an assortment of pretty dimpled bay windows, tiny leaded light openings and highly irregular overhanging rooftops, which almost meet overhead.

It is perhaps in the Springtime that the City of York looks most spectacular. This is when the deep grassy banks, which stretch right up to the base of the imposing high stone walls surrounding the perimeter of the City, are ablaze with a mass of golden daffodils. It is a magnificent sight and one definitely worth seeing.

Out in the rolling countryside, I loved admiring the abundance of dry stone walls and pretty York stone cottages, nestled in little hamlets. The vast rugged open expanses and changing moods of the dramatic North Yorkshire Moors always captivated me. And if you go off the beaten track a bit, you can explore the twisting narrow lanes around Goathland and discover the cascading Mallyon Spout waterfall as it tumbles down onto the rocky river bed below.

Then, heading for the coast, it's easy to spend a day or so investigating the quaint fishing villages with their cottages hugging the steeply cobbled streets. The pretty coastline is a joy too, boasting lovely sandy beaches, so reminiscent of my carefree childhood holidays at Elmer Sands.

Yes, we both adored North Yorkshire. It felt like *home* and we were both so happy we'd moved to this beautiful county.

New jobs

At first, we rented a tiny terraced cottage in a secluded hamlet near the brewery town of Tadcaster, half way between Leeds and York. I worked in Leeds *during the day,* travelling in my lovely little yellow Honda.   And Michael worked in Leeds *throughout the night,* travelling in his company car, a sporty Ford Capri, which was a welcome *perk* with his new Management position.

My new boss was the Chief Building Architect for Hepworths, the men's outfitters, and he was very kind and easy to get on with. My desk was beside one of the many windows in this expansive architects' office, filled with men sitting on high stools and silently leaning over their individual drawing tables, intently working on their current designs.

It was a lovely bright airy office and I had the latest electric typewriter, a status symbol to any secretary. The 'better the job' and the more 'senior' the position, the better the typewriter. But in this case, neither the typewriter nor the smart office impressed me for long, because the job wasn't very busy and I soon became incredibly bored.

I had been used to challenges and being kept constantly on the go but now, spending hours with little or nothing to do, was a challenge I didn't enjoy. In fact, I used to spend much of my time wistfully looking out of my high-rise office window and, just for fun, count the number of Jaguar XJS sports cars driving around the roundabout below me.

I'm afraid I didn't warm to Leeds city centre very much either and hated having to contend with the lengthy traffic jams every day. It was always such a relief to leave this busy city behind me and get back out into the open countryside. I was rapidly becoming restless and decided I had to leave both Leeds and my boring job. And so the search began for a more interesting one, this time nearer to York.

But jobs were few and far between and I only attended one interview. It was for a vacancy in the Registrar's Department at York University, which seemed hopeful. Shortly afterwards though, I received a letter informing me that I hadn't been successful.

Once again, I was on the verge of giving up when quite unexpectedly, *a telegram* arrived one day from the University. They had changed their minds and were now offering me the job. They wanted me to start *immediately.*

However, this urgent request wasn't exactly flattering, as I was quite obviously their second choice or even their last resort. But with no other options open to me, I reluctantly accepted and began immediately as they requested.

The York University complex was modern and architecturally interesting but the area in the historic main building where I worked was old and really grotty. I didn't even have an office, just a draughty space in a lino covered passageway. Not exactly the nicest place to spend your day.

My new boss

From the outset, my boss and I didn't really get on and very soon, we did our best to patiently endure each other. I still wasn't used to the Yorkshire accent and when he dictated certain words to me that I didn't understand or even know, he refused to help me and just said, *"Look it up!"* So I did and when I typed the letter, he would strike it through with a biro and say, *"Wrong word. Type it again!"*

Well, I'm a pretty calm and patient sort of person, but this was pushing me to my limits. *Never* had I come across anyone so rude or antagonistic before. I soon became convinced that he spent every evening researching the longest and most unpronounceable words he could find, so he could try them out on me the next day.

It wasn't long before I really began to detest this job and my only light relief every day was to enjoy a delicious cooked lunch in the subsidized students' canteen.

It was now mid-February 1979

And I hit *thirty* years of age. Oh! what a shock to the system. It seemed like a real *landmark*. *A time line* that I didn't particularly welcome. When I was in my late teens, I can distinctly remember thinking that anyone who was *thirty*, was absolutely *ancient.* And yet here I was, *thirty years of age.*

With this mental landmark challenging me, surely it was time to take stock of my life? Time to weigh up the *pros* and *cons* of our present situation. As I mulled over these thoughts, I decided I was thankful that Michael had a good, well-paid job as a Floor Manager in Ladbrokes' casino in Leeds, together with a company car, a generous petrol allowance and excellent healthcare cover.

Besides these obvious *benefits,* we had also just bought ourselves a very nice three bedroomed detached bungalow in a quiet cul-de-sac in Wheldrake, an attractive village on the outskirts of York. So all in all, I was feeling pretty pleased with life generally, except for one, big nagging negative. I absolutely *loathed* my job.

"Surely," I pondered, *"this has to be the perfect time to start a family."* Suddenly, I felt convinced that if I didn't have a baby right *now*, I might never have one. I carefully chose the moment to discuss my feelings and thoughts with Michael and, to my relief and great surprise, he didn't fight with me or disagree at all. So with one mind and in mutual agreement, we planned to start a family at long last. And quite amazingly, *I became pregnant almost immediately.*

Getting larger by the day!

I wasn't too well during the first few months of my pregnancy and often needed time off work. This, understandably, caused some annoyance for my boss and one day, when I rang him to explain that I was still feeling unwell, he suddenly ended our conversation by triumphantly declaring, *"Shall we call it a day then?"* It was blunt and to the point, but he couldn't have said a nicer thing to me and I gladly never went back.

Meanwhile, Michael carefully checked the fine print of his healthcare benefits and we were delighted to find out that I was entitled to private maternity care, absolutely free. This was great news and I was even more delighted when my Specialist told me that the epidural I wanted during my labour, would be included too.

Pregnant and so happy!

So with plenty of time on my hands, I got out my Singer sewing machine, a wonderful twenty-first birthday present from my parents, and began making some much needed maternity clothes as, without doubt, *I was getting larger by the day!* I also took great delight in making some pretty drapes, quilts and padded side panels for our new and beautiful wooden rocking crib, together with matching curtains for the nursery. Then, I began teaching myself how to cook a little better. I made a tremendous effort to produce presentable meals for our many casino friends who visited us several times a week. I was certainly never bored and was always busy doing something.

I kept cheerful and well for the rest of my pregnancy, except for one problem. I suffered with softening of my ligaments, which made walking around slow and difficult. Even sitting on a foam cushion in our car didn't ease the pain and I had discomfort with every jolt and bump on the road.

Thankfully, we had some wonderful neighbours, Mac and Margaret, who visited me every day and helped me in any way they could. How grateful I was for their friendship and kindness. They became my second Mum and Dad.

My first visit to church

I was determined that our baby would have the chance to be Christened. The chance I didn't have. The chance to be dedicated to the Lord. So I began attending our village church. This was another *major landmark* for me, as it was *the very first time* I had ever gone to a Sunday church service in my whole life! Although Michael always refused to accompany me, I still kept going. I so wanted to do the right thing for our baby.

Then one day, our local Vicar bicycled round to our home to go through the proposed Christening service. I pleaded with Michael not to be difficult and mess up my hopes and plans, by expressing his strong atheistic views. Thankfully, the Vicar overlooked Michael's opinions and agreed to conduct the Christening ceremony.

I was so excited

Two weeks had passed since my *due-date,* and there was still no sign of baby. When a few more days went by, I was hastily booked into the small, but friendly Fulford Maternity Hospital on the outskirts of York, to get things moving.

The previous night, I had been so excited, I couldn't sleep a wink and all the next day, I was hyper too. But once I'd been admitted and undergone all the usual medical treatments, I could relax for a few hours and look forward to soon becoming a Mum. Then, in the wee small hours of that night, *our baby's journey began.*

The next morning, Michael arrived cheerful and excited at the prospect of becoming a Dad and stayed with me the whole time, encouraging me and giving me much needed emotional support.

But progress became complicated, when after fourteen hours of labour, my Specialist was still unable to turn our baby's head to face in the right direction. He tried everything possible, without success. With no sleep for two nights, I was becoming tired and distressed. And so was our baby. The epidural was wearing off too and so the decision was made to give me an emergency Caesarean section, something I'd never expected and never wanted.   As I was wheeled into the operating theatre, exhausted and in pain, the last thing I can remember is the kindly nurse telling me to expect some pressure on my throat.

Our beloved first son Leon

And so our beloved son *Leon* was born, healthy and well, just two days before our tenth wedding anniversary. What a perfect gift he was! Michael and I were both ecstatic with *joy.*

Throughout my pregnancy, I'd been longing for our new baby, but I was totally unprepared for the *depth of love* and

163

intense *joy* I felt as I held my precious, beautiful son for the

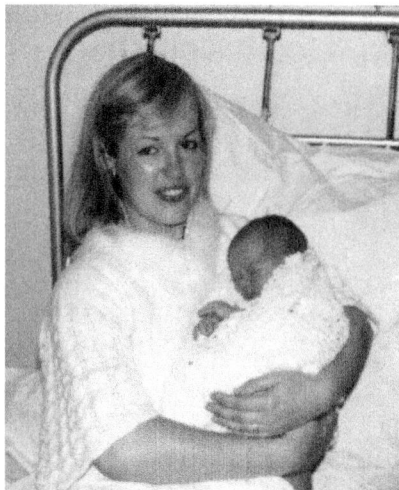

very first time. It was indescribable and I was completely overwhelmed with emotion. Never had I realized it was humanly possible to experience *such love.*

As I held this tiny new life close to me, a new life that God had formed and created inside my own body, it was so incredible, so awesome, that I

Baby Leon just born!

knew it was far too wonderful to experience only once. I knew without doubt, even then, that I wanted to experience this miracle of new life again. Hopefully, one day, I would be able to have another baby.

Grandparents

O ur parents too, were overjoyed to become Grandparents at last. And both our Mums had been busy knitting baby clothes for months. My Mum had crocheted a wonderful large round woollen

shawl and, on her knitting machine, had made some *miniscule* pure woollen vests which were perfect to keep baby Leon warm all winter.

164

Michael's mother, who became known as *Grandma,* had knitted the most intricate and most beautiful fine woollen long Christening robe with a matching bonnet, bootees and delicate shawl. Leon wore these lovely clothes for his Christening service on Mothering Sunday, when he was just three months old. It was such a joyful occasion and I was thrilled that all our parents, cousins and friends travelled from afar to celebrate with us. My dear friend Fran came too, and she was delighted to be Leon's Godmother. It was truly the most perfect and memorable day, and a wonderful family get-together.

"And how was Leon?" Oh, he behaved perfectly as was passed from one admiring arm to another and never cried once, not even during the church service.

But I have often wondered whether the firm and sincere advice that the nurses gave me before leaving Fulford Hospital, had anything to do with baby Leon's calm and placid nature. You see, I drank a pint or so of *Guinness shandy every day for five months* whilst breastfeeding him. Now that's sound nurses' advice for you!

A friend's yacht at Menton

I loved being a Mum, even more than I expected, and I had never been happier. Life just seemed so perfect, so idyllic. And when Leon was just six months old, some dear friends offered us the opportunity to spend two blissful weeks on their beautiful yacht moored at Menton, on the French Riviera. *An invitation definitely too good to miss.*

Having decided we would drive all the way to the South of France in Michael's Capri, we enjoyed the most wonderful journey. We passed through some spectacular scenery and stunning mountain villages such as Rocamadour, clinging precariously to the steep face of a gorge, overlooking the valley far below. It was fun too, staying in different small hotels every night, attempting to speak a smattering of French and sampling the local cuisine.

"And how did baby Leon cope with the journey?" Perfectly. No problems at all. During the day, he either lay down sleeping in his carrycot, firmly secured to the back seat or sat up in his car seat, taking in everything. In the evenings, he went to sleep at 7.30 p.m. like clockwork and never woke till morning.

Perhaps I was just an incredibly happy new Mum. But to me, Leon was a perfect baby and we all had a magical and memorable holiday.

Chapter 17

It Seemed Unbelievable

T hey say, *"Ignorance is bliss"*. Maybe so, because little did I know that there was a storm on the horizon. We were about to receive a cruel blow and our present happiness and joy wasn't to last.

Quite unexpectedly, Ladbrokes lost their Gaming Licence and ALL their casinos were immediately closed down. *It seemed unbelievable that this could happen.* But it did. And overnight, ALL casino staff, including Michael, lost their jobs. Their careers and livelihood came to an abrupt end. An end that stunned everyone and left us all totally unprepared for the future. Michael, along with hundreds of others, now had to find not just a new job, but a whole new career, *a whole new lifestyle.*

But what could he do, after being in the casino business for so many years? As you can imagine, this dilemma resulted in considerable turmoil, especially as neither of us had a job now.

After a great deal of thought, Michael decided to go into partnership with an associate, who'd also just lost his job as a Casino Restaurant Manager. Between them, it was mutually agreed that both families would sell their homes in order to jointly buy and run *a restaurant.*

We were all excited and full of anticipation about this new venture and the perfect premises were soon found in a lovely location, with ample living accommodation for both families.

Having only recently modernized and completely redecorated our bungalow, it sold promptly. But our partners, on the other hand, failed to sell their home in Rutland, a good two hours' journey south. This caused serious financial difficulties, especially as their mortgage still had to be met each month. The financial pressure of this unexpected additional expense increased to such a crisis point, that it became essential to reduce the restaurant's overheads. It was clearly obvious the business could not support two families. One family would have to move out and *quickly.*

This is where I'm uncertain what Michael discussed and agreed with his partner. To my thinking, we'd sold our beautiful bungalow and invested all our capital into the restaurant. And yet, the outcome was that Michael, Leon and I moved out. *Why?* I honestly don't know. Our partners still had their family home to return to and were looking forward to the arrival of their second baby. *"So what was going on?"*

Was it perhaps, that Michael had had enough of running a restaurant? Or maybe he thought he had more chance of getting a job elsewhere to support us? Or did our partners refuse to move out? To this day, I don't know the answer.

At the time, my concern was for baby Leon, who was only twenty months old. With no income and no home to return to, we now had to make plans to move out of the restaurant.

Again, I'm not sure exactly how it all happened, but a kind surveyor friend managed to arrange a loan for us. With his help and expertise, we bought a really cheap, rundown two bedroomed Victorian terraced cottage in a pretty village near York. The whole place needed extensive renovation, which our friend organized for us.

Amazingly, this work was completed very quickly and we were able to move directly from the restaurant into our pretty new home. By now, Michael had also managed to secure a trainee sales position with a leading life assurance company and was, we hoped, in the process of being taught a completely new career.

Sadly, the couple who remained in the restaurant didn't make a success of the business and after it was sold, they returned to their family home in Rutland. Our once, *seemingly exciting venture* had ended in failure.

Somehow, and I don't understand how, we were held responsible for *ALL* of the restaurant's remaining debts. Perhaps it was some small print on an agreement Michael signed with his partner? Again, I don't know.   But I do know that *we picked up the entire tab.* It was a horrible and deeply devastating experience.

Depression

U p until now, I'd always been a positive and generally cheerful person, but this last blow hit me really hard and I began to sink into depression. I felt drained and exhausted and quickly became a recluse. I didn't want to talk or mix with anyone. Even though we had our pretty cottage to live in, I'd lost my hope and vision, and felt like giving up. Thankfully though, I eventually understood what was happening to me and found the will to pull through, if not for my own sake, for my precious young son's sake.

Michael became concerned for me too and daily encouraged me to get outside into the fresh air and go walking. This proved to be wise advice and good therapy, helping to lift my spirits. At least once a day, I pushed little Leon in his buggy along pretty riverside paths, through quiet woodland glades, down peaceful country lanes and around our small village.

I found that focusing my thoughts and energies on Leon instead of on myself, or worrying about our debts and problems, helped a great deal too. Gradually, I got stronger and stronger, regaining my *hope,* until my strength was restored and I was fully recovered.

From this difficult experience, I have realized that every form of oppression, despondency, melancholy and *blues* is a ruthless and cruel attack from the devil himself. Depression, along with self-pity and deep hopelessness can creep up on you and then, in your weakest moment, quickly consume and overtake you, *robbing you of your hope and vision.*

What I have learnt over the years since then, is that *putting my faith and trust in Jesus Christ, and not just in my own strength and effort, has really helped me to overcome any attacks of oppression and hopelessness.* Jesus is, after all, the Great Physician who can heal us, help us and give us *the will*
170

we desperately need to keep on going. In our time of greatest weakness, *HE is faithful and strong,* and is always ready and willing to help us through every battle. HE listens day and night for our heartfelt cries, whenever we cry out to Him.

Only Jesus can give us the hope and the courage to carry on. *Only Jesus* can give us the strength to overcome everything we are facing ... *even suicidal depression. Whenever we call out and ASK HIM to help us, be assured HE WILL.*

Time to move on

Yes, Michael and I were licking our wounds. We had suffered a failed business venture, lost our cherished home and were staggering under a mountain of huge debts. But it was time to dust ourselves down and move forward. So we decided to sell our attractive olde worlde cottage with its oak beams, large flagstone fireplace and pretty dimpled bow front window, and made a good profit. This helped to pay off some debts and yet provide us with enough cash to put down a minimum deposit on our next home.

I knew Michael was a fighter, full of energy and he wasn't going to let our failed business venture stop him. Admirably, over the next few years, he paid off every penny of the restaurant debt to the bank.

There was no doubt about it, we'd been through yet another really tough patch, this time financially, but we'd survived. I still had great faith in Michael and finally, after undergoing a period of training, he entered the world of financial investment, mortgages and life assurance. Now, once again, his *salesmanship* talents came to the fore and stood him in good stead.

Enthusiastically, he turned one of our bedrooms into an office and purchased one of the first available *Apple* home computers. Full of ambition to succeed in this new career, he eagerly gained some computer experience, which proved to be an invaluable asset in the financial investment business.

Eventually, with a substantial portfolio of new investment clients to his credit, he decided to bravely launch out and rent his own commercial business premises. Very soon, he found just what he wanted. A small town-centre converted cottage. The upstairs office had its own entrance and separate stairway, and the ground floor was a shop. It had the added advantage of being in a prominent high street location and at a reasonable rent. *It was perfect.* Within just a few weeks, Michael opened the doors to the public and his mortgage and financial investment business had begun.

Michael's own business

Michael was so proud of his new office premises and used the space wisely. Upstairs provided him with a large comfortable office with ample space to receive his clients. Downstairs to the rear, with a window overlooking the back courtyard, was a pleasant area where Michael's assistant worked. To the front was the main shop, where we ran an agency for a major building society. This was *my* responsibility.

Although I was well used to running an office, this was a completely new and very welcome challenge, which I really enjoyed. In order to promote an efficient and professional air, I provided smart navy suits and navy trimmed white blouses for my capable team of three women to wear, including myself. I really enjoyed running our agency and was always surprised how busy we were. In our rare quiet moments, any one of us was capable of helping Michael with his secretarial requirements.

A working Mum

As any working Mum will know, working full-time is like a juggling act. Leon attended a small private school when he was just three years old and loved it. By three and a half, he was happily attending full-time, broken only by a half-day on Wednesdays. He thrived on it. His joy was made complete when, every lunchtime, the Headmaster kindly offered to personally teach him how to swim in the school's indoor pool.

This act of kindness paid off and Leon developed a love for swimming. In fact, his next two primary schools each had an indoor swimming pool and, by the time he was only eight years old, he had passed *all* his life-saving exams and had successfully managed to swim *one mile*. His primary school teachers could hardly believe it, and neither could I.

A year later, Leon began swimming in earnest. Three times a week, he attended two-hour swimming training sessions and, at weekends, he was busy competing in local galas. He became proficient in swimming breast stroke, front and back crawl and even butterfly. *Yes, I was a delighted and totally amazed Mum. Well done Leon!*

Finding good after-school care for Leon was essential and I was fortunate to find an excellent childminder who adored him and became like a second Mum to him. Sometimes, she invited him to stay with her family over the weekend, to play with her young daughter and keep her company. Other times, they took him for outings to the sea with them, while I was busy working on Saturday mornings.   I was so very thankful for her friendship and help, as it was such a comfort knowing that Leon was being really well cared for and enjoying himself so much too.

Our business was flourishing

It was also comforting and very satisfying to see how well our business was growing and flourishing.   And yet, this prosperous period proved to be some of our toughest years. With this success, Michael's unfaithfulness began again. He was having one affair after another. Each time, it brought me more hurt and more grief.

One especially painful occasion happened one day in Tadcaster, while I was out shopping. Quite unexpectedly, I saw Michael walking towards me and I cheerily went forward to greet him, expecting him to stop for a chat. But instead, his features hardened and he looked straight through me, walking on without saying a word. I was left standing on the pavement in a daze of rejection and humiliation, unable to quite grasp his unkindness. I had to face the cruel realization that he was yet again, having another affair and being unfaithful to me.

This wave of infidelity continued. Sometimes Michael told me himself. Sometimes, a worried work associate would ring me, asking if I was aware of his present mistress. Once, a letter arrived at our home from his current conquest and he jovially read it out to me. *Unbelievable.* Sometimes, I just guessed.

Michael's drinking escalated too, until eventually he was breathalysed whilst driving his powerful Mazda RX7 sports car. He lost his driving licence for a year. But this didn't slow him down one bit. He simply employed his own company chauffeur to drive him around and carried on regardless.

Being prosperous is a blessing

Having money and being prosperous is a blessing. In fact, it's a great blessing. And there's nothing wrong with that. But it can only be a real blessing if it's handled correctly and you don't let it go to your head or rule your heart. It can, very sadly, become a curse if it leads to pride, arrogance, selfishness and greed. The Bible tells us, *"It is more blessed to give than to receive"* (Acts Chapter 20 : verse 35b) and this is very true.

This means that we should always try to have an open and kind heart *to give to others*, especially those in need. But so often, the more money someone has, the meaner they end up and the *less* they want to think about the struggles of others. They just want to think about themselves. *I was guilty of this.*

Michael and I spent so much money on entertaining ourselves when we worked in the casino business in London, without the slightest thought or concern for the poor and needy. It took me a long time to learn that God wants us all to be willing *givers* and to receive the *blessing and joy* of helping others. The good news is, it's *never* too late to start.

I had to tread carefully

Michael might have been the life and soul of the party in the pub, but his behaviour when he arrived home every night was quite the opposite. He was often so abusive and so violent, that I became full of dread and fear.

In his nightly intoxicated state, I had to tread very carefully. If he felt I'd spoken to him in the wrong tone of voice, he would glare at me with cold, menacing eyes. When I saw those hostile eyes bearing down on me, I knew it would be only seconds before I would be hit and punched, and knocked around.

He'd wildly pick me up by my hair and throw me across the room, ignoring my struggles and frantic screams. Often, my face was left swollen and bruised. One night, in a fit of uncontrollable rage, he grabbed me by my hair and threw me out the back door. He locked me outside in the freezing cold weather for several hours, with no shoes on, no coat and no money. Not even a few coins to make a phone call from the village phone box. I was absolutely petrified of him.

I never knew from one day to the next when these fearful fits of unprovoked hostility would begin and, during a particularly violent struggle, the curved blunt end of a metal coat hanger got pushed into my forearm. I still have the scar. Our furniture suffered too. A dining chair would be viciously smashed, flying objects would hurtle through the air indenting a wall. I was particularly upset when he deliberately punched dents into the side of a brand new fridge-freezer that I'd just saved up for. His anger and rage was fearful, even demonic in its ferocity.

It was my dear friend Yolanda who helped me through these long tough years. Often she accepted *a reverse charge call* when I rang her from a telephone box and she sympathetically listened to my impassioned and tormented cries. Her kindness always calmed me and gave me the strength to carry on. I will always cherish her devotion and endearing love to me.

Why did I not leave?

E ventually, I became *a prisoner to fear*. Too frightened to even leave Michael. And to make sure I didn't, he threatened to take Leon away from me if I did, and I knew he meant it.

Twice though, I packed up my car ready to leave him. I planned to take Leon with me on the five-hour drive down through London (no M25 motorway back then to shorten the journey) and stay with my parents for a while, in order to recover and rethink. But each time when I rang my Mum, she refused to let me come. She just kept scolding me, *"Stay! Make your marriage work."*

I had nowhere else to go. So when Mum rejected me so harshly, I stayed and resolved to persevere and do my very best. But to be rejected so severely and so unkindly *twice* by my mother, was really hard to bear. I wondered if my Dad ever knew about my pleas for help. It's hard to believe that he would have turned me away. She just didn't seem to understand, or even want to understand, my desperate situation and how much I needed her affection and compassion. But I deeply loved both my parents and I wasn't going to let these rejections come between us.

I became totally anti-God

With so much pain and suffering, and living without any foundation or knowledge of God's love, forgiveness and guidance in my life, I became totally *anti-God*. I didn't want to *know anything* or *hear anything* about God or religion. My heart was hardened, my ears were closed and my eyes were tightly shut.

Never once, did it cross my mind that I was rejecting the most wonderful and powerful source of LOVE and HELP imaginable. An *unconditional love* that would never waver, reject me or let me down. A love I could *trust* in. A *faithful love* that would never, ever deceive me or hurt me. A *perfect love* that would always love me and never fail me. But sadly, the only time my lips spoke about God, was as a swear word.

I was so painfully ignorant. Ignorant that I was closing the door on *the answer* to my living hell. Ignorant that Michael and I were foolishly *running* in leaps and bounds along the *broad road to destruction* ...

> *"For wide is the gate and*
> *broad is the road that leads to destruction,*
> *and many enter through it."*
> (Matthew 7:13)

Yes, we were part of the *many,* and we weren't interested in hearing *the truth.*   The truth that could have saved us so much pain and suffering.

As Frank Sinatra's famous song goes, *"I did it my way!"* and that's just what we were doing. We were going to do it ... **our way.**

Chapter 18

Seven years Later

I t was another seven long, agonizing and testing years before our life seemed to settle down again. It took a great deal of perseverance, patience and genuine *forgiveness* but quite amazingly, our marriage had survived through the storms yet again.

And now, with our life so much calmer, we *both* decided we would like a second child. Wonderfully, within just a few months, I found I was pregnant. Now, at last, I was going to have a second baby. The baby I had so longed for. Michael and I were *both* overjoyed and Leon was thrilled too. No longer would he be *an only child* and now he had the promise of a new baby brother or sister to look forward to.

With our cherished baby on the way, we soon realized we needed another bedroom, so the search began for a new home. Before long, we found an idyllic house overlooking a green, in a pretty village just outside York. With peace and harmony back in our lives, and so much to plan and look forward to, I once again began attending the local village church. This was the first time I'd stepped inside a church, since Leon's Christening *seven* years ago.

However, during the third month of my pregnancy, just a few days after having an amniocentesis test, a *standard* procedure for older expectant mums, I was rushed into York Hospital with a suspected miscarriage. Being all too aware of my mother's sad history of miscarriages, I was really concerned for the safety of my unborn child. I'd waited seven long years for this second *window of opportunity* and I knew I might never get another chance.

It was on the evening of 5th May 1987, during my strict two-week period of bed rest in hospital, that a nurse brought me some heartbreaking news. *The news that my dear, lovely, kind Dad had just died.*

I could hardly take it in at first and my senses were numbed. She spoke words that didn't seem to belong to *me*. But as her brief and rather curt message sank in and began to penetrate my consciousness, my resistance to receive her words weakened. Searing pain of grief and disbelief now overwhelmed me, as I sat alone in my dimly lit hospital room. Memories, such dear memories of my precious Dad with his warm smile and twinkling eyes, flooded back to me. And I let the tears flow.

A jolly teddy bear of a man

My Dad had been ill for a very long time with hardening of the arteries of the brain. He was a large and jolly *teddy bear* of a man who enjoyed his food, always had a kind word for everyone and displayed impeccable manners. He was indeed a *gentle*-man but now, recently, in his early eighties, he had been a shadow of himself. Weak and unsteady on his feet, he spent most of every day sitting in his big comfy armchair, with Mum doting on his every need.

He never read much, except perhaps the local newspaper and if he watched television, it confused him as he thought it was *real life* happening all around him. If any violence came on the TV, he became frightened and alarmed. But his deep love for my mother never wavered and Mum lovingly and devotedly nursed him for many years, as long as she possibly could.   Eventually, his condition became so acute, that she could no longer control his increasingly frequent fits of extreme strength.

During these fits, my father was completely uncontrollable and totally unaware of his immense *superhuman* power and physical strength. Too often, he would storm up and down their bungalow like a steam train and it was impossible to stop him.   Or, on other occasions, he would seize my mother in a bear hug and virtually squeeze the life out of her. He would stand squeezing her like this for up to two hours, until at last, she was able to free herself. These fits became increasingly frightening and dangerous until finally, Dad was admitted into hospital where he was kept sedated most of the time.

Poor distraught Mum. She was totally and utterly broken-hearted and spent nearly every waking moment at his bedside, where he lay in a hammock. She never gave up the hope and belief that he would one day make a miraculous recovery and return home with her. So much so, that in Dad's last moments on this earth, when the nurse gently told her, *"It'll be any minute now,"* she still hung on to the desperate hope that *any minute now* meant that Dad was about to *recover.* She just refused to accept what the nurse really meant until, before her very eyes, Dad breathed his last and was gone from her. The *love of her life* and the reason she lived had just left her. She couldn't believe it. She couldn't take it in and the shock was too much. She was *alone*, so very *alone,* so unbearably *alone.* All she wanted to do was to die with him.

"Why *NOW* Dad?"

A s I lay in my hospital bed, I could hardly take it in either. It's the sort of news you never want to hear. At first, I was stunned and shocked, but gradually these emotions gave way to agitated annoyance at my helplessness. Here I was in hospital, not allowed to put a foot out of bed, with the news that my dear father had just died and I wanted to cry out, *"Oh Dad! Why did you have to die right now? Why did you die while I'm in hospital and can't get out of bed? You've been ill for so long. Why NOW Dad?"*

These tortured thoughts attacked my senses as the true meaning of the nurse's words sunk in. I would *never* see my Dad on this earth again. My lovely Dad, my dearest Dad was dead, gone from me. As pain and grief engulfed me, my heart was screaming inside me, *"No! Please no. I can't bear it."*

Yolanda

E arly the next morning, after being cruelly scolded by a nurse for not eating my breakfast (she was

183

unaware of my circumstances and emotional state), I sat dazed and motionless in my bed, in a state of shock. Through the open door of my room, I looked out into the ward with blinkered eyes, never once seeing my best friend who was standing beside the Nurses' Desk.

Then very softly, Yolanda stepped through the open doorway into my room and, with outstretched arms, hugged me. Suddenly, my dearest friend was right beside me when I needed her so badly. A wave of joy bathed my agonizing heart as I looked up and saw the love and kindness in her eyes. I could hardly believe it. *"How did she know? How did she get here so quickly?"*

Drawing up a chair, she explained that Michael had rung her the previous evening with the news of my father's death. Knowing that I was alone in hospital with no-one to talk to, she wanted to be with me. But this wasn't an easy task for her to fulfil. Firstly, she didn't have a car to drive, and secondly, she lived far away in the county of Hertfordshire. So, with no free car available for her to use, *"How did she get here?"*

Well, Yolanda wasn't about to give up that easily. Although she didn't manage to get a car, she did manage to beg the use of a friend's *rickety old van!* And then, to my added amazement, she told me how she'd left home at dawn and been driving hours up the motorway in this old jalopy to be with me by breakfast time, a journey of nearly four hours.

Oh, what pure delight it was to see her now, amidst my grief and pain. For the last seventeen years, we'd shared our joys and sorrows, and been like sisters to each other. How privileged I was to have such a kind and faithful friend.

184

I would always love him

My father's funeral was delayed for ten days until 15th May 1987, by which time I was back home after my two weeks of successful bed rest. Naturally, my mother wanted me to travel south for my father's funeral but alas, my doctors firmly refused, saying the risk of a miscarriage was still too great. I found myself in an agonizing situation.

I desperately wanted another child and the baby I was carrying was really precious to me. I'd just lost my father and although I really wanted to attend his funeral, I didn't want to take even the slightest chance of losing my baby. I had a new life living inside me, a new life I'd waited nearly eight years for and a new life I needed to protect. Some may think I was selfish and even callous, but if I miscarried and lost this baby, it would be terrible.

My Dad had been richly blessed with a devoted wife, my dear mother. He had lived to a ripe old age and if I decided *not* to go to his funeral, it would never lessen my love for him and never take away my treasured memories of him. He'd been my beautiful Dad and *I would always love him.* I knew my Dad would understand, but would the rest of my family?

A fond farewell to my Dad

I was faced with a terrible decision. Mum's brother, my dear uncle Frederick, very kindly offered to drive me slowly and carefully down to my father's funeral, but my doctors still refused to give their consent for me to travel. I remained really fearful of taking even the remotest chance of losing my precious baby. In the end, Michael offered to go in my place, making the five-hour journey south alone. During the service, he read a lovely poem that we'd both chosen, hoping it would bring some comfort to my grieving Mum. A little later, we had this poem beautifully scripted and framed, as a present for her.

To ease the pain of not being at my father's funeral, which was held at the Crematorium in Leatherhead, Surrey, my friendly local Vicar agreed to my special and deeply personal request. Very kindly, he opened our village church and held a private service for me and Yolanda, just the two of us to-gether, at exactly the same time as the service was being held in Surrey.   Lovingly and prayerfully, we committed my dearest Dad to the Lord.

She just wanted to die

Very soon, my forlorn and heartbroken Mum came to stay with us for two weeks. She was grieving desperately and just wanted to die. She simply couldn't bear the thought of living without my Dad and her life had no meaning or purpose any longer. It was truly terrible to see her so wracked with grief and listen to her pitiful heart-rending sobbing every night. When she returned home, I tried my best to telephone her every day to cheer and encourage her and give her the hope to carry on living.

Regrettably, I don't know if my parents at some point in their lives, ever invited Jesus into their hearts to be their Lord and Saviour. If they did, they never mentioned it. But at the time, I didn't know the Lord either. We were all so ignorant of the truth.   I mistakenly thought that just because we believed there was a God in Heaven and that Jesus Christ was His Son (the Bible says even Satan knows this), plus perhaps going to church occasionally, singing some hymns and saying a few ritual and even possibly *empty* prayers, that would be enough to get us all into Heaven. How very wrong we were to think like this and how Satan had deceived us to believe this lie. A wicked lie that many, many people still believe.

Looking back now, at that time of extreme anguish, I can only wish I'd known *the truth* about the love of Jesus. A pure, perfect love that my Mum and all of us needed so badly. A love that understands our pain and tears.   A love that heals the most desolate of hearts. A love that replaces the deepest sorrow and emptiness, with peace and tranquillity. A love that promises hope for the future and an eternity in Heaven. And a love that offers the will and strength to keep on living. A wonderful love ... ***a love greater than any pain!***

But sadly, without this *divine* love in her heart, Mum remained inconsolable. Even years later, she still wanted to die. She had nothing to live for anymore, no hope, no future, except death itself. And yet, she lived for another seventeen years, locked up in her misery.

A second blessing

Following the sadness of my father's death and the scare of a miscarriage, I gave up my job working for Michael and stayed at home. Thankfully, I enjoyed a trouble-free pregnancy without even a tinge of ligament problems. And, having just moved into our larger new home, there was plenty to keep me busy as I prepared for our treasured new arrival, due in late October. So, without further ado, out came my Singer sewing machine again. I had new crib drapes and curtains to make for the nursery, plus curtains and Austrian blinds for many of the other rooms. And, whenever I had a free moment, there was always a lovely garden needing attention.

Throughout this pregnancy, I was well cared for under the National Health Service and, to my surprise and great delight, I had the same Specialist to look after me this time, as I did when Leon was born. This was a tremendous blessing and a huge comfort to me.   However, due to my age and the time lapse since my last pregnancy, he insisted that I have another Caesarean section.   This time though, he told me, it would be planned and under an epidural, which would be so much kinder to me.

As my *due-date* approached, the Specialist brought forward the date for my Caesarean section by two weeks and our excitement levels rose. Hurriedly, we completed all the last minute preparations to get our home and new nursery ready. And, as an unexpected kindness, a good friend of mine offered to look after Leon for us. So, with everything ready and organized, I was admitted into York Hospital as planned. Then, one afternoon in early October 1987, we were truly blessed when our second and most precious son *Ross was born!*

Our beloved second son Ross

At last, the moment I'd been waiting for so long had arrived. Ross was so tiny, so beautiful, so perfect and we were all overjoyed. Tenderly, I nursed my new baby son, holding him so close to me.   Oh, what joy, what ecstasy, as his minute fingers clasped one of mine. I felt so incredibly blessed to be able, once again, to experience the unfathomable *love* and *joy* of nursing my very own newborn baby.

Leon, now almost eight years old, was filled with a tenderness I'd never seen in him before and he was totally *over the moon* to have his own tiny brother to love and care for. He simply adored baby Ross and the love expressed in his face as he cradled his new brother was absolutely priceless. This bond of brotherly love continued to grow and strengthen between them. And as soon as Ross was able to climb out of his cot by himself, I found him asleep every night snuggled up beside Leon in his bed. To my amazement and joy, this continued for many years.

I really loved being a Mum for the second time, and revelled in having another baby of my own to care for. Having a planned Caesarean section, by epidural, was indeed much kinder to me and I recovered very quickly. But to my surprise and disappointment, Ross absolutely refused to breastfeed. It was too slow for him.   And when the nurses finally advised me to use a bottle, Ross sank back into my arms in relief and drank hungrily.

189

I hadn't felt as happy as this since Leon was born and I genuinely thought our life was now settled and complete. We had a lovely home, my husband's business was still flourishing, or so I believed, and I loved being at home with our two children. At last, I was wonderfully and blissfully happy and content. Life had never been so good.

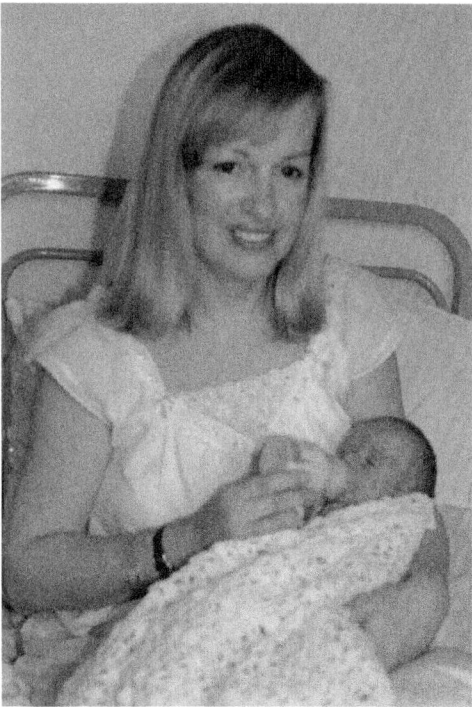

Ross was now two months old and already a lively bundle of fun. Always smiling and laughing and a pure joy to us. Leon doted over him while I, a proud and happy Mum looked on, brimming with joy and happiness.

Then one day, during one of our visits to the baby clinic, the nurse was alarmed at Ross's irregular arm movements and an inward-turning eye. So alarmed in fact, that she rang the Paediatric Department at York Hospital *immediately.*

Stunned, I struggled to understand the nurse's urgent concern over my baby. Very gently, she told me that she thought Ross was having fits. She was so concerned, that in just three days' time, Ross was admitted into York Hospital for a week of intensive tests.

By the time we arrived at hospital, his condition had deteriorated so dramatically, that he had gone completely *blind.* He didn't see anything and he didn't register anything or anyone. His eyes would not look at me, even if I held his head to face me. *"Whatever had happened to my precious baby? Whatever was wrong?"*

Ross and I shared a room together in the hospital and during that week, our poor baby was subjected to innumerable tests, some of which I wasn't allowed to see or even be present at. It was agonizing. Heartbreaking. And yet I never gave up hope.

I adored my baby

Ross was unfeeling, unloving, unresponsive. He was silent and he was *blind.* And yet I firmly believed that LOVE would break through the barriers into his silent world. I believed that if I showered him with LOVE, he would *copy* my affection. Between the daily tests, I cuddled him, kissed him, hugged him and twirled round our room with him wrapped up in my arms. I loved him. I adored my baby. *Love* gave me the strength I needed to *hope.* I firmly believed in the *POWER of love* and although I didn't know it at the time, the Bible gives all of us this great encouragement.

> *"Love ... always protects, always trusts,*
> *always hopes, always perseveres.*
> *Love never fails"*
> (1 Corinthians 13:7-8)

Wow! The Bible says *LOVE* never fails. That means, *LOVE ALWAYS WINS!* And I was more than willing to believe it.

Would Ross ever get better?

At the end of that week, I had a meeting with the Head Paediatrician. He told me that two of his doctors thought Ross had Autism. This was not a surprise, as I had already suspected that this was his condition. He paused, while I digested the news.   Then he continued to tell me that he, personally, believed Ross had a more serious condition. A condition that would, in all probability, leave him with a severely diminished mental aptitude.

Horror and panic flooded my senses and a profusion of questions cried out for answers. *"What did he mean? Was there no hope? Would Ross never get better?"*

Anxiously, I asked his opinion about Ross's future mental capabilities and truthfully, but gently, he told me that his prognosis was far from promising. I left his office that day totally stunned. Numb. Unable at that moment to comprehend what my ears had just heard. But I wasn't going to give up. I just kept on loving Ross, more and more.

Silently, baby Ross continued in his *unseeing* and *unresponsive* world for the next couple of months until *one special day*. *ONE DAY* when I suddenly noticed something. *ONE DAY* which still excites me even now, whenever I think about it.   So let me tell you exactly what happened.

Oh! What joy

Ross's baby car seat was fastened to the front passenger seat in my car, facing towards the back seats. That way, I could see him easily as I drove along, and could chat and sing to him. This particular day, I left him

192

sitting in his seat in the front of my car, while I nipped into the chemist shop to buy some new teats for his drinking bottles. When I returned a few minutes later, I opened the passenger car door and stooped down to throw in the bag of teats. But as I shut the car door again, something extraordinary happened.

As I closed the car door, *ROSS TURNED TO LOOK AT ME.* He didn't smile, his eyes didn't light up, *but he turned his head towards me.* He had *recognized* my actions and *responded* the way any baby would have done. In fact, his behaviour seemed so natural, that it took me a minute to realize what he'd just done. Then suddenly, it dawned on me. I'd just seen a miracle. *Ross could see!* He was communicating again with the outside world. *Oh! What joy.* We were on the road to recovery.

A miracle baby

R oss continued to recover rapidly and, with the help of Wendy, a devoted eye specialist and the dedicated assistance of a physiotherapist, he improved greatly. The whole right side of his body was weak and the physiotherapist taught me the necessary exercises to help rectify this. She gave me a seat designed to support and strengthen him and a little later, a special walking frame to strengthen his whole body. By the time he was two years old, he had nearly regained all of his body strength. *It was wonderful.*

During a further meeting with the Head Paediatrician, he was simply amazed at Ross's progress. In *his* eyes, *Ross was a miracle baby*. He only regretted not having made a video film of baby Ross *to give hope and encouragement* to other parents in similar situations.

With further advice and help from other specialists, I was able to understand and handle Ross's often difficult and irrational behaviour. Once I had learnt this, it helped me to be patient, yet firm, and be able to help him in a constructive way.

"And love? Did Ross learn to copy?" Yes he did, but not until he was about five years old. Yet I never gave up hope and firmly believed that if I showed him LOVE and affection, he would eventually *copy* me. And he did and became the most loving and adoring child ever.

Little by little, Ross grew stronger and stronger and as he grew older, he learnt how to manage any minor problems he still had with his vision. He didn't even have to wear glasses. And by his mid-teens, he didn't need any more check-ups with the eye specialist.

Today, I am delighted to tell you that he is a perfectly healthy, very intelligent, super fit, six foot one inch tall hand-some young man. *"Well done Ross! You're a fighter and a winner."* But I shall forever praise the Lord, for His amazing miracle in baby Ross's life.

> **"Thank You Lord, for Your divine favour,**
> **healing power, mercy and love,**
> **in baby Ross's young life ...**
> **even when we didn't know it was YOU**
> **who was blessing us."**

Chapter 19

My Worst Nightmare

One fine Spring afternoon, when Ross was only six months old, our friendly village Vicar called to see us. I never forgot his kindness to me when my father died and he was always welcome in our home.

We were relaxing in our living room, chatting over some tea, when Michael very casually chose that moment to break some staggering news. The news that since the previous year's stock market crash on *Black Monday,* 19th October 1987, just thirteen days after the birth of baby Ross, his business had, unbeknown to me, been struggling.

Michael continued to calmly announce that we would have to sell our beautiful home and move on. Stunned at his unexpected outburst, I tried hard to remain composed, but as this devastating news sunk in, I burst into tears. I knew the stock market crash had been serious, but never realized it had affected us to this extent.

I tried hard to control my tears and emotions in front of our Vicar, but being told we must sell our home in such a casual and blasé manner, was a very cruel blow. I'd put my heart and soul into our dream home, working so hard throughout my pregnancy to get it just perfect and I really loved every corner of it. The very thought of having to pack up and move on *again,* tore me apart.

And yet, I had to face the fact that since Ross's birth, I'd been so wrapped up in my own cocoon of happiness, plus coping with his recent medical problems, that I was totally unaware of the serious implications of this stock market crash. It seemed a minor detail to me. But now, I was forced to accept the serious consequences that this economic crisis had been having upon my husband's investment business.

Nevertheless, the facts remained the same. We had no choice but to move from our lovely home and then, it turned out, we had to move from our next home too, all within a year. Thankfully, the housing market was still buoyant at this stage and we managed to raise large amounts of valuable capital from each of the sales, investing almost all of the profits back into my husband's Company. Finally, we moved to a rural village near the coast, over an hour's drive away from York, where houses were much cheaper.

Michael had long since moved his business too, from the cottage premises with the building society agency I once run, to some spacious first floor offices in a nearby town. Several men, plus an accountant, now worked for him and I thought his business was thriving. I also believed our large injection of cash had rectified his pressing financial problems, so it was really harrowing to learn otherwise. But it was even more disappointing to realize that our efforts were not enough to make a significant and lasting difference.

Yet at weekends, Michael often took me out for dinner which, of course, I enjoyed. But if ever I should question him about the expense, his reply was always the same, *"I've worked really hard and I deserve it."* I didn't doubt that he worked hard, but I did doubt that we could afford it. My doubts were confirmed when we remortgaged our house to the absolute *max,* to create extra cash for his business. However, for the next two years, his Company still struggled under ever increasing debts. And through it all, he kept on drinking and spending, with no apparent restraint.

Suicidal

I t was during this tense and difficult two year period that Michael constantly talked about committing suicide.

His drinking was constant, depression was always at the door and his thoughts were always about death. But it was really a cry from his heart to *live.* He didn't really want to die, he just wanted his problems to end and he thought alcohol and committing suicide was the answer. He was full of self-pity and felt trapped in his economic stranglehold.

Then one day, when I couldn't take any more of his drinking, his violent behaviour and his morbid talk, I snapped. He pushed me too far and I boldly let rip, *"If you're going to commit suicide, then just get on with it!"*

I shocked myself, as much as I shocked Michael, with my uncharacteristic outburst. But amazingly, and thankfully, he never mentioned suicide again.

Serious economic crisis

The UK faced yet another stock market crash on *Black Friday,* 13th October 1989, when little Ross was just two years old. There was hardly a person living in the country who didn't seem to be affected in some way. It appeared to grip the entire nation.

Almost immediately, the bottom fell out of the buoyant property market. Fear was rampant as homes were increasingly being repossessed, shops boarded up and businesses forced to close down. Livelihoods were torn apart right across the nation.

By this time, my husband's investment business had become so seriously and uncontrollably in debt, that it had no hope of surviving any longer. The recklessness and pretence was over. With his office closed down, his Company car gone, and his credit cards exhausted, Michael's business was forced into *liquidation.* Due to it being an *'unlimited' Company* and with his *personal guarantee liability* for his business debts, we knew it would only be a matter of time before he would be called to appear in court, to be officially declared *bankrupt.*

Suddenly, our life was in utter turmoil again and, to my added horror, I found out that *our* extensive personal debts and bills now became *my* debts and *my* bills. I could hardly believe what was happening, as everything seemed to *automatically* be put into *my* name. Bills began arriving addressed to *me.* How could I possibly pay all these debts? I didn't have a job or any prospect of getting one, as northern England was particularly crippled in this economic crisis.

Michael left for Northern Ireland

Daily, I fought off despair. While Michael, in the hope of giving us a better life, left for Carrickfergus in Northern Ireland. He went to join some of his previous business clients who were planning to set-up a new manufacturing Company. At first, I thought this sounded hopeful and even promising, especially when they invited me and the boys to spend a week visiting them in Northern Ireland, all expenses paid.

As much as I relished the thought of this short break, I was nervous about it too. The TV News was constantly reporting bombings and atrocities taking place in Northern Ireland. But our hosts promised to take good care of us and very kindly showed us the most attractive tourist sights including Belfast Zoo and Carrickfergus Castle.

Then they took us for a breathtaking tour of Co. Antrim's wonderful Causeway coastline. We admired little sandy bays, dramatic mountains and lush valleys as the beautiful Glens of Antrim rose beside us. We passed through the pretty coastal towns of Cushendall and Cushendun before reaching the incredibly narrow, steep and quite scary road up to Torr Head. If you haven't been there, it's a stunning headland with amazing views across to Scotland.

But the highlight of our tour was when we reached the Giants Causeway, the National Trust's *top* tourist attraction. And no wonder. It was a spectacular sight. We'd never seen anything like this before and marvelled at the awesome sight of 38,000 towering basalt columns, consisting of hexagonal shaped stones, naturally formed, one upon the other.

Cautiously, we walked the narrow path around the base of these mighty cliffs and were able to view the incredible twelve metre high rock formations of the *Organ Pipes* and *Chimney Pipes,* which were both stunning and quite extraordinary.

This enjoyable trip, together with meeting our future business partners, had certainly been very encouraging. It was interesting too, to see their proposed business premises and, although the plans for this new manufacturing opportunity seemed rather ambitious to me, the men involved were all confident of success.

Michael was very enthusiastic about the whole project and it soon became clear he wanted me and the boys to join him in Northern Ireland. I could fully understand his desire to latch onto this new and hopeful *lifeline,* but to actually leave my home in England and come to *live* in Northern Ireland, so far away from my family and friends, felt like a step too far. I have to admit too, that when we returned from Northern Ireland, I took a deep sigh of relief to be standing back on Yorkshire soil. It was a place I knew and loved so well. A place where I felt secure.

So with Michael now living in Carrickfergus, I was left alone with the boys to carry on as best we could. I was pleased that my husband had such faith in these new partners and their brave business proposal, but I wasn't prepared for what came next. Michael began telephoning me from Northern Ireland to ask me to become a Director of this new Company, *in his place,* as he knew he was about to be declared bankrupt. This put a totally different slant on things, and I was far from happy about it. In fact, I refused point blank.

But his *asking* soon became *serious threats* and, in the end, he forced me against my will to become a Company Director of this new venture.

Helplessness and frustration, mixed with anger, engulfed me as I quickly became an unwilling pawn in Michael's plans. More importantly, I didn't want and certainly didn't need any more financial responsibility or possible debts.

So you may wonder, *"Was I wise agreeing to Michael's demands?"* No, of course I wasn't. But when you are left alone with two young children to look after, with no money, bills and legal demands arriving daily in the post *in your name,* and your husband about to be made bankrupt, it is not so easy to be wise. Ross was still only two years old and my main concern was to have a roof over our heads and some food to eat. Yes, with hindsight, it's always easier to look back with wisdom and judge things differently. But yet again, I found myself stretched to the limit.

The court case

L egal proceedings were progressing quickly now, and it wasn't too long before my worst nightmare became a reality. *The court case to declare Michael bankrupt.*

Somehow, it never occurred to me that he wouldn't attend his own court hearing. But, when he rejected my urgent appeals to return from Northern Ireland to attend he, along with his solicitor, insisted that I had *no choice* but to take my husband's place in court. I protested vehemently, *"You have to be joking!"* and flatly refused. But his solicitor was adamant, *"You must attend."* I pleaded and argued with him, but to no avail. I had to go to court, *alone*, like a lamb to the slaughter.

I can still see the court room now, even after all these years. It seemed huge to me and full to capacity. I just saw this *sea* of people sitting in front of me as I stood in the witness box, doing my best to defend my husband. I fought for him as hard as I knew how, answering all the questions fired at me but finally, an unexpected legal clause silenced me and I was unable to reply. An awful sinking feeling swept over me as I knew I had failed. It was over and I'd lost my defence. The Judge, moved by my tenacity, looked down at me sympathetically before firmly declaring *Bankruptcy* upon my husband.

Deflated and humiliated, I stepped out of the witness box with the judgement of "*Bankruptcy*" ringing in my ears. As I solemnly walked the length of the Court Room, a Legal Assistant who'd been listening to my defence came up to me and said, *"You did really well!"* I'd been amazingly brave up to that point, as I fought so ferociously on Michael's behalf. But as I raised my downward gaze to look up into her face, and saw her warm and friendly smile, her kind words broke me. I burst into tears, like a little girl. But there was no-one there to hug me. No-one to comfort me.

Out on the street, alone and feeling totally lost and utterly broken, I found a phone box and rang Michael to tell him the news. Shock was setting in fast now and I shook so badly, I could hardly speak through my tears into the heavy, black receiver, as I held it up to my ear. Somehow, I managed the long drive back to our home, over an hour away. I cried uncontrollably for hours.   Years later, I still suffered with dreadful nightmares from this deeply traumatic experience.

One cauliflower

M ichael, however, stayed away in Northern Ireland for nearly a year after this and there was little or no money to send home to me and the boys. My widowed Mum was very anxious about us and sent me some money whenever she could.   Buying food was always a pressing concern and feeding the boys was my priority. But one week in particular, we were so very poor, all I had left to eat was *one cauliflower.*

Thankfully, I met a kind lady in our village who befriended me and my boys. She enjoyed growing vegetables in her nearby allotment and every night she would bring some of her produce to our home. Whatever food we both had, we shared it and always ate our evening meal together. Then, while I bathed and put young Ross to bed, she thoughtfully did the washing-up for me.

Her name was Nancy and she was like an angel to us. She was a truly caring and faithful companion and I shall never, ever forget her. I thank God too, that in His love and mercy, He sent us such a kind and compassionate friend to help and comfort us, just when we really needed one.

We weren't the only ones

H ouses were being repossessed *everywhere* in the country, during this financially tough period in the nation. Eventually, it was our turn. And I had yet another humiliating ordeal to go through, *alone as before,* as I dutifully attended another court hearing. My struggle to stay in our home, by paying paltry sums to the mortgage lender every month, had finally failed. I left the hearing holding a Court Order, giving us the statutory one month's notice to vacate our home. But my biggest concern was, *"Where are the boys and I to go?"*

Michael had been away for nearly a year by now and I'd been left to cope with the mortgage demands and ever increasing bills. I didn't want to leave my home and go to Northern Ireland where I knew no-one and where there was so much hostility.

Also, I didn't like being part of a Company I knew little or nothing about. I hated it even more when Michael and one of his new business partners began telephoning me daily from Northern Ireland. Together, they *verbally threatened me very viciously,* saying that as a Director, I *must* sign the necessary legal agreements to buy some *very expensive machinery* for their new factory. I was being used as a pawn again and felt trapped and frightened.   It was horrible and I didn't like it one bit.

I needed help *urgently* and instinctively turned to my widowed mother. I wanted to ask her if the boys and I could come and live with her. She was alone now, since my father's death, and still lived in our family home in East Horsley, south of London. I knew this was a huge commitment, but I was desperate. I reckoned, *"If Mum could just help me look after the boys, I could try to get a job."* Being an experienced and capable Secretary/PA, I was more confident of getting a job in London or perhaps Guildford, than in the impoverished north where we presently lived.

I took the plunge and telephoned my Mum, and was absolutely overjoyed when she responded, *"Yes, you can come."* Oh fantastic! I was so very thankful and so very relieved, and wonderfully happy.

However, early the very next morning, my joy totally disappeared. My hopes and plans completely shattered. Mum rang me and all too clearly, I heard her say, *"No! You can't come. It's too much for me to cope with. I can't take on the responsibility."*

My mother had been my one and only hope and I pleaded with her to change her mind, but I guess I was too much of a liability and worry. Although totally heartbroken and deeply disappointed at the time, I tried hard to understand how she must have felt. She was, with no doubt, frightened too of the financial responsibility I could have been to her.

We had to go to Northern Ireland

I t seemed there was only one thing left to do. *We had to go to Northern Ireland. We had no other choice.* But first, there was still one great blessing, one great mercy open to us. My boys and I had four weeks left before the dreaded eviction date and this would give us the opportunity to spend three of them visiting my cousin Derek and his family, my best friend Yolanda and her husband and especially my Mum, whom I loved and missed so much.

I really wanted to be able to say *"good-bye"* personally to them all. And I'm so glad we did this, as it was another nine years before we would make a return visit to England.

No option left

T here was no time to lose, so we quickly packed a few bags, jumped into my little red Renault 5 car and off we sped. The boys thought it was a great adventure and were so excited to be visiting everyone, especially when we planned to spend two of the weeks with their Granny. *Two very special, precious weeks.*

Leon and Ross looked so happy, their faces radiant with delight. But all the time, I was putting on a brave front, trying to control my fears of being made homeless in just a few short weeks.

In addition, every time Michael rang me, he was continuing to pressurize me into signing my consent to purchase the machinery they wanted. So far, I'd managed to resist signing these financial documents in the faintest hope that even at the last moment, Mum would change her mind and let us stay with her. But sadly, with only two days of our visit remaining, the invitation to stay never came.

With time rapidly running out and my back against the wall, I could see no way out of this dilemma. Michael was really laying on the verbal pressure thick and fast, until it increased to such a pitch, I felt there was no option left but to surrender to his demands. With the prospect looming closer and closer of no roof over our heads, no money and endless debts, I just didn't know what else to do. How could I look after our children? How could we survive?

Mum wasn't prepared to help us, so who else would? I felt *abandoned* and desperate. *Desperate to keep my children.*

Michael, jubilant in his victory over *my submission to his demands*, immediately arranged for a representative from the finance company to meet me at a nearby restaurant, *Thatchers.* Here, I was to sign the necessary documents to purchase the highly specialized and expensive machinery for the new factory. As I lifted the pen to sign my signature on the dotted line, it felt as if I was signing my own death warrant.

Farewell, my dearest Mum

With our last day upon us, I was faced with the marathon drive back to our home in North Yorkshire, plus an unknown future in Northern Ireland. I never did let Mum know how disappointed and heartbroken I was and remained as cheerful and jolly as I could, appreciating every last second of her company.

Saying *"good-bye"* is never easy. But this was a particularly difficult and distressing one, since what lay ahead was so unknown. Mercifully, I had no idea that this would be *the very last time I would ever see my Mum alive on this earth.* The very last time I would ever hug her and kiss her, and see her lovely face. The last time too, that my boys would ever see their Granny. It was time to leave and I drove away slowly. We wanted to catch *the last glimpses of my Mum,* as she stood waving at the end of her driveway.   Even now, I can still see her smiling face.   I can still see her right arm raised high, waving a fond *good-bye* to us.   *I never ever saw my dear, beloved Mum again.*

Part Two

My Life

In

Northern Ireland

Chapter 20

No turning Back

T he bailiffs had already warned me, *"Get out of your house in time or we'll throw you out!"* And they weren't joking.

With the thought of this threat haunting me and with only a few days left, we hurriedly packed our belongings into a self-drive van that Michael had brought back with him from Northern Ireland. *Bluey,* our Sheltie dog, went with Michael in the van and the boys travelled with me in my car, with every inch around them packed to capacity. *It was time to go.*

And time to leave our home. Time to say farewell to our kind neighbours. Time to head off for the ferry terminal at Stranraer, Scotland. Time to tackle the daunting seven-hour drive to catch the last sailing of the day. Time to face an unknown future in our new homeland. *We were ready to leave. Ready to leave Yorkshire and our memories behind us.*

The journey up to Stranraer was one of the most tiring, stressful and exhausting drives I've ever done and it took us much longer than expected. Trucks and lorries, nose to tail, stretched mile upon mile with barely a passing point between them.   Thankfully, I was able to drive speedier than Michael in his fully loaded van and arrived at the terminal first, just as the ferry was about to leave.   Frantically I cried out,   *"Oh please, wait for us!"*

In sheer desperation, I pleaded with the ferrymen to delay sailing until Michael arrived.   Graciously, they agreed to give us ten minutes or so.   Every minute felt like an hour as I searched the darkness for the van's headlights to appear.   The thought of spending a cold and chilly night on the dockside cooped up in my little car till morning was an unbearable thought, especially after such a long hard drive.

Then suddenly, I saw Michael speeding towards us.   *I don't think I'd ever been so pleased to see him!*   Oh, what a relief as he literally drove straight onto the ferry, with me right behind him. *Just seconds later, the ship pulled away.*

It was really late by the time we docked at Larne and when we finally arrived at our farmhouse B & B, we had to wake the owners up to let us in. I'm not sure whether Michael personally made this booking, but when we were taken upstairs, there were only three small single beds, one of them being in the attic. Michael collapsed into the attic bed and fell asleep immediately.   I tried to make the best of a bad job by pushing the other two narrow beds together.

After settling the boys, both totally exhausted at this late hour, I curled up across the ends of their beds, fully clothed and tried to get some sleep. With no spare pillows or blankets to keep me warm, it was a miserable end to an emotionally and physically draining day. *"Surely, tomorrow would be better?"*

212

Hello, Northern Ireland

Michael had rented a nice, semi-detached house for us in Enniskillen, Co. Fermanagh, but little did I realize that this was another two and a half hours' drive away. I could hardly face another long drive after so little sleep and I struggled to suppress rising feelings of annoyance and irritability.

Eventually, we arrived at our pleasant new home on the edge of a quiet housing development, with a lovely view of a small lake in the distance.   At last, I could breath a sigh of relief and relax, or could I?   The van needed unloading, beds making, Ross's cot erecting and everyone was hungry and tired.   But at least we'd made it.   Now, we could all say, *"Hello, Northern Ireland!"*

The *'Troubles'* were still on

Without any doubt, Enniskillen is an attractive town set on the banks of the River Erne. This pic-turesque river meanders its way between the Upper and Lower Lough Erne, Co. Fermanagh's famous and stunning waterways.   But being a *border* town next to Co. Donegal, which is part of the Republic of Ireland or *the South* as it's known locally, it meant there was an English Army base stationed in Enniskillen, with intense security all around the town.   This was now early April 1991 and the *'Troubles'* were still on.

Not having seen any security measures during our previous *holiday* visit, it all came as quite a shock.   There was so much I wasn't used to, so much I hadn't been told and so

213

much I hadn't been made aware of. For instance, the constant security check points when a driver is stopped and questioned by *armed* patrols. I found this quite alarming at first and quickly realized the importance of carrying ID on me at all times, something I'd never done before. *'Controlled Zone Parking'* areas in town centres was completely new to me too. I remember being totally horrified when Michael explained to me that if I left my car unattended in one of these areas, the police or army could blow it up if they suspected it contained a bomb. *Oh, my goodness!*

Driving at night was fearsome too. I dreaded seeing a *red torchlight* waving back and forth at me in the dark, when the police or army would beckon me to stop. Sometimes, on a lonely stretch of road, it was so dark that all I could see was a piercing red light shining at me and it was impossible to see who it was, until I slowed right down. And yet, it was too dangerous not to. How my heart used to miss a beat when this happened.

I wasn't used either, to seeing guns pointing out of ditches along the roadside. Or patrols of armoured riot police vehicles and convoys of army jeeps with soldiers holding rifles and machine guns at the ready. No! No-one had warned me about all of this.

Very soon, I became acutely aware that my Renault 5 car, having an English number plate, together with my unmistakable *English* accent, made people automatically presume I was an *English Army wife*. I realized too, with some trepidation, that this could put me and the boys in some danger. I felt uneasy and fearful, especially when out shopping, and began using sign language at pay tills instead of speaking.

Each night, I peeked out of drawn curtains before going to bed, just to make sure *everything looked OK outside.*

How easily and very quickly *fear* can grip you.   Oh, it's easy to laugh at this now, when there's peace in Northern Ireland.   But it was no laughing matter at the time.   I wasn't used to being *fearful* of my surroundings or *nervous* about where I parked to do my shopping.   Additionally, almost every day the TV news was full of recent bombings, atrocities and deaths, which only increased my apprehension.   Before long, I chose not to listen to such depressing and upsetting news.   It was too disturbing.

Everything here seemed so very different and sometimes very scary.   Let me tell you about one incident ...

Our third day in Enniskillen

I will always remember our third day in Enniskillen.   I had been used to shopping in large supermarkets back in Yorkshire, like Sainsbury's, Tesco's, Asda etc.   But here, back in early 1991, there were only small shops, usually attached to a petrol station.   Even the Wellworths store in Enniskillen was small and unimpressive.

To add to my mounting frustration, there were many grocery items I bought every week at home in Yorkshire which were not available here, nor had they even been heard of.   Plus, fruit and vegetables were an extortionate price compared to England.   For instance, I could buy almost 1 lb. of apples in Yorkshire for the same price as *one* apple here.   I had never seen apples and other fruit priced *individually.*   I couldn't believe it.

So on our third day, I decided to go hunting for a supermarket, a large one. *"Surely,"* I thought, *"there must be one here somewhere?"*

With only a rough map and very few signposts on the roads to guide me, I drove and drove until I found myself in a quiet country lane behind a queue of about six cars. Ahead of me, I thought I could see what looked like towers and barbed wire. How very *strange.*

I sat waiting patiently, but the cars in front of me didn't seem to be moving. After a while, with still no progress, I finally decided, *"There are no supermarkets this way."* So, without further ado, I did a three-point turn in the road and drove off on my mission.

I never did find the supermarket I was looking for. And finally, when I arrived back at our rented house, I just sat alone in my car. Too disheartened, too disappointed, and too dejected to get out. With my face buried in my hands, I sobbed desolate tears. Tears of frustration. Tears of self-pity. Tears of pain and rejection. Endless tears. My heart was breaking in this *foreign* land.

I felt totally distraught, deceived, *abandoned* and so alone. I was already desperately homesick, but now, *I had no home to go back to.* I was far from my friends and my Mum, and I just wanted to go back to England. As picturesque as Enniskillen was, and still is, it was *not* home to me. As I sat weeping and feeling hopelessly sorry for myself, I passionately cried out, *"I would rather be in the Outer Hebrides than here!"*

Later that same evening, while chatting and getting to know my next door neighbour, a friendly single mum with four children, I told her about my escapades earlier in the day. She was totally shocked and horrified at what I'd done. She exclaimed, *"You could have been shot doing a three-point turn at a check point. You just don't do that. If a car turns round at a check point, they can shoot you!"*

Oh help! I had no idea. No-one had explained anything to me. I didn't even realize I was at a check point. *I was only looking for a supermarket!*

It was sink or swim

When we first drove off the ferry at Larne, I was quite unaware that the historic town of Enniskillen is situated on the *far western* side of Northern Ireland, where we planned to live.

It was only when we arrived, that I realized Carrickfergus, where Michael continued living and working all week, is on the *far eastern* coast of Northern Ireland. A two and a half hour drive between us. As he explained, *"I need to be near the factory."* Well OK, I can understand that. *"But,"* I argued, *"I'm a Company Director of this factory and yet you've placed me as far away from it as possible!"*

I was doing my best not to feel suspicious, angry and upset and made the effort to drive to the factory once a week to attend meetings. I was, after all, a Director with personal guarantees and felt it was vitally important to keep a tab on what was going on and see for myself the progress being made. But the glaring fact remained, *the boys and I were living alone again.* So here we were, in a *new* country so to speak, with no choice of going back to England. It was *sink or swim.* So, as optimistically as I could, I made a firm, positive decision to give our new life in Northern Ireland the best chance I could. And, gradually, the boys and I adjusted and settled in, facing one day at a time.

We learnt how to laugh again

I found an excellent primary school for Leon and a great playschool for Ross, both within walking distance from our new home. It was wonderful to see them adapting so well, which enabled our lives to fall into a reassuring routine. As the weeks passed and we felt more secure, *we learnt how to laugh again.*

After school, the boys and I enjoyed going for a drive. This was like a mini adventure for us, as we explored our new surroundings. During our investigations, we soon found some really beautiful lakeside walks where we took our dog *Bluey* for a run. When we felt really energetic, we tackled a seriously steep mountain path up through the woods to a splendid viewing point above Blaney. Arriving panting and breathless, we were rewarded with the most awesome far reaching views over the profusion of lakes below us. A fabulous sight.

In a surprisingly short time, the boys and I grew accustomed to life in Enniskillen and came to love the beautiful countryside all around us. Life was becoming fun again and we found we were laughing more and more. When we look back on these times, the boys and I still have very fond memories of these *fun times* spent together.

Eleven Plus exam

T here were many things that were still so different to us, and one of them was the *Eleven Plus* exam. It had been abolished years ago in England and now, as Leon was about to leave his new primary school, we found out that he had missed taking this important exam earlier in the year, while we were still living in Yorkshire. Being wisely advised to contact the Education Board for their help and advice, they took my details but were unable to offer me much hope of rectifying this predicament. Then, at 2 p.m. one Friday afternoon, we all got a surprise.

To the astonishment of Leon's Head Master, the Education Board rang him with some unexpected news. They informed him that a *special* Eleven Plus Exam had been arranged for my son, plus two other children at 11 a.m. on Monday. *Just three days away.* This created a minor panic to say the least.

Promptly, Leon was whisked out of his class and hastily given a two-hour cramming course by his flustered Head Master and Maths teacher, before the close of school. Besides the two sample Eleven Plus exam papers they gave Leon to study over the weekend, that was all the preparation he had. *And yet he passed. "Well done Leon, you did great!"*

Scrimping and saving

D uring the previous year, back home in our beloved Yorkshire, my sons and I had got used to scrimping and saving, and living virtually *on air.* So, when I began to receive a salary as a Director of this new manufacturing company, I was delighted and saved almost all of it.

219

Although we had warmed to our rented house and Enniskillen too, I disliked paying such a high rent and felt sure that a mortgage wouldn't cost much more. So, after only four months of carefully saving every penny I could, *a miracle happened.* I managed to save just enough money to put a minimum 5% deposit down on a small house and *get a mortgage in my own name.* I was absolutely thrilled!

But it had been a real fight to get it. I'd endured several nerve-wracking interviews at the Head Offices of two different major Building Societies in Belfast's City centre before I was successful. My dogged perseverance to give my sons a new home had paid off. Now, thankfully, every bit of this effort proved to be worthwhile *and we soon had our own home again.*

Our pretty new home

B y now, the boys and I had become quite attached to Enniskillen and actually regretted leaving this historic town with its lovely surroundings. And yet, only four months earlier, I had hated being there. Thankfully, we'd all adjusted really well to our new life and learnt to adapt quickly to the many differences, *even grocery shopping.*

But house prices in Enniskillen were quite high in this attractive and desirable location and we were unable to find anything we liked at the right price. We continued our search, beginning around Carrickfergus and the factory, but properties were still too expensive. We moved further and further out towards Ballymena, but still had no success.

Finally, after much diligence, we found just what we were looking for. A really lovely detached cottage, beside a village primary school, set in a small, rural farming community with quiet country lanes all around. It was also close to the River Bann and the beautiful Portglenone Woods, where we loved walking our dog. Amazingly, it was everything I had hoped and wished for. And when I look back now, I realize *I'd wished for an awful lot.*

During our searching, if anyone had ever asked me what type of home I was looking for, I very boldly replied, *"A period detached house with lots of character."* But I also wanted three bedrooms and three reception rooms, one to be an office for Michael, plus a large garden and lovely country views. Oh, and it had to be cheap too. Quite a tall order you might say.

And yet we found an old Headmaster's house, full of character, in a quiet village with far reaching views over the Sperrin Mountains. It fitted the bill perfectly. *How wonderful.*

It had taken a great deal of determination and an enormous struggle to achieve it, but we'd triumphed over every obstacle against us. *"And do you know something?"* The house had been on the market for two and a half years. It seemed as if it had been waiting just for us. It was so perfect in every detail, *and we all loved our new home.*

But it was many years later before I realized *why* and *how* we found this lovely, little hidden gem. I had so boldly *spoken* over and over again what I wanted. And I had held firmly to it, without compromising. I can see now, that it was *God Himself who heard me and fulfilled my ambitious wish list.* HE had kept this beautiful home especially for us, knowing it was just what I was hoping for. God certainly did give me *"the desires of my heart,"* even before I knew Him.

Just one week later

We were still on a *high* after moving into our new home when, just one week later, our joy disappeared, in an instant. *Michael lost his job at the factory.* He was, after all, *just an employee.*

For many years, he'd been *the big Boss,* running his own business and used to calling the shots. But now, as an employee, things were different and he couldn't just make every decision by himself. Whilst away on a business trip, he'd taken a liberty which was wrong and without the consent of his bosses, resulting in his dismissal. And their decision was final. They refused to listen and had no mercy.

This was really serious and it all happened behind my back. It became quite apparent that I was 'a Company Director' *only when it suited them. Only when* they wanted me to sign financial documents and *only when* they wanted me to accept personal liability. I had simply been *used* to fulfil their legal conditions.   Now, they didn't need me any more and treated me like a *sleeping* Director, as if I simply didn't exist. I was angry.

But I had to control my anger. *Without* my husband at the factory to keep me informed of the day-to-day affairs, I had no way of knowing what was going on *or what I could be held responsible for.* This was an alarming situation and I had to decide quickly what to do.

However, there seemed to be little choice open to me. I had to try and sell my shares to the other Directors, thereby releasing myself from any possible financial liabilities that I so dreaded. After an intensely difficult and highly charged Directors' Board Meeting, chaired by Aiden, the factory's independent accountant, the other Directors agreed to my request. They offered to pay me a monthly sum to purchase my shares, which I gladly accepted. Step *one* was successfully over.

Step *two*, was to get myself legally discharged as a Company Director. Something I knew nothing about. But Aiden very kindly offered to help me and organized it all. I was so grateful for his help and advice, and over the next few years, he became a faithful friend who helped me on several occasions.

This whole episode had been a deeply distressing experience. Yet I was so thankful to be free from the financial burden and any personal liability of this Company.   Feeling happy and content with the final outcome, I felt at least we had some money coming in each month to live on. This would give us a breathing space to sort ourselves out and give Michael a chance to find another job. But it was not to be. Just a few months later, the other Directors broke their agreement to me and stopped the payments. Our stress levels soared again.

I wasn't laughing now, I can tell you. I thought I'd been so clever getting ourselves a lovely new home. But now here I was, responsible for a mortgage, two young children to look after and no money coming in. Things just weren't going the way I had hoped and little did I know, that another challenge was just around the corner.

Another new business venture

Can you believe it? Michael persuaded me again to start a new business. This time, an *office stationery* business and before I knew it, he was off and away in my Renault 5 car for several days at a time, selling our stationery products. *"So far so good,"* I thought. *"At least he's trying to earn us a living."*

After a few weeks, I asked him how he was getting on and he said, *"Fine."* I was relieved to hear this and replied, *"That's great. Where's the money from your sales?"*

However, I wasn't expecting his flippant and completely irresponsible reply, *"I've drunk it!"* I couldn't believe my ears. Yes, he had literally spent every single penny on drinking whisky and having a fine old time.

"Oh, my goodness. Was this really happening to me?" I was still struggling under a load of debts from our home in Yorkshire and now this. I was absolutely *furious* and ready to *explode*. But what could I do about it? It was too late. There was no money left. *It was all gone.*

I felt weary and disillusioned. I had no-one to turn to as Michael rapidly plunged us deeper and deeper into debt. *I felt like giving up.* But I knew if I didn't stay calm and try to think clearly, we couldn't possibly survive this crisis. I had to do something and very quickly, before he sold even more of our goods to fuel his insatiable desire for whisky.

Mercifully, the manufacturers let us return all of our remaining stock. But I was horrified when they told us that nearly *four thousand pounds* was still owing for the goods already sold. Yes, Michael had blown four thousand pounds, *plus the profit,* on enjoying himself. Four thousand pounds that *I owed, not him.*

My hopes and expectations of a new start were now a distant memory and once again I felt cheated, deceived and *very* angry.

Michael simply shrugged it off and then tried, unsuccessfully, to find a job to bring in some money. As the weeks passed, our financial situation worsened until it became critical. Finally, he decided to return to England to look for a job and went back to live with his widowed mother in southern England. He did manage to find some work here and there, but it didn't bring in sufficient money to send us any. *Not even one penny did he send us.* Eventually, he came to the conclusion that he didn't like Northern Ireland any more and wanted to remain in England.

This may sound like *good news,* but I was hurting beyond measure. The boys and I were left to cope alone yet again, under the burden of a mortgage and massive debts. We felt humiliated, deeply wounded, discouraged and very vulnerable, with no friends or family to help us.

I was literally teetering on the verge of *sheer panic,* more desperate than words can ever express. The pain and agony of every waking moment seared my senses and I was on the brink of a total nervous breakdown. If only this was a dream, but it wasn't. It was real and *I didn't know what to do.*

Thankfully, a caring neighbour stepped in to comfort me. She came to visit us often, sometimes every day. Just having someone else in the house to talk to helped so much, as she quietly listened to my tormented woes and endless crying. She had compassion on me and I shall never forget her friendship and kindness when I really needed it. Her name was Linden.

But by now, my problems were mountainous, and I needed help. More help than a kind and listening ear could offer.

Chapter 21

Winter was upon us

I was terrified of losing our home again. But more than that, I was petrified of having my children taken away from me and put into care if I couldn't look after them. With Michael living back in England with his mother, the boys and I were left nearly penniless. I had hardly any money left and no income. Nothing, except my weekly Child Benefit allowance. *Absolutely nothing.*

How sad, that at this point of dire need, I was quite unaware that we may have been entitled to some other assistance from the Government. I suppose I was still hanging on to the hope that Michael would send us some money to help us. But none ever came. It seemed it was up to me to support us somehow.

Winter was now upon us and the boys and I went to Portglenone Woods to collect fallen sticks to burn in our fireplace. We had no heating and hardly any food. We didn't have enough pieces of carpet to cover the old and very draughty floor boards in our living room and were forced to keep our coats on all the time. So we just laid sheets of

227

newspaper down over the bare floorboards to keep the cold out. It was many years later before we could afford the luxury of a new fitted carpet.

But both Leon and little Ross were fantastic. They had gone through so much and yet they never complained. We worked together as a team helping each other and even collecting sticks in the forest became fun.

Community Visitor

B ut we needed cash urgently to buy some food and the barest essentials. After searching the local newspapers, I applied for a part-time job with MADCA, the local Community Association based in Maghera. Having the stated necessary requirement of a car, I was accepted as a local Community Visitor.

Every day, I now drove around visiting elderly people in their homes, in the two villages nearest our home. This proved to be a good way to meet people and find out about rural village life and local culture. I had a lot to learn.

One of the first things I was taught by my new companions was the local *lingo.* For instance, they taught me that *pretties* are potatoes, *scallions* are Spring onions and a *whin-bush* is gorse. They introduced me to soda farls, soda bread and wheaten bread, all unheard of in England. Then one day, I was met with the greeting, *"You're failed!"* I was puzzled and couldn't understand what I'd done wrong. Then they explained to me that I was looking tired and pale, and not my usual cheery self.

These dear old folks were all so kind and friendly and welcomed me into their homes. Their warm hospitality certainly helped me to adjust more quickly to their rural way of life and I enjoyed getting out of the house to meet new people.

My workday of visiting finished conveniently by 3 p.m., just in time to collect Ross, now barely four years old, from his primary school. I know this job didn't bring in much money, but at least it was something and *we were very grateful for it.*

Debts

Debts, debts, debts! And bills, bills, bills! *"Do you know what I mean?"* Final bills, warning letter bills, legal action bills, recorded delivery bills, bills of every description and endless demands. Those brown envelopes just kept coming through our letter box, with yet another deadline for payment.

Bills that stretched back before my husband's bankruptcy and had become *mine.* Bills that accrued during the year Michael left me and our children alone in Yorkshire, while he lived in Northern Ireland. Yes, he knew of our struggles and terrible need, but he never sent us a penny. Bills that followed us from North Yorkshire to Northern Ireland and now, over two years later, seemed bigger and more fearsome by the day.

I was swamped, overwhelmed and I wanted to run away and escape. But I had nowhere to go and no-one to help me. *"Desperate?"* That was an understatement. *"I was frantic!"*

We had barely any money and I still hadn't paid the solicitors their fees for handling the legalities to purchase our new home. I decided to make them a settlement offer. An offer to pay just *half* of their total bill. Reluctantly, they accepted, which was great news. I was now one bill less, but with plenty to go. There were loads and loads of them. Fifteen, twenty, twenty-five? I almost lost count.

Methodically, I began writing a letter to each one. First, I explained my situation and then I respectfully asked if they would accept a couple of pounds per month, against my total debt. Amazingly, they all agreed to my meagre offer and not one of them added a penny extra interest.

Christmas visit

After Michael had been back in England a few months, he planned to visit us over Christmas, but I couldn't help wondering, *"Had he changed? Had he stopped drinking?"*

I was dreading his visit and became really nervous about it. Full of trepidation, I collected him from the airport and when I didn't give him the rapturous, passionate welcome he wanted, he flew into an hysterical rage. Within an hour of coming home, he stormed out of the house, walking several miles to the nearest pub. He was in such a violent temper, that I rang the nice couple who owned the pub, to warn them that he was home and on his way.

I was *really* frightened after this horrendous home-coming, knowing that he would surely return in a few hours' time full of whisky, which was certain to be very dangerous. As I contemplated the situation, I knew locking him out was not a wise option, unless I wanted the windows and doors smashed in. So when he finally arrived back, I cheerily opened the front door to welcome him. But, what I hadn't realized, was that young Leon had been excitedly waiting up to see his Daddy. Sadly, he was standing up the stairs and witnessed his father's violent behaviour, as he hit me and threw me across the hallway.

Regrettably, he hadn't changed at all and his drinking was still a serious problem and so was the terrifying physical violence. Every night during his visit, he went off to the pub. One evening, after he returned home, he threw me down onto the couch and literally tried to strangle me. Then, very deliberately and very calmly, he delightedly poured his glass of whisky over my head.

This was the last straw. I'd had enough. I just couldn't take any more. No more stress, no more fear, no more violence, no more debts. *No more.*

It was such a tense and difficult ten days and I was a complete nervous wreck by the time he left. He made suggestions about coming back to live with us, *but I was too frightened to encourage him to return.* I just couldn't take any more of his drinking, his fearful violence or risk having any more debts. *I simply couldn't trust him.*

"Did he really want to come back to us?" I'm not sure, because he didn't press the point or even mention that he missed his children.

When his visit ended, I drove him to the airport and we said our final farewell to each other. Although it may sound strange, it was actually painful saying *"good-bye"* to him.

We'd been married for twenty-one years and weathered so many storms together and yet it seemed like an unspoken understanding between us that he would *not* return. Even though I was far from perfect myself, I'd tried really hard to keep our marriage together. But now, as we parted, I knew it was irrevocably over. It seemed so very, very sad. So very final. And I cried all the way home.

Enough was enough

W ithin a few weeks of his leaving, I came to dread the unexpected knocks on our front door, as yet another irritated man called to collect his money. Money that Michael had borrowed from him while at the pub, during his recent Christmas visit. Money that he had no way of repaying, plus no intention of doing so. It seemed to me, that every debt my husband incurred became *my debt*. Debts that I had no choice but to repay. And I did. *"But would it ever end?"*

I was already under extreme pressure, more than I could hardly bear and this seemed like the final insult. My life of fear, abuse and intense stress, *had to stop.* I just couldn't take any more. *Enough was enough* and a year later, we were divorced.

Divorce

I didn't realize it at the time, but being divorced carried a social stigma in Northern Ireland. For quite a while, it made me feel like a social outcast, which was very hurtful and did nothing to help my self-esteem and confidence. It seemed so unfair. But what I have now learnt, from my own personal experience, is that *divorce* touches so many lives and almost always causes untold pain.   Your children can especially suffer. Whether they are young or much older, the pain is still the same, and it can affect them for the rest of their lives.

Divorce is a serious decision and an action not to be entered into lightly.   The burden of being a single parent is a huge responsibility and one that is often overwhelmingly heavy to bear. My advice to anyone considering divorce is to *stop* and think *very* carefully, and don't make any hasty decisions. Swallow your pride, be ready to forgive, and be prepared to give your marriage another chance if you possibly can, especially if you have children. I wouldn't wish divorce on anyone.

Also, when you meet a divorced person, please think twice before stepping in to judge them.   Whatever the situation may be, and whoever is to blame, *both parties* will probably have been hurt along the way and gone through much pain.

Please be understanding too, and show mercy because, *"There, by the grace of God, go I"* is a very true saying.   That *divorced* person could be you or one of your children.   So please, think carefully, before judging anyone else's downfall and pain.

Chapter 22

Facing life Alone

H ere I was, alone again, and deeply hurting. Often totally desperate and living in a country at war with itself. So far from my family, friends and my dear Mum. Oh, how I missed my Mum. If ever I needed her, I needed her now. I was grieving and so were my sons. We felt like orphans *abandoned* in a strange land. We were so very lonely, so very vulnerable, and so very poor.

Facing life alone, without a husband to share the responsibilities with, *was much harder than I could ever have imagined.* Getting divorced had seemed the answer to many of my fears. But now I faced new fears, terrifying ones. Fears that overwhelmed me.

My eldest son Leon, now twelve years old, suffered in silence, in secret. For a long time, he cried himself to sleep, night after night. When years later I found this out, it really tore at my heart. He'd been close to his Daddy and missed him very much. Every time he spoke to him on the telephone, it upset him terribly and took him days to recover. This left a legacy of pain throughout his young life.

234

My youngest son Ross was only four, but not too young to understand that his Daddy didn't live with us anymore. He vented his grieving in behavioural problems, much to the dismay of his teachers. In fact, they told me he was the worst behaved pupil they had ever had.

It was only when I was discussing this matter with his primary school teacher, that she made a passing comment. A comment that helped us understand the situation, *"Ross is always writing stories about going places and doing things with his Daddy. Even last weekend, he wrote about doing this and that with his Daddy!"*

His teacher was totally unaware of our personal situation and never realized that Ross was living in a fantasy world. A make-believe world that was cushioning his grieving little heart. How deeply this upset me.

But thankfully, now that his kind and very patient teacher and I both understood what was happening, we were able to work together to help him. Very slowly, carefully and lovingly, we handled this problem until gradually, Ross's behaviour improved.

Little by little, Leon and Ross settled down. They made new friends and began to enjoy themselves. They played happily in our lovely back garden and enjoyed biking for miles around the quiet lanes. They also had fun climbing the sturdy rope ladder up to their roomy timber tree-house, set high in the branches of a large sycamore tree at the end of our garden, with incredible views towards the Glens of Antrim. This tree-house made a great hiding place and a marvellous *den* for them and their friends.

It was definitely a comfort and a pleasure too, to watch my children enjoying themselves, and to hear their happy laughter as they played. But for me, life was unbearably tough trying to make ends meet. I cried my own solitary, secret tears too, from a broken heart.

Yes, *divorce* may have appeared a welcome relief to my problems. But *nothing* could have prepared me for the life I was facing now. *Nothing* could have prepared me for the horrors and rigours of bringing up two children by myself, particularly with no family to help us. Now I had an incredibly hard task on my hands, as day by day I was finding out.

Years of silence

Nevertheless, just a year later, when Leon was twelve years old, he went to stay with his Daddy for one week in London. This was the last time they saw each other for six years.

Michael never came to visit us again and never managed to send us a penny maintenance. Contact between him and both our sons gradually waned and he rarely ever sent them Christmas or Birthday cards.

Years of silence went by, until Leon finished his schooling and then, at eighteen years of age, he understandably wanted to trace his father.

Through contacting Grandma, he received his Dad's phone number and rang him. And what a surprise he got. *His Dad had just remarried three weeks previously.* A marriage that sadly ended in divorce several years later.

First trip back to England

R oss was much older now too, and I felt it was finally time for him to meet his father again, along with his father's new wife and her teenage son. This was very important for Ross, *as he couldn't even remember what his Daddy looked like.*

This was our first trip back to England in nine years and Ross's first ride on a train. After visiting my cousin Derek and his family for a few days, we travelled south by rail to stay with my best friend Yolanda and her husband. She very kindly took Ross and me down to London to meet Michael and what a nerve-wracking day we had. Passing young Ross over to the care of his father for the day was so difficult. Michael had become a complete stranger to all of us and watching him walk away with Ross, his estranged son, was really hard.

Yolanda and I had planned a *girlie* day out together, looking round shops and sight-seeing. But however hard we tried, we just couldn't seem to relax and were both anxious for Ross all day.

When at last, it was time to meet up with them again, I was disappointed to see that a bond hadn't formed between father and son. They just stood apart saying their *"good-byes"* and I had to prompt Ross to give his Daddy a farewell hug. A hug that had to last them for many, many years to come.

But I've gone ahead of myself again. So lets go back to *My Story ...*

I was in business

Following Michael's stressful Christmas visit to us, I applied for some help from the Social Services. Month after month went by, with no news. In the meantime, I continued working for MADCA, even though the wage was so small until, sadly, it finally closed down due to Government cut backs.

Life seemed increasingly impossible as our paltry finances were stretched to the limit, especially when it came to buying groceries. Every week was a constant battle trying to make ends meet and have some food for my boys. I was completely and utterly distraught and crying was my only relief. But *tears* didn't pay the bills or put food on the table. I had to *do* something and *do* it quickly, if I was to keep my children and our home together.

I thought long and hard before remembering that my *now ex-husband* had set up our office stationery business in *my name,* together with a business bank account. So I decided to resurrect it. I knew it would take a lot of hard work, but I felt it was worth a try. So I threw myself into it and started working *round the clock.*

Every evening, and often late into the night, I typed up price lists for all the stationery items that I could sell. I had an excellent and very modern electric typewriter (no computers or laptops in those days) plus a photocopier that I'd brought with me from Yorkshire and suddenly, amazingly ... *I was in business!*

I managed to find a good and very caring childminder to collect Ross from school every day and look after him for me, while I went off to try my hand at selling. Something new and something I'd never ever done before.

I just kept knocking on doors

I targeted all the largest towns near our home and literally walked the streets for hours. I knocked on every office and shop door trying to sell boxes of envelopes, photocopying paper, fax rolls, till rolls, etc.

At first, I found this really hard to do. But the desperate need to care for my children drove me on and on and wouldn't let me give up. I just kept knocking on doors until I got some firm orders. And when I did, I drove down to the wholesalers in Belfast to buy the goods. But I had no money and certainly no credit facility, *so what could I do?*

I decided I had only one option. Write a business cheque, even though my account was empty. This meant I needed to receive immediate payment for my goods, hopefully in cash. So I had a race on my hands to deposit funds into my bank account, to cover the cheque I'd already written.

Phew! It was a bit frantic at times and not always enjoyable, but I just had to swallow my pride and overcome any fear, and get on with it.

Perhaps some of my customers felt sorry for me, I don't know, but through sheer hard work and determination, I thankfully managed to build up a good clientele with regular orders. My suppliers eventually gave me a monthly credit account too, which made life so much easier.

A welcome surprise

T hen one day, I received a long-awaited surprise. I was granted some Government help and it was back-dated eight months. *Wow, what an incredible surprise!*

Well, it didn't take me long to decide how to spend our *miracle* money. We badly needed to replace the old solid fuel furnace that heated our house. Yes, I'm serious. We had a *furnace*, not a central heating boiler. This horrible *furnace* gobbled up solid-fuel, belched out thick black smoke and daily covered our window sills and back yard with a layer of soot. It was a terrible contraption and I hated it.

It was a health hazard too, and I was getting bronchitis from all the dirt and soot in the atmosphere. This furnace was really only suitable for burning old tyres and *it just had to go.* To my amazement, someone actually wanted it and gave me £5 for it. Oh, what a delight to get rid of this filthy, grimy monster that could eat up a whole bag of coal in one mouth-ful.

So, with my unexpected windfall, I managed to buy and install a *brand new,* clean and beautiful oil central heating boiler. Plus, a *brand new* 600 gallon oil tank and completely fill it too. All for £800. *Exactly the amount of money I had.* It was like a wonderful dream come true and now we could have heat whenever we needed it, *at the flick of a switch.*

I was so very thankful

A mazingly, my new little business now flourished too, and I was able to keep our home, look after my sons and begin clearing some of the many debts. I was so grateful to the kindness of every customer who faithfully supported me, and for their friendship and encouragement through this really tough period.

Certainly, it was worth every bit of the enormous effort and perseverance because, after just two years, *I managed to repay all my debts from Yorkshire.* I knew this was nothing short of *a miracle* and I was so very thankful.

A young girl's prayers

N ow, as I recall this miracle, I know that God was watching over us. I know that God was helping us, *in answer to a young girl's prayers.*   A young girl who lived in the farm opposite our home, and who had compassion on us. Without our knowledge, she kept praying for us year after year until finally, one day towards the end of April 1997, she told me about her daily prayers for us all.

You see, written in the holy Bible, God promises to *"never leave us nor forsake us"* and He kept His promise, even though I didn't know Him or know of His goodness. *But God heard young Donna's prayers,* and in His love and faithfulness, He helped me.   Now I can confidently say ...

- *HE gave me* the idea and the courage to resurrect our stationery business.
- *HE helped me* overcome my fear of cold-calling and selling.
- *HE equipped me* with good health and plenty of energy.
- *HE found me* a loving family who offered to care for Ross every day after school.

- *HE enabled* my little Renault 5 car to be totally reliable and trouble-free throughout all my long journeys.
- *HE provided* sufficient profit from my sales to repay all my debts, except *one,* but keep reading.
- *HE provided me* with wisdom to manage my business.
- *GOD bestowed upon me* His grace and His divine favour *to succeed.*

It was GOD, and God alone, who blessed me like this. Why? Because HE loved me, even when I didn't know HIM. And He loves me now and forever. That means, if God loved me so much even while I was unaware of His love, *then God loves you too, just as much.* And that can only be *good* news.

Change on the way

After I'd settled all my debts from Yorkshire, my circumstances began to change again. The new stationery giant *Viking Direct* arrived in Northern Ireland, slashing prices and offering next-day delivery. It became almost impossible to compete against them and eventually, I lost all but a handful of my customers. This was really disappointing and, however hard I tried, I couldn't beat most of their prices or match their special offers.

As one by one I lost my customers, our finances declined rapidly and I found it harder and harder to continue making monthly payments to reduce my one last remaining debt. The massive single debt of £4,000, when Michael drank all the proceeds from selling our stock. This debt seemed so huge, so mountainous in my eyes and *how on earth could I ever pay it off?* It was just too big for me and I felt swamped again. But little did I know that God was still on my side and had *another miracle* waiting for me, just around the corner.

Another miracle

With our income yet again stretched to its absolute limit, I was totally unable to make even the smallest monthly payment against this last debt. It was at this crisis point of extreme helplessness, that I telephoned Aiden, the accountant who'd helped me a few years earlier. When I explained my predicament to him, he burst out laughing.   I was momentarily taken aback by his jovial reaction and almost felt a tinge of antagonism rising within me. *"What are you laughing at? I'm serious. I can't pay another penny!"*

Then gleefully, he shared the most fantastic news with me. *"The Finance Company has gone into liquidation, taking your debt with them. There's no need to pay another penny!"*

WOW! This was unbelievable news and I couldn't help asking Aiden, *"Say that again please. It sounds so good. So incredible."*   And now, I was laughing too. Surely, this was God's divine favour? And another answer to Donna's prayers to bless us. And Oh! How I needed it.

This debt had seemed totally insurmountable in my eyes, but to God, it was not difficult at all. This was, without any doubt, the best news possible and what an enormous relief to me.

It meant that finally, *I was free! Free* from every single one of Michael's debts. And I was so thrilled. *This was a miracle indeed!*

243

Careful budgeting

At long last, I could begin to budget our weekly money without the added stress of debts to repay. And how thankful I was that my Mum had taught me this wisdom. Without delay, I put this skill to good use and devised a chart that listed every expense that we would incur throughout the year. This included Christmas and birthday presents, pocket-money, school uniforms and shoes, haircuts, telephone and rates, TV licence, car maintenance, car tax and MOT, house and car insurance, plus central heating oil and electricity. Whatever we had left, was spent on food. And that wasn't much, barely enough for two growing lads.

Literally, *every single last penny* we received was allocated and recorded on this chart against these expenses. Whenever I could, I would save towards a future expense like Leon's eighteenth birthday, even if it was only 5p per week. But it paid off, because those few pennies saved each week amounted to £200 by the time his eighteenth birthday arrived. I did the same for Ross too, and how thrilled I was when I was able to buy them both a memorable present.

All those years of disciplined budgeting had been worth *every single penny*. This is how we managed and survived through such tough times and not a single penny was ever wasted or squandered. We never took anything for granted and we learnt to appreciate everything we were blessed with.

New friends helped us

It was really hard on my sons growing up with no father, no grandparents, aunts, uncles or cousins. We had no relatives we could visit or family to share special occasions with like birthdays, Christmas and Easter.   Leon and Ross grew up never having cousins to play with, aunts and uncles to encourage and guide them, grandparents to spoil or make a fuss of them and harder still, no Daddy to love and hug them.   No Daddy to kick a ball with them, take them fishing, teach them basic handyman skills or cheer them on.

All our relations lived back in England and they were too frightened to visit us, due to the *Troubles,* as incidents of bombings and murders were regularly reported in the News.   However, Christmas and Easter were particularly difficult for us and although I did my best to give them some treats and small surprises, we often felt very lonely.

Thankfully, over the next few years, we made some wonderful new friends who helped and encouraged us and became our *new* family.   They will always remain dear to my heart and I'm so thankful to them all for their loving kindness, deep friendship and welcome support.

But I shall be forever thankful too, to my wonderful sons who never ever grumbled about anything.   They were always grateful for whatever we had, even when it was so very little.   They were the most loving and adoring sons, and a real blessing and a constant joy to me.

However, life never stands still and little did I know that mine was about to be changed *forever.*   Yes.   Changed for *good* this time.   So, let's fast forward a little bit, to find out what happened.

It was amazing!

Chapter 23

The night that changed my life...
forever!

We were at last beginning to feel part of our local village community. We'd even begun to regularly attend church on Sundays. But there was one particular Autumn Sunday morning that I will always remember.

Dr. Helen Roseveare, a missionary, came to tell us about her trials and challenges as a doctor in a remote hospital in the Democratic Republic of the Congo, in Central Africa. We learnt that she had gone out to the Congo through a Christian Organization called WEC International to practice medicine from 1953 – 1973.

As Helen began speaking to us, I realized she was *different*. I mean she was full of joy and enthusiasm. She was vibrant and full of *life*, and spoke with *passion*. I was captivated by her every word and sat up straight on the hard wooden church pew, to give her my undivided attention.

She told us about an amazing *miracle* that happened to her in the remote jungle hospital in the Congo where she worked and, for the first time in my life, I was *stirred*. I mean, I was *really stirred*. The true life story she told us that morning left such a deep, lasting impression upon me, I just couldn't forget it.

A story of how a group of children in England had taken great care over packing a parcel to send out to Helen. A parcel that contained a vital life-saving gift. A parcel that arrived at Helen's hospital at just the very moment it was urgently needed. In time to help a newborn baby whose mother had tragically died during the birth.

Helen continued to tell us that she and her nurses were anxious to do all they could to keep this frail, premature baby alive by keeping it warm and away from the chilly night-time draughts. Yet with no incubator, this would not be an easy task and their only option was to rely upon a hot water bottle.

But to the nurses' dismay, they discovered the rubber on their very last hot water bottle had perished and it burst open when one of them tried to fill it. They needed a new one, and *quickly. Right now.* But being situated in a remote African jungle, far away from any towns, this seemed an impossibility. So all that night, the nurses took turns to keep this tiny baby warm beside the fire.

The next day, while Helen was praying with some of the children from the local orphanage, she told them about the burst hot water bottle and the desperate need to keep this premature baby warm. One orphan girl was so moved by the urgent problem that she prayed for God to send a new hot water bottle. Moreover, she prayed that *it must arrive today or the baby could die.* Then, even more boldly, she prayed for *a dolly* to comfort this baby's older two-year-old sister, who was crying and missing her mummy. Everyone, including Helen, was tempted to say this was an impossible prayer, even for God to answer. But we have a truly amazing God who hears our *every* prayer, however impossible it may seem. And God was about to answer this little girl's prayer, in an incredible way.

Within hours of praying, a large parcel arrived. It was the *first* parcel Helen had received in the Congo for almost *four* years. And when they carefully unwrapped it and looked inside, guess what it contained? *A new hot water bottle!* And right at the bottom of the box ... *a dolly!*

This hot water bottle and dolly had been travelling for five long months from England, to arrive at Helen's hospital on just the very day they were needed, *in answer to the trusting and believing prayer of a child.*

Is Jesus really real?

Wow! I'd never heard a story like this before. A real-life, present-day miracle and I began to ask myself, *"Is Jesus really real? Is He alive today ... now?"* I was beginning to realize that *"THE GOD"* I had rejected and scorned all my life was, in fact, an amazing, caring and faithful God. A *living* God. A *NOW* God.

But wait a minute. *"Hadn't I experienced miracles too?"* Yes I had. And not just one, but several. How blinded I'd been to God's faithfulness and love to me, over so many years.

As these stirring thoughts sparked a new curiosity within me, I began asking searching questions, *"How do you get saved?"* and *"Could I ever get saved?"* Each Sunday now, I listened extra hard to the sermons, but *nothing* happened and I felt just the same. By Christmas time, my enthusiasm had waned to such a point, that I defiantly said, *"I don't think I'll ever get saved. Nothing ever seems to go IN."* And yet, I still couldn't forget how *stirred* I'd felt while listening to Helen, and quietly pondered what *'being saved'* must be like. I mean, *really* like.

(This wonderful true life miracle of the *hot water bottle* can be read in more detail, along with many other faith stirring stories in Dr. Helen Roseveare's book, 'Living Faith'.)

She's coming back

About six months later, I heard that Dr. Helen Roseveare was coming back to speak at a women's meeting in a nearby town. And I knew without a doubt, *I just had to be there.* I just had to hear her again. It was the evening of Monday, 21st April, 1997. The night that changed my life, *forever!*

I was excited and expectant and really looking forward to hearing Helen speak again, and I was not disappointed. She spoke about *Jesus* and how He loves each one of us and immediately, I knew that even meant *me.* She told us how He died and shed His blood on the cross to forgive us our sins. Then miraculously, on the third day, He rose victorious from the tomb to *live forever,* as the *Lord of Lords* and *King of Kings.*

Helen was speaking with the same captivating sincerity and passion as the last time, and I could feel myself changing, tingling and getting *stirred*. Suddenly, my whole body, my senses, everything within me, came *alive*. Yes! This was what I'd been waiting for. And all at once, as I continued listening to her, *I knew Jesus was real!*

Yes, He's alive today, NOW!
And forever and ever

Oh, how humbled I felt as I realized how little I knew about Jesus. Besides learning some Bible stories and singing a few hymns, He'd never been a part of my life. And yet tonight, for the very first time, I was learning that *Jesus loves all of us, even me.* And more than that, He is *always* at our side to hear our cries, and *always* ready to help us when we call out to Him.

So, as I listened intently, Helen began telling us a story about a *bicycle wheel.* She told us how she had received some further parcels at her hospital in the Congo, but this time, they contained much needed bicycles, only they were in kit form. In fact, there were so many bicycle pieces and parts, she hardly knew where or how to start assembling them. But she was willing to give it a try.

Well, after spending three days trying to assemble just one wheel, by pushing the spokes into the rim and then trying to fit them into the hub, it simply wouldn't work. However hard she tried, the wheel kept collapsing into pieces. With her patience wearing thin, she threw it all down in frustration and was about to give up when she heard the Holy Spirit whisper to her, "*Start from the HUB!*"

250

So, in obedience to God's prompting, she tried again. But this time, she began from the *hub,* the *central* point, and before she knew it, the first wheel was assembled and *ready to roll!* (You can read more about '*The hub*' in Helen's book, 'Living Fellowship.')

Helen then explained how the *hub* is the *CENTRE* of the wheel, holding all the spokes and the rim together. And without the hub, the wheel is *not* complete and cannot function, falling apart into pieces. She continued by explaining,

When Jesus is *NOT* the *CENTRE*
or the *HUB* of our lives,
we are not *complete* either,
and our lives can fall apart too

Instantly, these words literally *exploded* in my spirit. It was as if a brilliant searchlight had been turned on inside me and I could clearly *see* and *feel* and *know* for the first time ever, *WHY* I'd messed up all my life. I felt like shouting out ...

THAT'S IT!
That's just how I feel
I'M BROKEN. Broken in pieces

"Was I complete?" No. Definitely not. I'd spent my whole life *without* Jesus and what a mess I'd made of it. Now at last, I knew *WHY* I'd gone wrong all my life. Helen then gave an invitation, *"If anyone here tonight feels* **incomplete,** *please don't go home without coming to speak to one of us."* Immediately, I inwardly responded, ***"Yes, that's me!"***

Well wild horses couldn't have kept me back. I knew without a doubt, what I *had* to do. Turning to the

251

Christian friend beside me, who'd kindly brought me, I eagerly asked her, *"Is it alright for me to go up there?"* Smiling broadly, she nodded her approval. In a flash, I was out of my seat and being led by Helen to a private area of the hall. This was definitely one of those rare moments of *spontaneity,* when you just *know* you must *do* something, but you're not sure exactly *what.*

As we sat together, Helen hardly spoke, just listened. But to me, it was as if she was Jesus Christ Himself sitting opposite me. Her kindness and love, compassion and gentleness overwhelmed me as I instinctively poured out my heart to her. I hadn't planned to do this, it just happened. All my defences and every objection simply disappeared. My hardened heart burst open, my soul was exposed and all my pain literally *poured* out.

I just hadn't realized how much hurt, anger, bitterness and unforgiveness was still stored up inside me. I had years and years of suffering, fear and rejection hidden deep inside me and like a suppressed spring, I couldn't hold it in any longer.

JESUS **was the perfect** ***KEY***
The *only key* **that knew the combination**
to unlock my stony heart.
The *only key*
that could release my pain

And, as Jesus turned the key, He released the floodgates to set me free. I totally forgot all about my pride and respectability as I humbled myself before Helen *and* the Lord.

Jesus kept turning the key, and as my heart broke open, all my pain spilled out. I was crying and shaking. My lips were trembling so much that I could hardly get my words out. I must have looked a terrible sight, but I didn't care.

It was as if every word I spoke, was literally
PULLING ALL THE PAIN OUT OF ME

Helen sat listening, not rushing me, as all my deepest torment, fear and agony came flooding out, until there was no more pain left inside me. Just *peace.* A wonderful *peace.* The peace of Jesus Christ and the blessed Holy Spirit. That evening, as I opened my heart to receive Jesus ...

ALL MY PAIN
was literally washed away.
ALL my deepest hurt, anger and resentment
JUST VANISHED!

Very softly Helen said, *"God has chosen YOU tonight!"* I was in awe at this. I could hardly take it in that God, the Creator of the whole Universe, the One and Only true God, had chosen *me* tonight. It was almost too wonderful to comprehend. But I knew it was true. As her words began to penetrate, I felt a wave of warmth and utter peace, followed by intense JOY, flow over me.

Oh! The JOY I felt was unbelievable!
Incredible!
My heart was at peace.
Yes, No more pain inside me,
GOD HIMSELF had done a miracle ... for ME!

I'd rejected God all my life and knew nothing or very little about Him and yet *He knew me.* That blew me away. I'd never realized what a heavy burden I'd been carrying for so long. But this evening, Jesus unlocked my heart and set me *free* and I felt I was walking on air.

> ***JESUS loves me! Really loves me.***
> ***He died for me.***
> ***He chose me tonight!***

I was bubbling over.   And I thought my heart would burst with *JOY.* I wanted to laugh and shout. I was getting drunk. Intoxicated on *the Holy Spirit of God.* Wow! I'd never felt like this before and it was *fantastic.* Now I knew what being 'saved' was *really* like. And, by the grace of God, I left that meeting a completely changed person. Changed for *good.* ***Changed from the inside out!***

Leon was waiting up for me

When I arrived home that night, I was surprised to find Leon, now seventeen years old, waiting up for me. I was so very happy and yet he looked so very serious. *"Whatever was the matter? I'd only been gone a few hours."*

Then in great distress, he blurted out, *"Mum, I have something I want to talk to you about."* As we sat down together, Leon began to unburden his heart to me. He confessed that he had not taken my advice about a certain issue and deeply regretted hiding it. He felt convicted of his guilt and apologized, *"I'm so sorry Mum!"*

I was suddenly aware that his deep anxiety was possibly caused by my own lack of sensitivity to his needs. I'd been a

254

bit strict with him lately, perhaps too strict, and I quickly remembered how I too, had rebelled in my youth against my own mother.   My well-meaning advice to help him, it now seemed, had been too constraining.   But as any single parent well knows, it's not easy being both *mother* and *father* to your children.

Leon had prepared himself for my angry reaction, anticipating I would be furious with him.   Yet to his utter amazement, I lovingly asked him, *"Are you happy about your decision Leon?"*   Sensing a tone of compassion in my voice, instead of the anger he was expecting, he replied, *"Yes, I am Mum."*

Then taking hold of his hand, I spoke to him as gently as Helen had been speaking to me, only one hour earlier, *"If God can forgive me my sins, who am I not to forgive you yours?"*

Leon could hardly believe the tenderness of my words and the marked change in me.   I was like a different person.   *But then I was.   All my anger and pain had gone.*   Peace filled me now and it showed instantly, even within the *first* hour of being *'saved'* and *'born again'* by the Holy Spirit.   Without any doubt, a miraculous transformation had taken place in my heart.

That night, Leon and I bonded closer together than ever before, as we sat up chatting happily for hours.   What *joy* we shared that night.   The night that changed my life *forever.*   And, the night that my dear son Leon also witnessed *the forgiveness of God* in his own young life, first hand.

The night that our Heavenly Father ... *forgave us both!*

Chapter 24

So what happened next?

I was bursting to tell everyone my *good* news ... that I was *saved!*

I must admit, I automatically expected everybody to be happy for me. But all too often, the exact opposite happened. To my dismay, some of my best friends, who were unsaved, cruelly scorned me and discouraged me. They taunted me and said things like, *"It's impossible. You can't be saved so quickly. You don't even know the names of the twelve disciples."*

I was so disappointed and when I kept hearing unkind, negative words spoken over me again and again, I became disheartened and actually started to doubt the miracle that God had done in my life. In my weakness and ignorance, as I listened to these words of unbelief, I began to waver in my new faith and, foolishly, began to believe them. I was letting go of Jesus' outstretched hand to me. I was letting go of my *second chance* of a new and better life. Instead, I was succumbing to Satan's seductive words to draw me back to him, back to my *old* life, as he filled me with doubt and fear.

I spent the next two months agonizing over what had just happened to me and caused myself, and others around me, a lot of needless pain. I knew God had miraculously touched my heart and yet, I didn't fully understand it. I kept questioning and doubting, *"Was I really saved?"* Then one afternoon, our village Minister said to me,

"You do know, don't you, that *ALL* your sins are forgiven?"

"No! I didn't know that." But it was just what I needed to *hear.* Just what I needed to *know.* Suddenly, *I was brought back to my senses.* Those few precious words cut right through the last cords of bondage clasping my heart. Satan had kept me caught in his grip of accusation and condemnation for far too long. But now, I was truly *free.* I was *forgiven.* I was *saved. And I was NOT turning back.*

The 'blinkers' I'd been wearing *all my life* had been torn off my eyes. Now I could *SEE.* Really *see,* for the first time ever. I could see the light of Jesus and His love for *me.* And I couldn't stop smiling and laughing. My heart was bursting with elation and I couldn't hold it in. I couldn't hide it. I was grinning *'like a Cheshire cat',* beaming from ear to ear. Oh, what priceless *JOY* I'd found.

My sins are forgiven

Wow! This was amazing. God, in His great *mercy* and *love* had forgiven me *ALL* of my sins, even though I didn't deserve it. Not only that, in His *goodness* and *grace,* He threw all my sins far away ... *"as far as the east is from the west"* (Psalm 103:12) and if that wasn't enough, He threw them *"into the depths of the deepest sea,"* NEVER to be remembered again. NEVER to be fished up and dangled in front of me with a scolding, wagging finger.

> *"You (God) will tread our sins underfoot*
> *and hurl all our iniquities (sins)*
> *into the depths of the sea."*
> (Micah 7:19)

Oh, wow! I was seeing God's amazing grace and un-deserved favour in my own *undeserving* life. Now, at last, I could understand the meaning of the first verse of John Newton's wonderful hymn ...

> **"Amazing Grace, how sweet the sound,**
> **That saved a wretch like me.**
> **I once was lost but now am found,**
> **Was blind, but now I see."**

That wretch was me, saved by God's amazing grace. He took me by the hand and led me into His glorious light, so I could *see.* *See* to step off the broad road that I'd been on, and *see* to step onto the narrow road leading to my new future, my *second chance ...*

> *"For wide is the gate and*
> *broad is the road that leads to destruction,*
> *and many enter through it."*
> (I said "good-bye" to this forever)

> *"But small is the gate and*
> *narrow the road that leads to life,*
> *and only a few find it."*
> (That's where I am now. Praise God)
> (Matthew 7:13-14)

258

I'd been through so much unhappiness, so much pain and endless suffering for years and years. My heart had wept and wept, but now I could see the way forward and my *new future* was waiting for me.

My Heavenly Father had touched my life with His goodness, grace, mercy and love **... *a love greater than any pain!***

I belong to Jesus now

S atan never loved me. He *hated* me and wanted to *destroy* me. And he nearly succeeded. He'd worked hard to keep me in darkness and hide *the truth of Jesus* from me all these years.

In my early twenties when I felt so *empty,* Satan hid Jesus from me and my heart hardened. He kept me away from *the love of my life.* But not for any longer. I'd found Jesus at last and broken free from the devil's evil clutches.

I was jubilant. I'd won a great victory over Satan's cunning schemes to hold on to me and keep me bound in my sinfulness. Bound in my fears and doubts that robbed me of *hope,* a *second chance* and *eternal life.*

With this battle won, it was high time to send the devil packing. I wasn't his property any longer. *I belonged to Jesus now.* Jesus who loved me and who would always protect me from Satan's evil schemes to harm me and his attempts to draw me back into my old ways and habits. So, filled with new courage, I boldly shouted ...

"OUT YOU GO SATAN!
You're not going to steal my future from me

I have a *new life* to look forward to,
and I want it. *ALL* of it.
I BELONG TO JESUS NOW!
And I command you devil ...
'In the mighty Name of Jesus Christ,
and in the power of the Holy Spirit,
TO GET OUT
and NEVER COME BACK!'"

No! I wouldn't listen to Satan's lies any more. I had the *still small voice* of the Holy Spirit living within me now, filling my *emptiness* with His comfort and strength. And at last, I knew without a shadow of doubt ...

I was saved!
Gloriously saved and complete
No more doubting.   No going back

I knew *for certain now* that Jesus truly *loved* me and that He had totally *forgiven* me for all the bad, sinful and shameful things I'd done in my life. That He'd forgiven me for all the years I'd rejected and scorned Him and used His Name in vain.   Now, I could visibly see the *miraculous change* in my life. With gladness and pure joy, I stepped from my *old* life into my *new* life. And it felt unbelievably wonderful.

The truth will set you free

At long last, I'd stopped rejecting and sneering at *the truth.*   *The divine truth* of God's free gift of salvation, through Jesus Christ. *The truth* that I'd ridiculed and scorned for so long. But now, I was learning something new.

"You will know the truth,
and the truth will set you free."
(John 8:32)

And that's just what I was ... *free!* I was delirious with joy and flooded with peace. *Never* would I let go of Jesus' hand again.

Jesus paid the price for *our* freedom

J esus, in His infinite love for all mankind, paid the ultimate price for *you* and for *me* by dying on the cross at Calvary 2000 years ago. He died to set us *free.*

"But why should Jesus be so faithful and loving to us? Why? When we are sinners and don't deserve it?" Well, Jesus explains this perfectly in the following verses ...

"For God so loved the world
(the world means you, me and everyone)
that He gave His only begotten Son, *(Jesus)*
that whosoever believeth in Him
should not perish
but have everlasting life.

For God sent not His Son into the world
to condemn *(accuse)* **the world,**
but that the world through Him *(Jesus)*
might be saved."
(John 3:16-17 KJV)

Yes, God loves ALL of us. He loves us so much that He sent His beloved Son, Jesus Christ, down to earth to die for *you* and for *me,* and for *everyone.* Jesus didn't come to condemn and judge us. *He came to save us and set us free.*

261

Jesus died for us all

G od watched His own Son being savagely scourged and lashed, as *stripes* of flesh were torn from His back. *God watched* His own Son, so full of love and *grace*, being humiliated and *disgraced* as soldiers stripped Him of his clothes. *God watched* His own Son being stretched out on the wooden cross as mocking, spiteful hands prepared to crucify Him. *God watched* His own Son pay the ultimate price for our sins. Yours and mine.

With massive nails, mercilessly hammered through his hands and feet, Jesus hung naked and bleeding on the cross at Calvary. He suffered excruciating agony and torment as He bore *in His own body ALL the sins, pain, sickness and suffering* on behalf of every man, woman and child in the world.

"He Himself *(Jesus)*
bore our sins in His body on the tree."
(1 Peter 2:24)

ALL the sins, guilt and shame of the whole world were heaped upon Jesus, as he hung bleeding and dying on the cross ... *until* ... Almighty God was completely satisfied that *ALL* of humanity's sins (past, present and *future)* had been paid for in full (redeemed) by the *sacrifice of Jesus' life* ...

"God made Him *(Jesus)* **who had no sin,**
to be sin *(with our sin)* **for us,**
so that in Him *(Jesus)*
we might become the righteousness of God."
(We might become right-standing with God)
(2 Corinthians 5:21)

A miraculous role reversal was taking place on the cross. Jesus took our filthy sins and paid the price for them by dying and shedding His own blood, so that we wouldn't have to. He gave His own body, as the sacrificial *Lamb of God* to set us free from our sins.   Then, to complete the role reversal, *He replaced our sinfulness with His righteousness,* so that we could become 'right-standing' before a holy and sinless God.

In *agony* of spirit, body and soul, *Jesus claimed the victory* over Satan's curse of sin over all humanity when He triumphantly cried out from the cross, *"IT IS FINISHED!"* Jesus bowed His bruised and bleeding head, so cruelly pierced by the vicious crown of thorns placed upon Him, and gave up His Spirit. He truly became *the Saviour of the whole world.*

JESUS MY SAVIOUR

Oh Jesus, Jesus! Jesus my Saviour,
Beaten and crucified, nailed to a tree,
Stripped of His clothing, for all to see,
And with only two thieves, for His company.

A crown of thorns, adorned His battered head,
And from nail wounds, His precious blood shed.
He died once for all, for you and for me,
Oh what a gift to mankind, was Calvary.

"IT IS FINISHED!" He cried from the cross on high,
As He gave up His spirit with a mighty sigh.
Then out from His side, flowed His precious blood,
To wash away man's sin, in a great cleansing flood.

Poem by Esther Barbara Dennison

This was Jesus' *once-only sacrifice. His 'finished work' on the cross* to give all mankind a second chance and the assurance of spending eternity in Heaven.

Only the sinless, spotless blood of Jesus has the *divine power* and *authority* to completely cleanse us from our sins and set us *free. Free* from all guilt, shame and condemnation. And that means every sin, however big.

NO SIN IS TOO BIG
for God *not* to forgive ...
when we truly and sincerely repent

This is God's awesome gift of *grace.* His *unmerited, undeserved favour* that He freely offers to each one of us.

Jesus rose victorious

Three days later, ***Jesus rose victorious from the grave!*** Jesus, in His own words, confirmed this eternal truth ...

"I am the resurrection and the life.
He who believes in Me (Jesus) will live,
even though he dies;
and whoever lives and believes in Me
will never die."
(John 11:25)

Jesus rose in glorious triumph and crushed Satan for all eternity. *Nothing and no-one,* and that includes Satan and all of his demons, *has any power over Jesus,* for ... **Jesus Christ is the Lord of Lords and the Kings of Kings, forever and ever!**

THE VICTORY WON

To sinful man, Jesus hung defeated and dead,
Unable to see that He'd died in our stead.
In only three days, He rose from the grave,
Victorious and glorious and ready to save.

For all mankind, He laid down His life,
To set us *free,* from Satan's sin and strife.
With His mission on earth, nearly complete,
He left man with promise, and not defeat.
So with Satan crushed and the Victory won,
We're delivered from sin by the Holy One.

So shout *"Praise the Lord!"*
for His grace and salvation,
And the gift of forgiveness
For every people and nation.

Poem by Esther Barbara Dennison

NO time limit

J esus shed His own *sinless* blood to wash away the sins of the whole world. And that includes *your* sins and mine too. In fact, *EVERY SIN* I have ever committed has been forgiven and forgotten, *forever.* No matter how bad, how big or how shameful they were. Jesus has forgiven me *completely.* That's why I am now *complete.* But you may be wondering, *"Surely, Jesus lived 2000 years ago.   That can't be true for today?"* Well the Bible tells us ...

*"Jesus Christ is the same yesterday
and today and for ever."*
(Hebrews 13:8)

265

That means there is **NO time limit** to His love, forgiveness and healing power, through the Holy Spirit. Jesus is as powerful *TODAY* as He was when He walked this earth 2000 years ago. And, praise the Lord, He *always* will be.

What is even more amazing, is that every time I confess my sins (whether in thought, attitude, word or deed), I have the full *assurance* that I will be forgiven. The full assurance that when I sincerely repent, whether today, tomorrow or in the *future*, my sins will be washed clean away by the cleansing power of Jesus' precious blood. This is Jesus' *finished work* on the cross for ALL who put their trust in Him. How amazing and simply *astounding* is that?

But what is even more *astounding,* is that so many of us *refuse to acknowledge* our own sinfulness and accept God's gift of love, grace and forgiveness. We refuse to accept Jesus into our lives. We just choose to keep on going the way we are. We don't want to change. It's too much bother, too much effort. *We want to stay with Satan who hates us* and who will one day, drag us down to eternal torment in hell.

"Hey! Doesn't that sound crazy to you?" Yes, of course it does. And yet, I was one of the *many* who refused to accept Jesus into my life. *"So WHY then, do we do it? When no-one is forcing us to stay with the devil?"* This is what seems really astounding to me. *We choose to do it.* And I was one of Satan's captives too, until I finally received *the truth* and broke free. Broke free to live *afresh* with Jesus.

I decided to choose *life* and not death. Choose *joy* and not tears of sorrow. *Truth* instead of lies. And the good news? This truth is *free* and it's *free* for you too. But it's your choice. Even the poorest person on this earth can say *"Yes!"* to the truth. It costs no money to come to Jesus.   It's simply a decision of the heart.   But, if you reject the truth, Jesus and His gospel message, **it will cost you your soul to stay with Satan.** *Jesus* is seriously worth thinking about.

But I didn't know

When I arrived in Northern Ireland back in 1991, I had never heard of being *saved* and *born again* or God's gift of *grace.* I thought attending church once a week was enough to get me into Heaven. Anyway, I considered myself a *good* person. *"And surely,"* I thought, *"ALL good people automatically go to Heaven when they die!"* That, of course, naturally included me and it never entered my head that I was a sinner, heading for hell.

Many of us make a conscious effort to get on well with those around us. We try to have a *good* attitude of kindness and gentleness, compassion for the poor and needy, and make donations to charities and good causes whenever we can, and be honest, upright and trustworthy citizens.

These are all good and admirable *virtues* that often earn us a commendable *reputation* and *great esteem* in the eyes of our family, friends and the people around us. But they will *not* automatically entitle us to enter Heaven after we've taken our last breath. Because, *"Being good, just isn't good enough."*

Why? Because God is a holy, righteous and perfect God and He cannot allow sin of any kind to enter into His kingdom. There is only one way we can be *acceptable* and *good enough* in the sight of Almighty God and that is through our faith in His beloved Son, Jesus Christ. We all need to be

267

washed in the precious, spotless blood of Jesus to cleanse us from our sins.   I learnt too, that all the *good* and even *benevolent* things I'd ever done in my life counted for *nothing* regarding my own salvation, if I didn't believe in Jesus. There is absolutely *nothing* any of us can do through our own good deeds, good virtue, wisdom or money to get us into Heaven. *Nothing.* Even if we are blessed to be the richest person in the whole world, no amount of money can *buy* the love of Jesus or *buy* ourselves a ticket into Heaven. **Jesus Christ is the *only* way into Heaven.** No other religion or belief can do it. Why? Because no-one else *died* for you and me. *Jesus died in our place. Only Jesus ...*

> *"I am the way*
> **and the *truth* and the *life.***
> *No-one comes to the Father* (Almighty God)
> ***except through Me"*** (Jesus Christ)
> (John 14:6)

I know having money is great. But being rich will not get you into Heaven. It's all to do with your *heart.* In fact, the most uneducated, most uncivilized and poorest person in the world who humbly gives his heart to Jesus, can actually be the *richest* person.

> ***"Has not God chosen those who are poor***
> ***in the eyes of the world***
> ***to be rich in faith and to inherit the kingdom***
> ***He promised those who love Him?"***
> (James 2:5)

How I love this verse. Because even if I am the poorest person in my town or neighbourhood, I am still rich. *Rich in faith.* And no-one will ever be able to take that away from me.

Gates of Heaven

W hen Jesus' mission on this earth was complete, He ascended in splendour and glory, and opened the gates of Heaven to us. The narrow pathway to Heaven was now OPEN. Open to everyone who repents of their sins and makes Jesus the hub or the centre of their life. *Open to everyone who asks Jesus to be their Lord and Saviour.* And as long as I have breath in this body of mine, I shall rejoice and shout ... *"Thank You Jesus for saving me!"*

Believe it and receive it

Y ou see, God's divine mercy and grace in my life has nothing to do with what I have done ... it is all to do with what *Jesus has already done.* His *once-only sacrifice of His life* for *you,* for me and for all of us. Jesus suffered and died on the cross, then rose victorious *to save* every man, woman and child, and that includes *you.* And all *you* have to do, is simply *believe it* and *receive the truth and good news of the gospel of Jesus Christ,* with a thankful and repentant heart. It's the most precious gift of all ...

"Thanks be to God for His indescribable gift."
(Jesus Christ)
(2 Corinthians 9:15)

D ear Reader, at this point in *My Story,* I would respectfully like to say that *everything* I am writing in this book about *faith in Jesus Christ* and the *Christian religion* is the truth and purely *Scriptural,* and is *not* a lie or a cult teaching. All the Scripture verses quoted in this book are the *Words of God* and printed in any version of the holy Bible.

Chapter 25

I was Eager to Learn

N ow with *new* hope and a fresh purpose in my life, I began to do things I'd never done before.   Indeed, just a few weeks later, after accepting that I was truly *saved,* I attended *New Horizon,* a week-long Christian conference held annually in early August, upon the campus of the University of Ulster in Coleraine, Northern Ireland.

It was Saturday night, the opening evening of the event. I arrived early and managed to find a quiet corner at the back of the huge marquee, where I could sit by myself and watch what was going on.

I felt rather uncomfortable and self-conscious at first, like a *fish out of water* in these unfamiliar surroundings. But as I listened to the beautiful hymns being sung, and the heart-stirring praise music rising from Dave Pope and his band up on the stage, I began to relax. The tent too, was filling rapidly by now and there was a tangible sense of expectancy, of excitement in the air as everyone took their seats. It certainly was a memorable and enjoyable occasion although, I have to admit, I didn't understand much of the Bible teaching that first evening. It sounded like a new language to me.

But I was eager to learn and attended the morning seminars too. Having never set foot inside a university before, it felt peculiar sitting in the steeply tiered lecture rooms, amongst so many strangers. It was all so *new* and so very different, but I was enjoying this *newness* and listened carefully to every word. Then, after a few days, I noticed I was making headway, as I gradually began to understand what they were talking about. To my surprise, I found it really stimulating and exciting and *not at all boring.*

Ross came with me every day and happily joined other children in a separate youth area. They were divided up into different groups and given encouragement to strengthen their faith in Jesus. They also received valuable help and advice with problems children often face in their young lives, such as bullying. But it wasn't all teaching. University students interacted with them, often playing their various musical instruments and, on many a day, they had lively sessions of singing and praise.

Then, in the evenings, the children met in the campus theatre and had some more fun. Even the shyest child blossomed and enjoyed actively participating in the dynamic drama sessions. When, at the end of each evening, I arrived to collect Ross, the drama was often still in progress and the children were enjoying themselves immensely. If I peeked inside the theatre, all I could see was a hundred plus smiling faces, amidst excited and joyful laughter. Their week was packed with loads of fun and Ross loved every minute.

Each evening, the pair of us left New Horizon more and more invigorated. We drove home as high as kites. *High on the joy of the Holy Spirit and the love of Jesus!*

Renewed vision

I was learning so much about Jesus *and* about myself too. By the end of that week, I was a *renewed* person with a *renewed* vision. I came away knowing *three* very important things. Things that were to change the rest of my life forever ...

- I loved God
- I wanted to serve Him all of my days
- I could do it by myself, with Jesus' help

The last point may sound very peculiar to you. But please remember, I had been so full of fear and pain for so many years, I hardly knew who I was. I'd lost my identity and yet, during that week, I began to *regain my self-confidence.*

Also, it had taken a lot of courage for me to go there *by myself*, find my way around and go into crowded teaching seminars, mixing and talking to new people. I quickly discovered that I had a *new inner strength, courage and determination* to move forward and change my life through trusting in Jesus. I could go to new places and do new things *by myself* without being afraid of being alone anymore. I had gained a *freedom* I'd never experienced before.

And it was not a dream. Nor was it *emotionalism* or *fantasy.* It was real. It was happening. *Happening to me.*

Why me?

Why did God choose me that particular April evening? *"I honestly don't know."* Because I hadn't done anything to deserve it, but I'm sure glad He did! But Jesus knows the answer:

> *"You did not choose Me,*
> *but I chose you ..."*
> (John 15:16).

How wonderful it is to feel *chosen by God.* What joy. What inner peace. He has chosen *you* too, if only you'll accept it and believe it. I have expressed my immense thankfulness for His loving goodness, mercy and grace to me, in these few verses ...

Every day is a joy, and a gift from His Hand,
Of mercy and forgiveness you understand.
With salvation He blessed me, along with His love,
And His grace overflows, from Heaven above.

So I look to my Saviour from morn till night,
Who gives me the strength to fight the good fight.
My heart keeps rejoicing, as I praise His Name,
Oh I'm so glad, to me He came!

(From the Poem "Hosanna!")
By Esther Barbara Dennison

Now I was truly rich

Yes, Jesus had taken my torn, battered, bruised and broken heart and given me a *brand new heart ...*

"He (God) heals the broken-hearted
and binds up their wounds."
(Psalm 147:3)

A *brand new heart* full of renewed hope, peace and joy. He was giving me a fresh new beginning, a second chance at life. And I was claiming it ... *all of it.* I had learnt a very important lesson. I had wavered and doubted, *but Jesus hadn't.* He still loved me and welcomed me with open arms.   And that's where I always want to stay, *close to Jesus.*

Now, I was truly *rich.* *Rich* with blessings of joy, peace and happiness.   *Rich* deep down in my heart, with a priceless love ... *a love greater than any pain!*

A LOVE GREATER THAN ANY PAIN!

Jesus, Jesus! Forever I'll love Him,
As I humbly repent, washed clean by His blood.
I'll shout *"Hallelujah! My sins are forgiven!"*
For He set me free ... by His grace, mercy and love.

I gave Him my life and my heart sings His praise,
And I'll trust and adore Him, all of my days.
Though nothing I've done, could warrant His grace,
I'll thank Him forever, for He died in my place.

To my knees do I fall, and my head do I bow,
For my pain is a memory, far from me now.
A new love have I found, Jesus is His Name,
A love greater than any pain!

Poem by Esther Barbara Dennison

My new and faithful Friend

I was learning how to start living again. In fact, my life was only just beginning. *My new life with Jesus. My new and faithful Friend.* A friend who would never lie to me, deceive me or let me down. A friend I could truly trust and who would never leave me alone.

> **"Never will I leave you,**
> **never will I forsake you."**
> (Hebrews 13:5)

My *friendship* with Jesus took the same course as any other friendship, because it takes time to get to know someone. As a relationship deepens, you learn to trust and even love them. And once they have become an important part of your life, you don't ever want to lose them.

My *friendship* with Jesus grew in just the same way and, little by little, I saw Him working in my life, changing it for the better. I learnt that His love for me was *unconditional,* because He didn't only love me when I was on my best behaviour. He loved me *all* the time. Even when I failed Him and let Him down, He still loved me. In fact, I could hardly grasp the depth of His love for me.

Bit by bit, *as He healed my pain,* I grew to love Him too and trust Him more and more. I learnt to receive His loving kindness, to rely upon His guidance and to trust in His faithful provision. My best Friend has never failed me, and I know He never will. *He loves me.*

Truthfully, the more I learnt to love and trust in Jesus, the more I realized what I'd been missing. I'd rejected Him all of my life and yet now, He was *healing* me, *restoring* me, *loving*

275

me and setting me *free* from Satan's bondage. At last, I felt loved and complete and I wanted to tell everyone about *my New Love.* I wasn't embarrassed or ashamed either, to tell anybody what Jesus was doing in my life. He was my best Friend and my Saviour.

"Do you long for a best friend too?" Someone you can talk to anywhere, anytime, day or night? Someone who will help you and not deceive you? Someone who really loves you and understands you?

Don't be embarrassed or think it's a sign of weakness to call out to Jesus. In fact, it's quite the reverse. For it's in your weakness, that you will see God's grace and strength in your life. God will replace *your* weakness with *His strength* ...

> **"My grace is sufficient for you,**
> **for My power**
> **is made perfect in weakness"**
> (2 Corinthians 12:8)

In fact, that's what I meant when I said, *"I can do it by myself,"* because God filled me with the strength I personally lacked. You see, in the natural I can be weak, nervous and timid.

> **"But the Lord stood at my side**
> **and gave me strength ..."** *(His strength)*
> (2 Timothy 4:17)

But now, with Jesus by my side and the Holy Spirit within me, I am filled with His strength, joy and courage *every time I need it.*

God had always been helping me

N ow, as I look back over my life, I realize that God had *always* been watching over me, *always* been helping and protecting me. *He didn't reject me,* the way I'd rejected Him and *He never gave up on me.* He was so patient, loving and kind, waiting for *me* to find *Him.* I just never knew it.

- HE had protected my life from death and serious injury as a teenager, during both of my accidents.
- HE had *closed the doors* on me living in England and brought me across the sea to Northern Ireland, to protect me from a violent husband.
- HE kept the perfect house waiting for me for two and a half years, until I was able to buy it.
- HE heard young Donna's prayers for me and faithfully answered them. (*Always remember, God will be faithful to your prayers too.*)
- HE enabled me to successfully run my own stationery business, so I could afford to pay off my debts.
- HE blessed me with *a miracle* to cancel my last debt of £4,000.
- HE touched my life with His mercy and grace, and opened my hardened heart to receive Him.
- HE humbled me ... and that took some doing.

And then? **HE SAVED ME** *Hallelujah!*

- **HE** *forgave* ALL of my sins.
- **HE** *healed* my brokenness and put *peace* and laughter back into my life.
- **HE** *loves me.* A sinner *saved* by His amazing grace.
- **HE** is my *Lord* and *Saviour,* and my best Friend!

MY PRECIOUS LORD AND SAVIOUR

Oh Jesus, Jesus! My precious Lord and Saviour,
He cast off my fear and my shameful behaviour.
He set me free from Satan's curse,
For to end up in hell, what could be worse?

So, with every breath, I'll praise His holy Name,
Oh wow, *My life will never be the same!*
From glory to glory as I tread The Way up
How thankful I am, that Jesus drank from His Cup.

Until one day, when to Heaven I'll go,
And His glorious face, I will see all aglow.
There will be beautiful angels and streets of gold,
A sight too awesome to behold.

To God, the Father, the Creator of All,
To my hands and my face, I will humbly fall;
On my knees will I bow, before His throne,
Then truly I'll know ... *I'm Home, I'm Home!*

Poem by Esther Barbara Dennison

I learnt to surrender

So a *gradual* learning process began, as I learnt to surrender *my plans* and *my will* to *God's plans* and *His will.* This may sound easy, but I can assure you it wasn't, and isn't. Most of us are very strong willed and want to do *what* we want, *when* we want and *how* we want. And I am no exception. But God very patiently led me away from the temptations and sins of the *broad road* that I'd walked on for far too long. Then, very gently but firmly, He set me down on

His *narrow road* that was to lead me to my new and better life.

So I'll walk the *narrow road* until life's end,
And remain hand in hand with my new Friend.
For He's promised to love me and beside me He'll stay
And I'll shout *"Hosanna!"* for I'm on The Way.

(From the poem "Hosanna!")
By Esther Barbara Dennison

You know, the *broad road* usually *looks* a good and fun road to be on, especially to young people who yearn for pastures new, freedom and excitement. The allure of experimenting with life's thrills and pleasures can seem so enticing and tempting.   And it is easy to kid yourself that you are happy and having a ball. And for a while, you probably are.

Yet at some point down this road, you will find out that it is pure deception, just froth and bubble. The devil is busy blinding you to *the truth* and the *real freedom,* the way he blinded me. This *broad road* is a big cunning LIE. Ultimately, it leads to destruction and *hell. So beware.*

Although the *narrow road* may initially appear to be very unappealing, boring and unattractive, you will discover that it really is the road to *true freedom, inner peace and joy.* The *only road* that leads to Heaven, the home that our Heavenly Father has so lovingly prepared for us to *enjoy.* Where we can *enjoy* His immense goodness and mercy to us. Where there's no pain, sickness, fear or torment. Just laughter, fun and joy forever and ever, in the glorious and eternal presence of our Lord and Saviour Jesus Christ.

Regrettably, I resisted taking this step for so long but, when I did, it was like taking a breath of fresh air as *my walk to freedom* began. I have never regretted it. And should you decide to take this step too, I know you won't regret it either.

Are you on the road to *freedom?*

So dear Reader, do you know which road you're walking on? Are *you* walking along the *narrow road to freedom* that leads to Heaven, or are you speeding along the *broad road* to destruction, just the way I was?

Have you hardened your heart and been rejecting God in your life? Have you closed your ears and won't listen, the way I did? Is your confidence in your own achievements or prosperity? Your own success or power? Your own intellect or logic? Or maybe you're just too busy doing things *your* way? Too busy to stop and think what life is really all about and *where* you're ultimately heading?

It's time to be honest *with yourself* and with God. You can hide nothing from Him anyway. He *sees* everything and He *knows* all things ... even your every thought (Psalm 139:1-4). *He is God,* who created you in your mother's womb and who knows you far better than you know yourself (Psalm 139:13-16). And that's scary, isn't it? But it needn't be. Not if you stop *running away* from Him. Not if you stop *ignoring* Him. He is your Heavenly Father, who loves you with a *father's adoring, compassionate and merciful heart.*

You see, for far too many years, I suffered a life of fear and torment and cried countless lonely tears. Often, I felt isolated and desolate in my heartbreak and sorrow, and yet all the while, I ignored, rejected and totally refused to take hold of God's outstretched hand. The only hand that could *really* help me. Is that what you're doing?

I got in a mess

P erhaps you're struggling right now and feel your life is going nowhere. Too many failed plans, too many pressing problems or towering debts. Been through too many disappointments or painful heartaches. Feel your life is in a mess and don't know how to change it or what to do. But hold on. You're not the only one to get in a mess you know, many have, including me ... *I got in a mess too.*

You see, I never asked God to help me. I never even once gave Him a thought. He wasn't part of my life and He barely existed as far as I was concerned. I thought I could do it all by myself. I thought I knew what was best. I made decisions that I later regretted and made plenty of mistakes too. Never did it cross my mind that God could help me.

"And anyway, why should He?" I hardly ever went to church, I prayed even less and used His Name in vain. But amazingly, it didn't stop God from loving me and wanting to help me. It didn't stop Him from offering me a second chance. I never knew or understood that God could help me, or would help me. *I never even gave Him a chance* ... **but He was willing to give ME a chance.**

In fact, no-one ever told me that I could *cry out to God* for His help. No-one ever told me that He would listen to me. No-one ever told me that He could do a miracle for me. No-one ever told me about the goodness and mercy of God. And, no-one ever told me that He loved me. But today, **I'm telling you.** I'm telling you right now ....

"GOD LOVES YOU!
You are PRECIOUS to Him
and He longs for you to know that."

I'm not joking and I'm not telling you a lie. He *will* hear your cry for help and He sees your every shed tear.   Don't despair or give up, because **God will make a way for you ... where there seems to be no way.** He loves you and has your best interests at heart.

God made a way for Leon

W hen Leon, my eldest son, broke the news to me back in 1997 that he planned to go to university, I knew I couldn't financially help him at all. I couldn't even manage to give him a few pounds spending money each week. We were so poor. In fact, the only money that Leon had, was what he'd earned during the school holidays doing gardening jobs.

Nevertheless, I had just given my life to Jesus, so I began asking HIM to help Leon and provide for his needs. You see, I couldn't help my son, *but I knew God could.* And HE was faithful and *made a way for him.* Within a few weeks, Leon managed to get a student loan. *Yes, God heard my prayers.*

Then, when Leon left home for university, I could barely give him enough cash to buy a hot drink on the ferry over to Scotland. But I was slowly learning the truth that *when* we trust God to help us, He is always in control. I was about to find this out ...

Leon's girlfriend was going to Dundee University too, and I was overjoyed when her father offered to drive them both all the way to Dundee. If he hadn't done this, I have no idea how Leon would have got there. But even in this small detail, God knew our urgent need and showed me that He was in control ... *He made a way, where there seemed to be no way.*

Leon arrived at university broke and needed a job quickly. So I began praying again and within a few weeks, he was offered a part-time catering job in the university, which provided him with the essential spending money he needed. In reality, there were plenty of other capable first year students wanting jobs, but Leon was chosen. You see ... *God made a way, where there seemed to be no way.*

I continued praying for Leon, and God continued hearing and answering my prayers. When Leon graduated, he was offered a job straight away in Dundee, where he stayed for several years. Many of his friends couldn't get jobs, but he did, and a good one too. *I never stopped praying, and God never stopped answering and faithfully providing for our needs.*

After a few years, God led Leon into some super jobs and he was able to pay off his huge student loan. And today, he has an amazingly well paid job in London.   And the good news? *God will hear your prayers too.*   For what He did for me, and for Leon, He will do for you too.   Just trust Him and **He will make a way for YOU, where there seems to be no way.**

"So what are you waiting for?"

T here has never been a better time to make Jesus the centre of your life. Only Jesus can *heal* your deepest grief and pain. Only Jesus can *remove* your fear and replace it with His wonderful peace and joy. Only Jesus can *fill* your emptiness and give you the *hope* you need. *Only Jesus can give you a second chance!* And that's the truth.

"So what are you waiting for?"

Consider this, "You've got nothing *eternally important to* **lose**, *have you? Just everything eternally important to* **gain!**"

Chapter 26

Early one morning

N ow, dear Reader, before I continue with *My Story,* and tell you some stories and amazing miracles that happened to me that were *beyond my wildest dreams,* I would like to *fast-forward* fourteen years to 2011, when something very important happened ...

Early one morning, in September 2011, I was happily sitting up in bed reading before the start of a new day. I was comfortable, with my pillows stacked up behind me and a hot mug of tea beside me. I was warm and cosy under the soft duvet and feeling relaxed when, quite suddenly, I felt an *inner stirring in my spirit,* an excitement and a sense of expectancy that something was about to happen. *And it did.*

Very clearly and very precisely, I heard my Heavenly Father begin speaking to me. *Yes, I heard God speaking to me.* But I wasn't anxious or fearful. I was delighted. You see, it is *not* peculiar or even unusual for the Holy Spirit to speak to *born again* Christians, because we are all God's children and *He,* the Holy Spirit, is living within us.

Full of *anticipation* and with my spirit *stirred and alert,* I eagerly grabbed a pen, a piece of paper and began to write down *exactly* what the Holy Spirit was saying to me. I quickly realized He was giving me a *very important* message, with a special purpose. A message to share with everyone who is still *doubting* God's immense love for them. A message to share with every person who has NOT, as yet, *invited Jesus Christ into their heart, to be their Lord and Saviour.*

I realized too, that this message was *'a warning in love'* from Almighty God. An earnest warning to everyone who habitually rejects, scorns or denies God and His Son Jesus Christ. A powerful, direct message, that I could not ignore.

For the Lord also gave me the clear instruction, *and the responsibility,* of passing His message on. Why? Because God wants *every person in the world to know the truth of His gift of salvation. And He wants everyone to be given the chance and indeed the opportunity, to willingly choose to be with Him in Heaven one day.*

Please understand, that Almighty God of the Bible, is a holy and righteous God. He is faithful and true and will never force us to do anything against our will. And, while we are living on *His* earth, however long that may be, He wants to give us the chance to invite His Son Jesus Christ into our hearts. Nevertheless, if we *persist* in rejecting Him until our final, dying breath, we simply cannot expect to *then* just boldly enter into His Heavenly home.

Imagine this: *"Would **you** open the door of your home and let your enemy in? Someone who dislikes you, detests or even hates you? Someone who ridicules, scorns or curses you and wants to do you harm? Would you welcome him (or her) in and*
286

tell him to put his feet up and make himself at home?" Of course not.   And yet, our Heavenly Father, *your* Heavenly Father is ready and willing to *OPEN the doors of his home* to us. To fling open the doors and welcome us in.   And all He asks us to do is **humbly repent of our sins and invite Jesus to come into our lives.** *God is so GOOD.*

So I can't help wondering, *"WHY is it so difficult to come to our senses and humbly accept His invitation?"*

Well for me, it was my own horrible, obstinate *pride* that held me back from accepting His invitation. *Nothing else.* But what *joy* I found when, at last, I finally responded to Him. What *freedom.*

And for all of us, once we have truly repented and humbled our hearts to the Lord, He will *never* remind us of our past sins and failures. *Never* chastise us for the scathing, disbelieving words we have cruelly spoken against Him. *Never* scold us for our hostile attitude or mocking accusations made against Him. *No. Our past is over. Totally forgiven.* And, instead of sharply reprimanding us as we deserve, He will bathe us in His mercy and love, and *WELCOME* us into His celestial, glorious home for all eternity.   Yes, this is indeed *amazing grace!*

Too good to be true?

However, you may still be feeling sceptical and doubting that God really cares about you or has any special interest in you.   Perhaps you are resisting or even outright rejecting Him and not believing a word I'm telling you. You may argue that God has done nothing to help you in your life so far and has nothing to offer you. Possibly, you are *blaming God* for allowing a specific hurt or loss in your life. Or maybe you're harbouring anger, unforgiveness or resentment deep in your heart, perhaps against someone you once loved and trusted, or maybe someone who rejected or abused you and caused you great pain and suffering.

If so, this can *block* you from being able to *believe* that you are dearly loved by God.   And *block* you from *believing* the truth that God loves you *just the way you are* and He wants the very best for you.   It can also prevent you from *believing* that ... *He can turn your pain into GOOD and heal you.*

It took me several years to learn this hard lesson, but when I did, I was amazed at how God used my painful past for *GOOD* to help others.

"All things work together for good
to those who love God"
(Romans 8:28 NKJV)

You see, even though *you* may not know or acknowledge this awesome Sovereign God and may have been rejecting His deep love for you, it does *not* mean *He doesn't love you.*   It does *not* mean He won't forgive you.   **HE loves you,** whether you accept His love or not.

Yes, *it is too good to be true.*   Because we are *all* sinful beings and not one of us deserves His unconditional mercy and divine love.   That's *WHY* I'm obeying Him and writing this book, *because you need to know this.   Because you need to know and believe that,* **"You are special to God and He loves you."**   And it's *because* you are so special to God, that He gave me **His Personal Message** to pass on to you.

GOD's Personal Message to YOU

N ow, I must tell you something. This is no wishy-washy message. It is a *strong* message. A *serious* message. A *scary* message. And it may well offend you and even make you angry. Yet it is the truth. The real hard facts of life and death. God wants you to understand and face up to this truth, because *He loves you MORE* than you can possibly imagine. And He wants you to make the *right* choice.

But you may be wondering, *"If God really loves me that much, WHY should His message be so severe and harsh?"* Simply, it's *because* He loves you so much, with an un-quenchable and limitless love, more than you can ever fathom or possibly imagine. And, *because* He wants YOU to fully realize the **serious implications** and **eternal consequences** should you decide to reject Him in your life. It's that **real.**

So dear Reader, please prepare yourself to receive this message, direct from GOD to YOU and let your life be changed, enriched and *renewed,* when you read it with an *open* heart ...

- A heart ready to *listen*
- A heart willing to be *humbled*
- A heart desiring to be *SAVED*

Here are the *exact* words, undiluted and unchanged, that the Holy Spirit gave to me early that morning back in September 2011. A *heart-searching* and *heart-challenging* message from our **Heavenly Father ...**

GOD'S PERSONAL MESSAGE
(through the Holy Spirit)

"The time has come My friends (that's you)
when I must speak out ... speak out for JESUS
and His gospel message.

For too long, the Lord of Lords and King of Kings
(Jesus)
has been ignored.
Have you ignored His message of Salvation?
Have you read His Word in the Bible recently?
When did you last pray to your
Heavenly Father?

Don't you know Jesus died on the cross
because HE LOVES YOU so much?
He died so that you can go to Heaven
and spend eternity with Him.

Why is it so hard to admit that you are a sinner
and *repent* of your sins?

Have you ever lied, even little fibs?
Used the Lord's Name in vain?
Are you doing that right now, as you read this?

REPENT now and be saved.
Ask Jesus into your heart *before it is too late.*

You may scoff and jeer at these words.
You may openly deny Jesus.
Even openly deny that there is an Almighty God
who created you,
the earth and the whole universe.

What is stopping you from accepting Jesus
as your Lord and Saviour?
What is stopping you from believing in Him?

PRIDE?

He died for you
and shed His precious blood for you.
Yes, *you.*

Don't let PRIDE stop you.
Don't wait any longer.

Jesus is waiting for your answer.
He has been waiting a long time.
He has been very patient.

But this is His warning to you
Time is running out.

Jesus LOVES you.
He always has and He always will.
He freely offers His love to you.

Will you accept it?
Will you repent now and be saved?"

(Jesus, through the Holy Spirit, continues ...)

I AM WAITING FOR YOUR REPLY
It is *your* choice ...
To spend eternity with ME in Heaven,
surrounded by love and joy,
fun and laughter, family and friends,
even pets
OR ...

**Reject ME ...
and spend eternity
in abject pain, fear and torture,
with no-one to help you or care about your cries
of torment and agony
as demons torture you mercilessly.**

They (the demons)
**will be the only ones laughing ...
laughing at you.**

**You had the chance to choose ...
*Heaven or hell.***

**Don't let *PRIDE* stop you
from making the *right* choice."**

(End of *God's Personal Message*,
which I received directly from the Holy Spirit)

Hey, JESUS has just spoken to you!

A nd you may well be feeling shocked and even a bit stunned at His stern message. But Jesus is not angry with you or wanting to punish you. *He loves you!* In fact, **His heart is breaking ... *breaking over you.*** He is longing for you to respond to Him. Longing for you to ask Him into your heart. Longing to be your best Friend and *not* your enemy. He is waiting ... **waiting for your reply.**

Dear Reader, the Lord gave me His Personal Message early that morning back in September 2011, to share with *anyone* who doesn't yet know Jesus as their Lord and Saviour or understand *the truth about eternity.*

Please don't ignore **God's urgent warning** to you, because ...

It's a *HEART CRY*
from JESUS CHRIST to YOU ...

A HEART CRY to REPENT
before it's too late

You see, while we are alive and living on *His* earth, God has graciously given each and every one of us *a free will* to choose our eternal destiny. But after we die, this opportunity is gone. Our chance to choose *Jesus* and *eternal life in Heaven* is gone. *It's too late.* And the gates of Heaven remain closed to us.

Please take your Heavenly Father's warning seriously by making the *right* choice. *Repent* and *humbly surrender your life to Jesus.* You'll never regret it.

"HOW do I do that?"

B egin by *talking* to Jesus. Just the way you would to a friend. Begin by telling Him *everything*. That means *every* worry, *every* concern, no matter how big or how small, or even how *silly* it may seem.

You see, Jesus *wants* you to tell Him about *all* your pain and grief and suffering. *All* your agony and fears. *All* your disappointments and struggles. *All* your emptiness and loneliness. Jesus *wants* you to share *everything* with Him. *"But why?"* you may ask. Quite simply, "If it's important to you and causing you stress, *then it's important to Him too."*

Now, when you do respond to Jesus and share even your most intimate and private secrets with Him, *remember it is between you and Jesus,* and no-one else. You don't have to do it in front of anybody else. It will be a *special* time, and a *personal* time, just the two of you together. And you can do it in private, *anywhere* you feel comfortable. But be totally *honest* and tell Him *everything* and don't ever lie about anything. **For Jesus is the only *go-between* or *mediator* between every living person and Father God.** Nothing and no-one can take His place ...

"For there is one God
and one mediator between God and men,
the man Christ Jesus,
who gave Himself as a ransom for all men"
(1 Timothy 2:5)

Jesus came to earth as *all-man* and *all-God* ... the Son of Man and the Son of God. We only need *Jesus.* No-one else.

Jesus is inviting you ...

To *come to Him.* But are you still *resisting* His invitation and *holding back?* Are you frightened of making this commitment? Perhaps you are still doubting, and even scornful that you *need* Jesus in your life.   Are you making excuses, *"I can't repent now. I need to clean up my life first. I need to STOP smoking, drinking, gambling, swearing, being promiscuous, etc, etc. ..."*

"NO YOU DON'T!" Jesus is inviting you to come to Him *just the way you are!*

He welcomed me *just the way I was* and *He'll welcome you too.* So don't hold back any longer. Don't be afraid of taking this step and making Him part of your life. For when you do, you'll experience the same unbelievable *joy* and incredible *peace* and wonderful *freedom* that I received the moment I gave my heart to Jesus. I promise you, *there is nothing more wonderful.*

"So, what will your answer be?"

Will you let Jesus *heal* you and be your best Friend? Will you let Him *bless* you with His love?

"Are you ready to receive your new future, filled with new hope?"

Your response to this question will be the *most important decision* that you'll ever make in your whole lifetime. It's a choice that will *rejuvenate* your heart, *transform* your mind and *renew* your whole outlook on life. It's a decision that will give you new strength and fresh courage to face every challenge and problem before you. It's a decision that will fill you with a radiant happiness and an amazing peace that you've never experienced before. Believe me, it's true.

If your answer is a genuine *"Yes!"* then come to Jesus *just the way you are* and get ready to be *blessed.*

"OK, Yes! But what exactly do I do now?"

Read the following Bible verses. They will tell you what to do next. But please, read them with an open *loving* heart and read them *aloud ...*

"That if you confess with your mouth,
(that means speaking out loud)
"Jesus is Lord,"
and believe in your heart
that God raised Him (Jesus) from the dead,
you will be saved.
For it is with your heart
that you believe and are justified
(made righteous and acceptable to God)
and it is with your mouth that you confess
and are saved.

For, "Everyone (that includes you)
who calls on the name of the Lord
will be saved.""
(Romans 10:9-10,13)

Wow! Isn't that good news? But please, read these verses again and again until you fully understand the *truth* in them. *The truth that will 'save' you and set you free.*

Why? Because *Jesus is waiting* right now for you to respond to Him and ask Him into your heart. And remember, you can do that *anywhere.* You don't *have* to be in a place of worship or special building or at a service or meeting. You can do it in the comfort and privacy of your own home. Perhaps by your fireside, at your kitchen table or at your bedside. You may even like to go to a special place in the country, or anywhere in fact, where you feel at ease. My son Leon was living in Dundee when he gave his life to the Lord and he went off to his favourite spot in the Scottish mountains. Just Leon and God, *alone together.* What a divine and memorable experience he had. But you too, can have this blessed experience, for God will meet with you *anywhere.*

Total commitment and promise to God

S o it's your choice *when* and *where* you give your heart to Jesus. You can do it alone or amongst your family and friends. But remember, this is all about a life-changing **heart commitment and heart relationship between you and God** and the place is *not* important. But what you decide to do about it, *is vitally important.*

That's *why* you should examine your own heart *before* you make this promise to God, and ask yourself if you can *honestly and sincerely* AGREE to the following points ...

- You truly *want* to give your heart to Jesus Christ and ask Him to be your Lord and Saviour.
- You *want* to make Jesus the *centre* of your life.
- You're prepared to *humble* yourself before Almighty God and *admit you're a sinner;* that you're not perfect.
- You *want* to *walk away* from the darkness of your old life and *enter into* the light of your new life ...

"I am the light of the world. (Jesus)
Whoever follows Me will never walk in darkness, (sin)
but will have the light of life."
(John 8:12)

As soon as you pray ...

A n amazing *miracle happens.* For at the very *moment* you sincerely repent of your sins and make your *heart commitment* to Jesus, your inner spirit and soul will be washed and cleansed by the **blood of Jesus** and you will be **saved from your sins.** At the same moment, Almighty God of the Bible, our Heavenly Father, will **forgive ALL of your sins,** *every single one* and you will be certain of spending eternity with Him in Heaven.

But that's not all. Now that you are *saved, cleansed* and *forgiven,* another miracle happens. You become **born again** when the **Holy Spirit** comes to live within you. Y*our inner spirit* is literally made 'brand new' by the power of the Holy Spirit (God's power, not yours) and you are now **saved and born again** *in the name of Jesus Christ.*

> **"I tell you the truth,**
> **no-one can see the kingdom of God**
> **unless he is born again."**
> (John 3:3)
>
> *(Please note, these are Jesus' words to all of us)*

Now dear Reader, please don't get alarmed or frightened of the Holy Spirit, as it is the *Spirit of Jesus* coming to live within you. Always remember, the Holy Spirit *loves* you and longs to comfort and help you.   All He wants you to do, is learn to trust and obey Him, and let Him *lead* and *guide* you every day of your life. *What an amazing blessing.*

But there's another surprise in store. Another miracle that happens when you pray and ask Jesus into your heart. You become a dearly loved *son or daughter of Father God* and a member of His eternal family. In fact, you will be part of a huge family. A worldwide family, with millions and millions of brothers and sisters, of all races and all tongues, *who all love Jesus ...*

> **"How great is the love**
> **the Father has lavished on us,**
> **that we should be called children of God."**
> (1 John 3:1)

So *never again,* need you ever feel rejected, illegitimate, an orphan, unwanted, an outcast or even aborted. You will be dearly loved and cherished forever and ever, *for all eternity* by your Heavenly Father and His beloved Son JESUS. This is *good news* indeed.

As soon as you feel ready ...

L et's pray together. But wait a minute, *"Are you unsure how to pray? And feeling a bit awkward and shy?"* Well for *me,* when I talk to Jesus, it always helps me to remember that He is my best Friend and I can tell Him *any-thing.* And, I can talk to Him anytime and anywhere, no matter what I'm doing. *"So why don't you try doing the same?"*

Now don't worry. You don't have to speak eloquent words to impress anyone with your prayer. You will be talking to Jesus, who is gentle and kind, and your new best Friend. He cherishes you and will never mock you or belittle you.

So come on, let's talk to Him, because *He is longing to hear from you.* And to give you a *helping hand*, here's a special prayer for you. But first, please read it through and if you want to add some very personal words then that's OK, go right ahead. Just remember, you are speaking to *Jesus,* who loves you so much that He died for you and He'll be the *best Friend* you'll ever have.

As soon as you feel ready to make this commitment, please pray genuinely *from the bottom of your heart,* speaking *aloud* and, if you want to, kneel down ...

PRAYER OF SALVATION

Dear Lord Jesus,

I come before You now and confess that I'm a sinner, and I sincerely repent of my sins.

I am truly sorry for all the wrong and hurtful things I've ever said and done in my life and I humbly ask You to come into my heart right now and be my Lord and Saviour.

Thank You Lord Jesus for dying in my place on the cross and for shedding Your sinless, spotless blood to wash me clean from ALL my sins.

I believe in my heart that after three days, Almighty God, in His Sovereign power, raised You from the dead to live forever. And that *You rose victorious from the grave* to crush Satan's curse of death and eternal damnation over me, and anyone else who will put their faith in You.

Thank You Lord, for Your finished work on the cross and for Your wonderful gift of *eternal life in Heaven,* which I now receive with a contrite and grateful heart.

Lord Jesus, I believe that You are the *Lord of Lords* and the *King of Kings* and the Son of the One and Only true God, the Lord God Almighty of the Bible.

I believe too, that the holy Bible is the truth and that every word is, *"Living and active. Sharper than any double-edged sword,"* (Hebrews 4:12) and that You are *alive today* and for evermore.

I'm so grateful to You Lord Jesus, for *saving me* and that Heaven is now my eternal home. Please fill me with the Holy Spirit, and lead and guide me all of my days.

I'm so thankful too Lord, that You chose me and that I can now say, *"I am saved and born again!"* Thank You Lord Jesus, for loving me.

Amen.

By GRACE

I f you have just prayed this *Prayer of Salvation* and sincerely asked Jesus into your heart to be your Lord and Saviour, you are now *saved* and *born again* by the GRACE of Almighty God and the Holy Spirit now lives *within* you.

"For it is by grace
you have been saved, through faith ...
it is the gift of God."
(Ephesians 2:8)

ALL OF HEAVEN

D id you know that *ALL of Heaven is rejoicing* over *you now?* Can you grasp that? Everyone in Heaven knows that you are now *saved and born again* and they are all celebrating!

"There will be more rejoicing in Heaven
over one sinner (that's you) who repents."
(Luke 15:7)

And I'm celebrating too. *Congratulations!*

Now ... DON'T DOUBT IT!

T ake care ... don't ever doubt that this miracle, *your miracle,* has just happened to you. Rest in what you have just done and be assured that it is enough. Know for certain that *YOU ARE SAVED* because you responded to Jesus' invitation by sincerely praying the Prayer of Salvation.   Even if you don't feel any different, *believe* in what God's Word tells you, for it is the *truth* ...

> *"For, "Everyone* (that includes you)
> *who calls on the name of the Lord*
> *will be saved.""*
> (Romans 10:13)

Claim this verse for yourself and *believe it.* TRUST in God's promises to you *more than your own feelings.* Your feelings and emotions can change like the wind, from day to day. But God's holy Word and His promises in the Bible *never change* ...

> *"God is not a man, that He should lie,*
> *nor a son of man, that He should change His mind.*
> *Does He speak and then not act?*
> *Does He promise and not fulfil?*
> (Numbers 23:19)

Always, put your trust in **God's unchanging, faithful Word** and NOT in your own fluctuating feelings and fickle emotions. Rest in this knowledge and DON'T DOUBT IT.

The TRUTH and the Way of Salvation

S o dear Reader, stand firm in your new faith and don't listen to anyone who tells you, *"It can't be that easy.*

You can't be saved that quickly!" But you can. And you have been, if you've genuinely prayed the Prayer of Salvation.

So don't weaken or backslide the way I did, and keep believing God's Word in the Bible, which is the TRUTH. Continue reading the following verses over and over again, because they are the Way of Salvation for all of us ...

"If you confess with your mouth,
"Jesus is Lord,"
and believe in your heart
that God raised Him from the dead,
you will be saved."

"For it is with your heart
that you believe and are justified
and it is with your mouth that you confess
and are saved.

For, "Everyone
who calls on the name of the Lord
will be saved""
(Romans 10:9-10,13)

So REJOICE with Heaven

R ejoice! That Jesus Christ is now your Lord and Saviour. *Rejoice* that He will care for you, for the rest of your life. *Rejoice* that you are now *saved* from your sins and set *free. Rejoice* that you will spend *eternity in Heaven. Rejoice* that you have a new future ... *in Jesus' mighty Name!*

"Rejoice in the Lord always.
I will say it again: Rejoice!"
(Philippians 4:4)

My sincere hope and prayer for you now, is that you will day-by-day ...

> **"Grow in the grace and knowledge of our**
> **Lord and Saviour Jesus Christ."**
> (2 Peter 3:18)

Whether you fully realize it or not, you have just stepped *out* of the devil's evil clutches and *into* the loving arms of Jesus. You have stepped *out* of the world's darkness and *into* God's glorious *light* and the promise of an eternity spent in Heaven. This is a *great step of faith,* because you are now *saved, forgiven and eternally blessed.*

> **"Whoever believes in the Son** *(Jesus)* **has eternal life,**
> **but whoever rejects the Son will not see life,**
> **for God's wrath** *(anger and unforgiveness)*
> **remains on him."**
> (John 3:36)

So dear Reader, keep on *rejoicing* in what God has graciously just done in your life. For you are now a *new person* and a *new creation.* God's holy Word in the Bible confirms this wonderful *miracle,* in the following verse ...

> **"Therefore, if anyone** *(that's you)* **is in Christ,**
> **he** *(or she)* **is a new creation;**
> **the old has gone, the new has come!"**
> (2 Corinthians 5:17)

This means that you are now a *new creation* and your inner spirit has literally been *born again* by the power of God's *Holy Spirit* coming to live within you.

God has given you a second chance and a new beginning, and that's a *mighty miracle. Your miracle!*

Chapter 27

My own journey of Forgiveness

T he more I began to realize *just how much God had forgiven me,* the more it helped me to begin my own journey of forgiveness ... *to forgive those who had hurt me so deeply.*

Jesus knew the depth of pain and unfair agony that I went through, as I learnt to forgive. He wanted to spare me the torment of this mental anguish and was ready and willing to take ALL of my pain off me ... but I couldn't let go of it. *I kept holding onto the past,* letting it replay over and over again in my mind, and causing myself needless emotional turmoil and stress. I was caught in a relentless cycle of bitter memories and blame.

Many a time, I thought I'd been successful and truly for-given everyone.   But sadly, just the mention of a name or recollection of a particular situation or occasion had unkind and hostile words spewing out of me. *No, I hadn't forgiven them at all.* All I had done was bury my hurt and pain. Bury my past and I couldn't seem to suppress or control when these emotional outbursts would surface in retaliation. Oh, I wanted to be free to fully forgive ... *but how?*

The answer I longed for lay in learning to **totally believe and totally trust in Jesus' love for me.**   Only His divine, perfect, faithful love in my heart could drive out my hidden pain. Only the limitless *power* of His love could heal my buried hurt. Only the *love of Jesus* could set me *free*.

You see, *Jesus' love for me was stronger than my hurt and pain.* His love reached down into the hidden recesses of my heart and healed the deepest scars in my memory. And, through believing and trusting in the *power* of Jesus' great love for me, I received His grace and His strength to do what I couldn't do in my own weakness ... *totally forgive.*

> **"My grace is sufficient for you,**
> **for My power is made perfect**
> **in weakness."**
> (2 Corinthians 12:9)

I'm not saying it was easy. It was really *hard* and it took me quite a while. But the more I learnt to *believe* in Jesus' love for me and live every day trusting in *His complete forgiveness,* the quicker my heavy burden of unforgiveness, anger and bitterness passed from me and *onto Him.*

Thankfully, I learnt this hard, but so very important lesson to forgive and when, at last, I obeyed *God's command to forgive,* I found I had a wonderful peace and a new freedom in my spirit. Yes, to my surprise, it was actually a great relief to finally succeed in truly forgiving everyone who had ever hurt me ...

> *"Forgive whatever grievances*
> *you may have against one another.*
> *Forgive as the Lord forgave you."*
> (Colossians 3:13)

Likewise ...

I am very aware that I too, must have inadvertently hurt and offended many others over the years, especially my own two dear sons and members of my family and, for that, I humbly apologise. Very sadly, we can all fail each other at some point in our lives, whether knowingly or unknowingly, and we all need God's saving grace and unconditional love to forgive each other ...

> *"For all have sinned*
> *and fall short of the glory of God."*
> (Romans 3:23)

Are you struggling?

So dear Reader, *"Are you holding onto unforgiveness and bitterness, or anger and even revenge in your heart against someone? Is there anyone you refuse, or find impossible to forgive? And you just can't let go?"*

If so, begin today to believe in **Jesus' great love for you.** Trust in His Sovereign power and the divine strength of the Holy Spirit within you, to give you the ability and the grace *to forgive everyone who has ever hurt you or caused you grief.* Don't hang on to your unforgiveness any longer. *Give it all to Jesus, in prayer.*

307

I know this may seem impossible or even unthinkable to some of you right now. And you may be thinking, *"Why should I forgive? I'm innocent. I didn't do anything wrong."* But the truth is, until you *totally forgive,* you will never be free from your painful, haunting memories and unhealed scars. You have to forgive *first,* before deep healing can begin.

And, do you realize that *unforgiveness is a serious sin?* Jesus firmly warns us of the harmful and even severe *eternal* consequences that we can bring upon ourselves by *not* totally forgiving, even if we are the innocent party.

> **"For if you forgive men when they sin against you,**
> **your Heavenly Father**
> **will also forgive you.**
>
> **But if you do not forgive men their sins,**
> **your Father will not forgive your sins."**
> (Matthew 6:14-15)

These are serious words indeed, especially when so many of us struggle to forgive. And I don't only mean our *past* wounds, but the day-to-day offences, insults, teasing and bullying that can hurt us so deeply and be difficult to forgive.

So you might be feeling that Jesus' words are unjust or even impossible to obey and wonder how a *loving* God could be so stern, so uncaring. Everything inside you may be screaming, *"That's not fair. I want an apology. I need to know that person (group, organization, etc.) is **sorry** for what they have done. **Sorry** for the pain they have caused me."*

But God, in His infinite wisdom, knows what is *best* for our mental and physical wellbeing. He knows that keeping pent-up volatile emotions of hurt, pain, anger and even revenge inside us is definitely *not good for us.* Whatever is in our heart, *comes out of our mouth.* If there is unforgiveness and bitterness stored up inside us, then words of bitterness and animosity will rise up and keep coming out of our mouth. On the other hand, if we have *totally forgiven* everyone who has hurt us and our heart has been *healed,* then words of forgiveness will come from our lips ...

> *"For out of the abundance of the heart*
> *the mouth speaketh."*
> (Matthew 12:34b KJV)

No-win situation

I n theory, you may agree that it is the best thing to pass your burden of unforgiveness over to Jesus, but in practice you simply *can't let go.* And, in reality, it's possible you actually *want* to hang onto your pain. But you need to understand that this is a *no-win* situation. And should you continue to resist your Heavenly Father's command to *forgive* and persist in holding onto your unforgiveness, you are only harming yourself and *not* the person who has wronged you. **All you are doing is hurting yourself.** This may seem like a cruel injustice, but it is the truth.   A truth that many of us have had to learn at some point in our lives, including myself.

So take heart dear Reader, and know that justice will ultimately be done, even if you don't see it or receive an apology in your lifetime. Trust God to be the Ultimate Judge in your particular situation and that He will avenge all evil, according to His holy Word: *"It is Mine to avenge; I will repay," says the Lord.* (Romans 12:19)

So please forgive. Stop struggling under a heavy burden you don't need to bear ... a burden that Jesus nailed to the cross and wants to carry for you. *Let Him* take the yoke of unforgiveness *off* your shoulders and place it on His own ...

> **"For My yoke is easy**
> **and My burden is light."**
> (Matthew 11:30)

Another unfair reality, is that very often the 'guilty' person is unaware of your pain and is *not* hurting at all and, in some circumstances, may already be dead. Yes. It is possible that you are holding onto unforgiveness against someone who has already died. *Please, let it go and forgive.* Believe in your heart and be assured that God is in control, even if it doesn't look like it. Know that He will *not* forgive any *unrepentant* or *hidden sin.* Know that He will *not* allow any evil to enter into Heaven for, **"God "will give to each person according to what he has done"".** (Romans 2:6) Moreover, never doubt that God is the *Righteous Judge* of the whole world ...

> **"The earth is the Lord's,**
> **and everything in it,**
> **the world, and all who live in it."**
> (Psalm 24:1)

And yet, I know it can be desperately hard to see so much cruelty and injustice in this world, especially when the corrupt and guilty perpetrators often seem to get away scot-free. They may even laugh and boast that they have dodged capture and punishment, but God sees their sin and *not a single one of them* will escape His Judgement ...

> *"For we will all stand before God's judgement seat ...*
> *Each of us will give an account*
> *of himself (or herself) to God."*
> (Romans 14:10,12)

TAKE CARE!

N ow please, take care *not* to bring God's judgement upon yourself by holding onto your unforgiveness. Jesus clearly warns us ...

> *"But if you do not forgive men their sins,*
> *your Father will not forgive*
> *your sins."*
> (Matthew 6:15)

This is a serious, *lifetime warning* that none of us can afford to ignore or disobey. We all need to continuously, day-by-day learn to forgive those who hurt or offend us.   And, if we do *not* forgive and store up the sin of unforgiveness in our hearts, we may ourselves come under the hand of Almighty God's judgement.   Judgement that could even cost us our eternity in Heaven. For the Bible tells us ...

> *"It is a dreadful thing*
> *to fall into the hands of the*
> *living God."*
> (Hebrews 10:31)
> (For those who are not in a right relationship with Him)

Please understand dear Reader, how very important it is to obey our Heavenly Father's command to truly *forgive. Forgive,* as God is so graciously willing to forgive every one of us our failures and sins, however great they may be.

Take courage

To help you leave your painful memories behind you, here is a short *Prayer of Forgiveness*. Please read this prayer through first and then, as you pray, keep trusting in Jesus to give you the strength that you lack, to be able to speak these words of forgiveness *with all of your heart* and *really mean* every word. And, as you pray, you will **release** and **cast out** the pain and burden of unforgiveness that has been hidden and buried deep within you and kept you in bondage. Know too, that as soon as you *sincerely* pray these few words, you will truly begin your new future with Jesus.

So come on, take courage, for it's time *to let go* of your painful past and sincerely pray this *Prayer of Forgiveness ...*

PRAYER OF FORGIVENESS

**In the *Name of Jesus Christ,*
Who forgave me all of my sins,
I now willingly and totally forgive
all who have ever sinned against me
and all who have ever caused me deep pain,
immense grief and intense suffering.
I now claim the *victory of forgiveness*
over my life.
Amen.**

Well done! You've just broken off the cruel shackles of *unforgiveness* that the devil has kept you bound in. You've thrown off the heavy burden of pain that has kept your wounds raw and your scars unhealed. *And you've won your own personal battle over unforgiveness.* This is a great victory, in Jesus' mighty Name. *So rejoice.* Your heart is now free to receive the wonderful peace and healing love of Jesus ... *a love greater than any pain!*

J esus knows our fears, temptations and weaknesses and that is why He gave us a daily prayer to strengthen and help us. *A prayer that encourages us to continually forgive* those who sin against us.   A prayer that you can read in the Bible.   I was brought up from an infant to pray this prayer every bedtime and, although I lapsed as I grew older, I never forgot Jesus' special prayer ...

THE LORD'S PRAYER

Our Father, who art in Heaven,
hallowed be Thy Name.

Thy kingdom come,
Thy will be done on earth as it is in Heaven.

Give us this day our daily bread
and forgive us our trespasses (sins)
as we forgive those
who trespass against us.

Lead us not into temptation,
but deliver us from evil.

For Thine is the Kingdom,
the power and the glory,
forever and ever.

Amen.

(You can read this Prayer in Luke 11:2-4)

Chapter 28

A Personal Victory

**"To win a victory,
a battle has to be fought first ..."**

I'd like to tell you about a very personal, emotional battle that I fought and *won*. A battle created by my own fluctuating feelings and emotions, keeping me in bondage and pain. But first, I need to share with you a little of what happened to me *before I was saved*, between the years of 1992 and 1997.

When Michael and I separated after his Christmas visit in 1991 and our divorce was underway, I became friends with a local farmer. He was a bachelor and, as our friendship developed, he became a close friend. He lived with his brother and elderly mother at their farm and I began helping them whenever I could.

Gradually, as their mother became increasingly immobile and unable to cope with the daily chores, I began helping more and more until, after a while, I was going every day to cook their midday meal. Then, after collecting my four-year-old son Ross from his primary school, we returned to the farm to care for their ailing mother, who had severely ulcerated legs. In fact, one of her legs was almost completely raw from her ankle up to her knee, causing intense suffering. It was horrible seeing her in such pain and I so wanted to help in any way I could.

After closely watching the visiting nurses that came to her home and then being taught by the nurses in the Dermatology Clinic at Coleraine Hospital, I was allowed to dress her legs, using the special dressings they supplied to us.

Nearly every afternoon, I would gently apply fine gauze squares soaked in soothing saline solution onto her raw legs. Thankfully, this seemed to ease her suffering. I would then, carefully and patiently, apply the special dressings under elasticated bandages. This dedicated care was rewarded, when her wounds began to noticeably heal and reduce.

This dear old lady and I became very close and I nursed her at the farm for many years as she became weaker and increasingly frail. Sometimes, when she was particularly poorly, I made special visits to help her get up in the morning. Then at night-time, I would return again to help her get into bed and make sure she was comfortable for the night.

Looking after this dear old lady was a labour of love, and yet one I enjoyed and never regretted. In fact, to be able to bring her a little relief from her terrible pain was reward enough. As the Bible says, *"Do to others what you would have them do to you."* (Matthew 7:12) I cared for her deeply and treated her as though she was my own mother. I did my very best for her, until she passed away early one morning in hospital.

We had never been on a farm before

L ittle Ross loved being at the farm with all the animals and having plenty of space to run around. I can still picture him enthusiastically pedalling at full speed down the farmyard in his sturdy green John Deere toy tractor, with a trailer full of hay behind him.

We particularly liked harvest time, when Ross and I loved standing up on the front of the combine harvester amidst clouds of rising dust, as the ripened barley was being harvested. Occasionally, we even volunteered to go out together into the fields to pick up stones, which was really tiring and back-breaking work.

But my donation to the household was to cook good wholesome food, especially at silage and harvest times, when there were many hungry mouths to feed.

Yes, I'm talking about me, who in my youth hated cooking. Although my new roles as *cook* and *nurse* were certainly very different to anything I'd known before, I really enjoyed this new lifestyle and found pleasure in being able to help.

But there was another important reason. I didn't feel threatened any more. You see, I was so used to being hit and punched by Michael, that if my new boyfriend suddenly moved or lifted his arm to reach for something, I immediately ducked or leapt backwards. He was alarmed at my defensive behaviour at first, until he realized the inner fear I was still carrying. Gradually, my defense mechanism died down and I learnt to relax and enjoy his company, without any fear that he would hurt me.

He had backslidden

Although my new friend did not go to church, chapel or any religious meeting, he explained to me that he had been genuinely *saved* as a teenager. But, for the past twenty years or more, he had backslidden. To me, at the time, this didn't present a problem at all, as *I wasn't saved either* and hardly understood what he was even talking about. It wasn't until several years later though, when I finally got *saved* and *born again* by the Holy Spirit, that I understood the gravity of the problem facing us, when I so wanted *him to return to the Lord.*

But sadly, he refused. And this is one of the reasons why I began to weaken and backslide myself, after that life-changing night in April 1997, as I struggled with this unexpected dilemma. However, several months later, I regained my faith when my local Minister told me, *"Don't you know that all your sins are forgiven!"* and shortly afterwards, I spent a whole week at *New Horizon.* I then knew for certain, that I wanted to serve the Lord for the rest of my life.

"But how could I serve the Lord Jesus with a backslidden boyfriend? Someone who utterly refused to accept the Lord back into his life?"   Sadly, I knew deep inside me, that our relationship was doomed.   It just wouldn't work any longer between us.

Unequally yoked

Nonetheless, we spent hours, days and into weeks discussing this ever-widening rift between us and although he wanted us to stay together, he refused to accept the Lord Jesus back into his life. I realized we had become what the Bible calls, *unequally yoked*. I was heartbroken and didn't want to leave him, but he simply refused to join me in the walk I had now chosen with the Lord.

At *New Horizon* I had willingly committed my life to God, to serve Him for the rest of my days. And I meant it. No-one was forcing me to do it, I wanted to do it. But now I was faced with this surprise test. A BIG test. *My boyfriend or Jesus?* I hadn't expected this, but God was testing my faith, my new commitment and love for Him.   It was a choice only I could make.

In reality, I was wavering and being double-minded. I wanted my old life as well as my new life. I wanted them *both*. I found out that while *I kept my eyes on Jesus,* I was strong and committed.   But as soon as *I looked away* and thought about my own personal desires and wants, I wavered and became weak and undecided, letting *fear* in. *Fear* that Satan wields as a cruel weapon against us. *Fear* that can so easily cripple our senses and distort our decisions. And in this state of indecision, my emotions were in complete turmoil.

My local Minister, together with certain friends, advised me against continuing this friendship and this caused me even more distress.   I agonized and wrestled over this predicament, and prayed for guidance from my Heavenly Father. But deep in my heart, I already knew the answer. I knew that God wanted me to separate from my boyfriend and begin my new life with Him.

I knew too, that My Heavenly Father wanted to use me in His Kingdom. But I was aware too, that it would be impossible

318

for me to fulfil His plans for my life *if* I couldn't make this one, important sacrifice for Him now. *If* I couldn't choose to walk unhindered and unburdened into my new life with Jesus. *This new life I so dearly wanted.* The Bible gave me a clear answer to my dilemma but, although I knew it was the truth, I found it so hard to obey.

> **"Do not be yoked together with unbelievers ...**
> **What does a believer have in common**
> **with an unbeliever?**
>
> **Therefore, come out from them**
> **and be separate,**
> **says the Lord."**
> (2 Corinthians 6:14-15,17)

More than anything, I wanted to please God. And tearfully, I ended our relationship. Yet over the following weeks, we kept passing each other on the road or bumping into each other while out shopping or, harder still, he kept calling to see me at my home, which extended the suffering. But he remained stubborn, refusing to change his mind. No matter how much I urged him to return to the Lord, he just wouldn't.

I agonized over ending our friendship and through all the pain, heartache and suffering, I cried out to the Lord to help me, to strengthen me. I found a Bible verse that gave me the hope and courage I needed *to keep my eyes on Jesus* and not be tempted to veer off and follow my own temporary desires.

> **"After you have suffered a little while,**
> *(Jesus)* **will Himself restore you**
> **and make you**
> **strong, firm and steadfast."**
> (1 Peter 5:10)

I claimed this verse for myself and prayed over it day after day, week after week. But when the torment in my heart didn't lessen, I kept asking the Lord, *"How much more suffering? How much more pain? How much longer Lord?"*

I was grieving over ending our friendship, losing my *new* family and fearing being left alone again. I just didn't have the strength to completely *let go*. What made it much harder, was that it wasn't as if we didn't get on, because we did. Over the years, we'd come to love each other and be very close friends.

But things had changed now ... *I had changed*. And I couldn't ever go back and live in my past again. I only wanted to go forwards and grasp my new future. *Jesus was my future, my life and my love now.* He was the true love that I'd been waiting and searching for all my life. He understood me and knew all my failings and weaknesses. He knew all my desires too, and my deep need to be loved.

Yet through this emotional battle, I learnt a big truth. *"Having the love of Jesus in your heart, is far deeper and immensely greater than any human love you can have or ever hope for."*

Upon realizing this truth, I knew for certain that, *"I could never give up Jesus."* If there had to be a choice between my boyfriend and Jesus, it would have to be *Jesus*. Jesus would win every time. THIS was the test.

God was helping me

This test may seem very severe to you, dear Reader. You may wonder how a loving God would ask me, or anyone, to leave their boyfriend or girlfriend. But really, *God*

320

was helping me. He was answering my prayers, but not in the way I wanted. God knew that if my friend was unwilling to return to Him and walk hand in hand with Him, our relationship would suffer disharmony and ultimately fail, causing even *more* pain.

You see, my boyfriend was already disapproving of the monthly OMF (Overseas Missionary Fellowship) prayer meetings that I was holding in my home. And, should we marry, as we had previously discussed, how could I ever serve God with all of my heart? How could I happily consider marrying someone who resisted Jesus and opposed my work for Him? And I was only just *beginning* to serve Him.

Although this test seemed so hard and painful at the time, *God knew what was best for me.* I had to learn to trust God's ways and not my own. I had to learn to let the Holy Spirit within me lead and guide me. I had to learn *not* to be *'the boss'* of my life any longer. A tough lesson maybe, but an essential one if I was to serve Jesus and *obey* Him.

So dear Reader, if you are considering getting married, please don't forget to earnestly pray and seek God's guidance *before* committing yourself. God really does know *who* is the right person for you.

However, should you find yourself already in a marriage where your spouse is *not* saved, just keep showing them *the love of Jesus* in your life. Keep patiently praying for them, always trusting God to save him or her. And this includes your children and all your loved ones too. This is an important ministry, *your ministry.* Remember, you are His precious child and you have the Holy Spirit within you ...

"The prayer of a righteous man (or woman)
is powerful and effective."
(James 5:16b)

That's true. Your prayers *are* powerful and God knows your heart's desire and sees your pain and tears. God is love and He is faithful. So don't ever give up ... *Jesus didn't give up on you. And He didn't give up on me.*

Leon left home for university

It was during this stressful time, in September 1997, that my heart was broken yet again when Leon left home to go to Dundee University. I dreaded the moment of giving him a last hug and saying *"good-bye"* to him, and just the very thought of it sent me into floods of tears, weeks before he even left. I just couldn't imagine life without him, without seeing his smiling face every day ... he was still my *baby.*

He was so dependable and capable and helped me around the house doing all the things I couldn't. Plus, he was so skilled at keeping our large garden in order. For so many years, we'd worked together as a team and I'd come to depend upon him for his help.

But now, it was time for Leon to leave us and the house seemed empty without him. Ross was still young, not quite eleven years old and yet he tried his best to help me when he could. Gradually, as he matured, he learned to become a reliable and sensible young man like his older brother, and a promising *new man of the house.*

The new man of the house

I was in an emotionally vulnerable state with Leon leaving home, especially having recently separated from my boyfriend. It really broke my heart seeing Leon leave and I missed him terribly. We didn't have mobile phones, email and Skype in those days to keep in regular contact with each other, just the occasional expensive phone call.

I was lonely and hurting, and desperately cried out to God for His help. Our finances were being stretched too, as I lost several benefits when Leon left for university and through it all, I was feeling extremely weak and battle-weary. In the end, it was young Ross who set me straight, *good and proper.* Here's how he did it ...

I arrived home one day distraught and in tears, after seeing my ex-boyfriend's friendly, smiling face as he passed me on the road. I was in deep pain and being sorely tested. Ross, in a flash of youthful wisdom and as the *new man of the house,* accurately assessed my deep heartache and extreme distress and took full control of the situation. He commanded me to sit down at our dining table and proceeded to sternly reprimand me ...

"Mummy. If you don't pull yourself together, you won't get through this. I am only ten years old, but even if I die at twenty, I will spend the rest of my life living for Jesus!"

Whaoo! What pearls of wisdom from a babe. My mouth fell open in shock and utter amazement at his decisive, authoritative outburst, which successfully gave me the shake-up I needed. I truly believe it was God *warning* me, through my ten-year-old son.

But I have told you all of this because God knows our deepest pain and weaknesses. He knows how we can be so strong one minute and then totally weak the next. He knows how difficult it is for us to do things in our own strength, and that is *why* He is always ready to help us by any means available, *even through the words and actions of a young son.*

That is *why* we all need the love and help of our Heavenly Father and the guidance of the Holy Spirit every day of our lives, *to give us the strength and wisdom we lack.*

And that is exactly what God did. He gave me the strength, the courage and the willpower I lacked, to win through to *victory.*

To win the victory

One Sunday morning, shortly after Ross's severe reprimand, I woke up full of energy, stress-free and feeling absolutely great. In fact, I felt like a brand new person and knew immediately what had happened. My agonizing burden had been lifted off me. It was completely gone.   I was free from all my pain and suffering over leaving my boyfriend. And it felt *wonderful.*

My Heavenly Father, in His amazing love and mercy, had heard my desperate prayers and cries for help and totally fulfilled His *every* word in my Bible verse ...

"After you have suffered a little while,
will Himself restore you
and make you
strong, firm and steadfast."
(1 Peter 5:10)

Almighty God, being forever true to His word, had *restored* me to full strength and made me *strong, firm and steadfast.* He had removed all my suffering and filled me with His wonderful peace and incredible joy. *It was a miracle* and I was in awe at God's goodness to me.

At last, *I'd won the battle* over Satan's plans and cruel attempts to completely weaken me and drag me back to my old life. Satan knew my *Achilles heel* was leaving my boyfriend and the fear of being alone again. He attacked me on these issues really viciously. *But my Saviour was fighting for me.* My Saviour who will always love me and protect me from my own weaknesses and temptations, by the power of the Holy Spirit living within me. My Saviour who has promised to *"never leave me nor forsake me."* And He kept His promise to me. And He'll faithfully keep His promise to *you* too, and to *all* who trust in Him.

Suddenly, I felt so *strong* and all the desire and longing for my ex-boyfriend had completely disappeared. *Totally gone.* It was miraculous and I felt as light as air now that my heavy burden had been lifted off me. I was free. *Restored, strong, firm and steadfast.* Yes, God is so good.

In my utter weakness, God had shown me His strength and His grace. And yet, only *when* I made the firm choice to put God's will above my own. Only *when* I made Jesus No. 1 in my life. Only *when* I learnt to *keep my eyes fixed on Jesus*, my precious Saviour.

"And afterwards?" Never once was I tempted to return to my ex-boyfriend. I was free now. Free to serve my Lord and Saviour with all of my strength, and all of my heart.

"And my ex-boyfriend?" We still bumped into each other occasionally, but whenever we did, it didn't hurt any more, the pain was gone.

But he was, and always will be, a very dear friend who will remain in my prayers ... *"May he return to You Lord one day, with all of his heart, and may that day be soon."*

You see, my Heavenly Father in His great faithfulness, compassion and deep love for me, delivered me and set me free from the last chains of bondage. HE strengthened and restored me, so I could look *forwards* with confidence to my new future and not backwards to my past. God fought my battle for me and graciously pulled me through *to claim the victory.*

> **"The Lord will fight for you;**
> **you need only to be still."**
> (Exodus 14:14)
>
> (Keep constantly trusting in the Lord, and be at peace)

A wonderful blessing

T hen in 2006, my loving Heavenly Father fulfilled the desires of my heart.   He gave me **a new husband, Paul.**   A wonderful, caring and loving husband *who loves the Lord as much as I do.   Thank You Jesus!*

> **"Delight yourself in the Lord**
> **and He will give you**
> **the desires of your heart."**
> (Psalm 37:4)

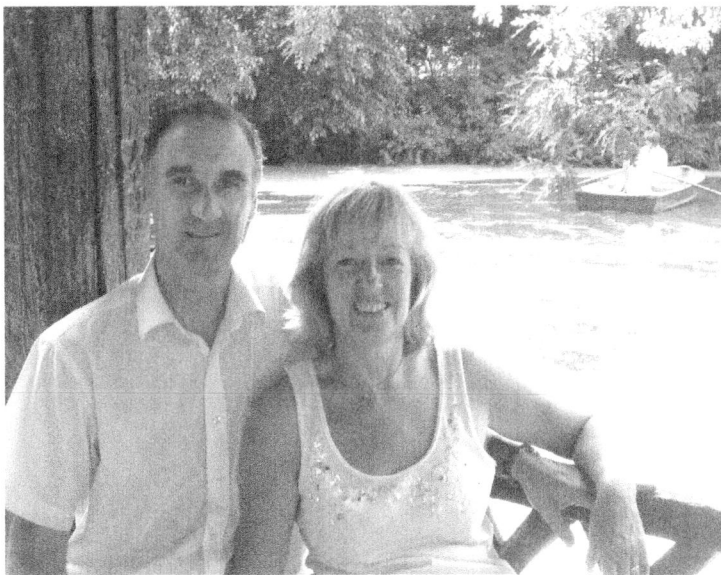

Chapter 29

Jesus' Power is Supreme

I t most certainly is! For when Jesus becomes our Lord and Saviour, **we are no longer left defenceless** to face life's many trials and tribulations.

Yes it's true, for whatever sorrows and troubles the future may hold, I now have the comfort and peace in my heart that Jesus will always *stand with me* through the toughest of times. And what a blessed assurance it is to know for *certain* that Jesus will *"never leave me nor forsake me"* (Hebrews 13:5) and that I can draw on *His supreme power* to help me through anything and everything.

Divine protection

J esus wants us to depend upon Him each and every day for *divine protection* over our lives and over our future. *"But how do I do that?"* you may ask. There are many ways, but first, you must sincerely *believe* that Jesus' power is supreme and that His Name is above all other names ...

"Therefore God exalted Him (Jesus)
to the highest place
and gave Him the Name that is above every name,
that at the Name of Jesus
every knee should bow,
in Heaven and on earth and under the earth,
and every tongue confess that
Jesus Christ is Lord,
to the glory of God the Father."
(Philippians 2:9-11)

This means that the **Name of Jesus** is powerful in itself, and when we finish our prayers, we should always end with the words, *in the Name of Jesus,* which adds divine power to our prayers, and *Amen* means *so be it* and seals our words. So we need to use our words wisely, as our prayers spoken *in Jesus' Name* are powerful and effective, and weapons in times of need, and as tools of thanksgiving, when praising the Lord.

Speaking **God's Word,** written in the holy Bible, is also a powerful weapon for us, as this verse confirms ...

"For the Word of God is living and active.
Sharper than any double-edged sword,
it penetrates even to dividing soul and spirit,
joints and marrow;
it judges the thoughts and attitudes
of the heart."
(Hebrews 4:12)

So, it is vitally important that we begin reading God's Word in the Bible, to learn more about our Heavenly Father and His beloved Son, Jesus Christ. Jesus, who sacrificed His sinless life on the cross to offer us eternal life, and shed His precious blood to wash away our sins. And it is the spotless **blood of Jesus** that is one of the *most powerful weapons* that God has given us. For, whenever, and wherever we pray *in faith,* and say the words, "***I plead the blood of Jesus over my life for divine protection",*** God will hear our sincere plea and be ready to help us.

However, whether we like it or not, our Heavenly Father knows our inner thoughts, so when we **plead the blood of Jesus over ourselve**s, we should pray with a sincere heart, and *not* speak flippantly or casually.

You can "***plead the blood of Jesus for divine protection"*** over yourself, your family and friends, your marriage and relationships, and your home and car or vehicle too. Plus, any of your journeys and travelling, sporting activities, medical treatments and operations and, of course, childbirth. You can even pray for the *divine protection of the blood of Jesus* over the welfare of your business, your staff, premises and stock, *plus* your farm livestock, crops and land. In fact, you can pray *the blood of Jesus for God's divine protection* over anyone and anything that is important to you. That means *any* situation or occasion, and at *any* time and *any* place, whenever you feel the need for some extra *divine* help and protection.

Now, you may be thinking to yourself, *"this all sounds a bit far-fetched. A bit over-the-top."* And to those who haven't yet accepted Jesus as their ***SAVE*-iour**, it most likely is. You may also be disputing, *"Show me in the Bible where I can read about the power and protection of blood?"* Well, I'm about to tell you ...

As you have already read, I didn't go to church as a child, but I still knew about the well-known Bible story of Moses crossing the Red Sea.   And today, I still marvel at God's awesome power to make a dry path through the mighty waters, which allowed the Israelites to leave Egypt in *safety.*   But first, in order for this *miracle* to happen, we can read in the Bible about the **power and protection of the blood of the lamb.**

God gave strict instructions that **unless the blood of the sacrificial lamb** was painted on the sides and tops of the door frames of the Israelites' homes, the firstborn of their children and animals would *die.*   Only the *blood of the lamb* could protect and save them from God's judgement passing through Egypt. For God clearly told them,

> *"When I see the blood, I will pass over you.*
> *No destructive plague will touch you*
> *when I strike Egypt."*
> (Exodus 12:7,12-13)

But instead of killing a live lamb, as they did in the Old Testament times, the *New* Testament records how **Jesus Christ became the sacrificial Lamb of God,** when He died on the cross at Calvary and shed His sinless blood to *save* us and *protect* us. The precious **blood of Jesus Christ, the Lamb of God,** is still our divine protection against all harm today, and it always will be, for ...

> *"Jesus Christ is the same yesterday*
> *and today and for ever."*
> (Hebrews 13:8)

We all need the *divine protection of the blood of Jesus* over our lives, because the devil is *real.*   We need to be *aware* that his spirit of evil and darkness is *active.*   Be

331

aware too, that he constantly wants to cause strife, disunity, sickness and disorder in our lives, whenever and wherever he can.   And we need to realize that Satan is cunning, deceitful, cruel and *our enemy ...*

> **"Your enemy the devil prowls around**
> **like a roaring lion**
> **looking for someone to devour."**
> (1 Peter 5:8)

You only have to watch or read the world news any day of the week to see his influence *everywhere,* as he stirs up dissention, hatred and violence between people and nations. His evil plans and conspiracies cause destruction, hostility and wars.

It is the devil who spreads his evil grip of poverty and famine across nations and yet, at the same time, feeds an insatiable greed for money and lust for power, often causing widespread corruption and injustice. He is the one responsible for all perversion and immorality, pornography and sex trafficking around the world. The devil inflames fury, hatred and revenge in hearts; ignites incensed murder, massacres and atrocities; and breeds every form of degradation and vice.

In 2007, my new husband Paul and I had the opportunity to visit *Auschwitz* in Poland, the notorious Nazi concentration camp where *over one million souls,* mostly Jews, were mercilessly tortured, starved and exterminated during World War II.

We saw for ourselves the huge mountains of *shoes, spectacles and human hair* taken from the prisoners at Auschwitz. This was indeed, a deeply distressing sight and, tragically, are the horrific remains of the devil's atrocities carried out during the Holocaust in World War II.   And, disturbingly today, Satan is inciting another wave of anti-Semitism and anti-Israel plus, in many countries, widespread persecution against Bible-believing Christians too.

But, as sure as day follows night, there will come a predestined time when the world will see the *Supreme Power of Jesus* and the *authority, wrath and judgement* of Almighty God, *"the Judge of all men"* (Hebrews 12:23) when He fulfils His Word of *warning* upon ALL nations and individuals who *condemn and persecute* Christians, Jews and *His* Nation of Israel ...

> *"I will bless those who bless you,*
> (the Nation of Israel, Jews and Christians)
> *and whoever curses you*
> *I will curse."*
> (Genesis 12:3)

All of us are susceptible

S atan is a *predator.*   Skillfully, he watches for every opportunity to attack us at our weakest and most vulnerable moments, when our emotions are irrational, delicate and unstable.   Often, it is when we are experiencing a time of crisis in our lives; when we are at an all-time emotional or physical low ... that is when the devil will choose to strike, without any mercy, to disrupt our lives.

And that is precisely the time when we need to *cry out* to the Lord for His help and ***plead the blood of Jesus*** over our lives for His divine strength and protection ...

"The Lord (Jesus) is faithful,
and He will strengthen and protect you
from the evil one." (Satan)
(2 Thessalonians 3:3)

None of us, *in our own strength,* can withstand attacks from the devil when he whispers his lies to us; when he expertly twists the truth in our minds, until we begin to believe his reasoning is logical and factual. When he slyly manipulates our thoughts, and cruelly tortures our minds by *reminding us* of every sin and failure in our lives.

But you are not alone when this happens, because *all* of us are susceptible to the devil. I know this, because the devil had plenty to remind me about. But we need to keep remembering that **Jesus is loving and kind, and He will never remind us of our failures and past sins. He died to save us from them and give us a second chance.** No, it's the devil who accuses us and tries to pull us backwards into our sinful past. *So fiercely resist the devil,* with all of your strength ... **"Resist the devil, and he will flee from you."** (James 4:7).

"But how can I do that?" you may ask. Keep reminding yourself that Jesus loves you and has forgiven you *all* of your sins. Stand firm in your new faith and whenever you have an urgent need or feel particularly anxious or stressful, **"plead the blood of Jesus"** over your life to protect you from all harm, and to protect your mind, your emotions and your thoughts. Be confident of the truth too, that ...

"The one (Holy Spirit) **who is in you**
is greater than the one (Satan)
who is in the world."
(1 John 4:4)

I too, learnt this great truth that *Jesus' power is Supreme*, and listened to the loving words of encouragement from the Holy Spirit within me, rather than the whispers of accusation from Satan, the great accuser. So every day, my new faith in Jesus became stronger and I claimed the glorious *victory* in my life ...

"But thanks be to God!
He gives us the victory through
our Lord Jesus Christ."
(1 Corinthians 15:57)

I felt I could face almost anything from now on, knowing that I had the strength of the Holy Spirit within me *to go* wherever He sent me, and *to do* whatever the Lord had planned for my life ...

"For I know the plans I have for you,"
declares the Lord,
"Plans to prosper you *(plans for good)*
and not to harm you,
plans to give you hope and a future."
(Jeremiah 29:11)

This particular Bible *promise* meant so very much to me when I was first saved. I even kept a copy of it beside my television. Then every day, I would see it and read it, sometimes many times. It gave me the *daily encouragement* and *hope* that I really needed, together with the *strength* and *courage* to overcome and face up to the many trials that I battled through as a single parent.

God knows the plans He has for *your* life too ... plans for *good* and not for harm.   And the more you keep *your eyes on*

Jesus and let His helping hand guide you day by day, the sooner you will have *His peace in your heart.*

Shalom! PEACE

N ow, with *my old life* put firmly behind me, I was filled with a new enthusiasm for the future and an incredible *peace.* But it was not a lazy, lackadaisical peace, but an *invigorating, stimulating* and *empowering* peace. A peace that only comes from the Holy Spirit and through keeping your eyes on Jesus. Peace and calm. That's what Jesus wants all of us to have in our hearts today and every day. Inner peace and *not* anxiety, tension and stress. Peace over every decision we make and every problem that confronts us ...

> *"Peace I leave with you,*
> *My peace I give you."*
> (John 14:27).

Always remember, if you *don't feel peace* in your heart and mind about something you are doing, or a decision you have made, then you may have made the *wrong* choice. If this is the case, *pray again for guidance* until your peace returns. If you have made the *right* choice, then you will be *at peace.* This is God's grace and daily guidance in your life. So let *peace* be your guide, always ...

> *"And let the peace of Christ*
> *rule in your hearts."*
> (Colossians 3:15)

Chapter 30

I never could have Dreamt

As my thoughts slip back now to the summer of 1997, when I meekly stepped inside New Horizon's huge tent meeting for over 3,000 people, and I fearfully hid in a dark corner on the first evening of their week-long Christian conference, I still marvel at what God did in my life during those seven days.

I *arrived* so timid and full of apprehension, insecure and unsure of myself as I ventured into those unfamiliar sur-roundings and yet, just one week later, I *departed* as bold as a lion. All my insecurity, fear and apprehension had gone and I was focused and *sure* that I wanted to serve Jesus Christ as my Lord and Saviour for the rest of my life. And never could I have dreamt how *exciting* that was going to be.

What a turnaround

Jesus came into my life and turned it *upside down and inside out.* And Oh! How I loved it. Suddenly, my life became vibrant and meaningful, and worth living. And I wanted to do something that would honour God and not just satisfy my own cravings and selfish desires. I wasn't scared any more to do something completely new and unfamiliar. I wasn't fearful any longer to meet new people and go to new places.

Suddenly, I felt full of energy and raring to go. And I was ready and eager to make a public declaration of my personal commitment to my Lord and Saviour, Jesus Christ ...

My public commitment

On Sunday, 9th November 1997, just a few weeks after Leon's departure to Dundee University, I made my public *vow* and very sincere heart commitment, to serve the Lord Jesus for the rest of my life.

To me, this was a really momentous occasion and, as this important day approached, I wondered, *"What shall I wear?"* You see, I hadn't been able to buy myself any brand new clothes for over *ten* years.

So I began searching through our cupboards. To my absolute delight, I found tucked away a lovely slim-fitting cream suit that I'd bought nearly fifteen years earlier in *Next,* back in Yorkshire. And quite amazingly, it still fitted me. It was just *perfect* for my special day.

I was thrilled at *my find* and delighted that I had something really *presentable* and nice to wear. But to my dismay, some dear elderly friends in Scotland *insisted* that I wore a hat on this memorable occasion. And, to make sure I did, they promised to send me one. *Oh help!* Whatever would my friends, who were already in their *eighties,* choose for me? I

338

tried to take courage from a Bible verse which wisely advises, *"Do not be anxious about anything."* (Philippians 4:6) But however hard I tried, *I was.*

Thankfully, my fears were soon put to rest when our postman delivered a great big box containing the *prettiest cream hat* I'd ever seen. It was absolutely *gorgeous.* So the Bible verse proved to be true after all.

I felt like a bride

D ressed up in all my finery, I felt like a *bride. A bride* about to embark upon her new life.

A bride whose *New Love, Jesus,* would never abuse her, never be unkind or cruel, and never lie to her. A *New Love* who would cherish and adore her, with a pure and faithful love, forever and ever, and even for all *eternity* in Heaven. *A love that would never die.*

I was immensely happy and aware of an inner glow, an *inner peace* that I'd never experienced before. My heart was overflowing with joy and thankfulness and at last, I felt *complete* and deeply loved for the first time in my life. My new *True Love* loved me through and through and accepted me *just the way I was,* and promised to **"never leave me nor forsake me."** (Hebrews 13:5)

Yes, with all of my heart, I was ready to make my vow to Jesus, rejoicing that my life *will never be the same again ...*

Oh Jesus, Jesus! My precious Lord and Saviour,
You cast off my fear and my shameful behaviour.
You set me free from Satan's curse,
For to end up in hell, what could be worse?

So with every breath, I worship Your holy Name,
Oh wow, *My life will never be the same!*
From Glory to Glory as I tread The Way up,
How thankful I am, that Jesus drank from His Cup.

(From: "My Precious Lord and Saviour")
By Esther Barbara Dennison

My Baptism

It was such a lovely mild, sunny morning on that Sunday back in early November 1997. And, with my navy blue leather bound Bible, a precious gift from my parents when I was only eleven years old tucked firmly under my arm, Ross and I set off for my *Baptism service* at our local church.

Although Ross was barely eleven years old, the service made a deep impression upon him and afterwards, as we walked back to our car, he turned and confidently declared, *"Mummy, I want to be baptized too and become a Christian!"* His jubilant outburst was not merely a childish, emotional whim for, by the Spring of the following year, Ross was ready to commit his young life to the Lord. So one Saturday afternoon, the two of us sat quietly together in our living room reading through some Bible passages and, after praying together, Ross gave his young life to the Lord Jesus. So simple, and yet so very meaningful. Ross was now *a child of the living God* and I was really thrilled for him.

A few years later, on Sunday 18ᵗʰ November 2001, Ross *rededicated* his life to Jesus at a Youth Rally, run by Steve Parsons of Logos Ministries. When he arrived home, he was *ecstatic*. Leaping about the place and beaming from ear to ear like 'a Cheshire cat.' He was bubbling over with joy, just the way I had been a few years earlier. And in his excitement, he kept shouting, *"I'm saved! I'm saved!"* Two of his friends, Robert and Jason also gave their lives to the Lord at that Rally, so *treble celebrations* were going on in Heaven that night.

Several years later, on 7ᵗʰ August 2005 in Eastern Europe, Ross and I were baptized by being *immersed* in water. We walked together, hand in hand, down into a flower-strewn lake. It was an immensely moving and emotional occasion. One that we shall always remember and deeply treasure.

I was ready and willing to go *anywhere*

With my whole heart, I knew that I wanted nothing else but to serve my Lord and Saviour Jesus Christ and *I was ready and willing to go anywhere and do anything.* And I really meant it. But I had absolutely no idea *what* I could do, *where* I could go or *how* to do it. I just knew I wanted to serve Him and was certain there must be *something* I could do.

That *something* was to start praying. And with Ross's full support and encouragement, I began praying with all of my heart for God to open new doors for me and to show me the work He wanted me to do. Full of enthusiasm and unabated zeal, I claimed the chorus from the praise song, *"I the Lord of Sea and Sky"* as my daily prayer and urgent plea to the Lord ...

"Here I am Lord! *Is it I Lord?*
I have heard You calling in the night.
I will go Lord, if You lead me,
I will hold Your people in my heart."

Yes, I meant every single word and wanted to get going *quickly.* I was totally fearless now. But month after month passed by, and nothing happened. I became increasingly impatient and prayed more earnestly, *"I really mean it Lord! I'll go anywhere and do anything!"*

It took me quite a while to realize that through this delay, God was teaching me some very important lessons ... *HIS ways* and *HIS timing.* I had to learn that *He was the master of my life now,* and not me. I had to learn to do things in *God's timing* and not my own. I had to learn to be *content* in all circumstances, whether I liked them or not. And until I learnt these vitally important lessons, *nothing would happen.*

These long months of training and *waiting on God* for my prayers to be answered, taught me *patience* and *perseverance.* Two extremely valuable, but very hard lessons to learn ...

"Who through faith and patience
inherit the promises."
(Hebrews 6:12 KJV)

Then, after *more than a year* of persistent prayer, the Lord began to open an unexpected door for me.

Was this what I'd been waiting for?

It was now November 1998 and, as on most days, I was busying myself around the house whilst listening to

UCB radio (United Christian Broadcasters) and happily singing along to the praise and worship songs. And today seemed to be the same as any other day or so I thought, *until* I was suddenly stopped in my tracks at what I heard on the radio.

For over the airwaves, came an agonizing appeal that tore at my heartstrings. It *stirred* me. It *compelled* me. It *moved* me to tears. And I began questioning, *"Was this appeal the answer to my prayers? Was this what I'd been waiting for?"*

Heart wrenching appeal

B elfast born broadcaster and author Pastor Bob Gass, a co-author of UCB's free, daily devotional booklet titled, *'Word for Today,'* was telling UCB listeners that for quite a while, he'd been visiting and helping needy orphanages in Romania. But, during his most recent visit to Eastern Europe, his interpreter had taken him to witness the shocking discovery of an *appalling* orphanage in the next-door country of *Moldova.*

Pastor Bob Gass continued to tell his listeners that he was horrified at what he found and could hardly believe his eyes at the dreadful sight that met him.   He found two hundred orphan children, who were barely surviving in the worst, sordid conditions imaginable. *It looked like a bleak concentration camp for children.* All the children were *grossly malnourished* and living in *stinking, filthy, inhumane, absolute squalor.*

Pastor Bob Gass's heart-wrenching appeal stirred many hearts, *including mine.* And immediately, like many others, I began making enquiries. I found out that *Romanian*

Connection, a humanitarian aid charity based in Belfast and already working with orphans in Romania, *had readily agreed* to help Pastor Bob Gass when he first approached them.

Responding instantly to his appeal, *Romanian Connection* loaded several huge trucks with vital aid and made the necessary preparations to tackle the very long journey, through icy winter conditions, into Eastern Europe.

"But how could I help? What could I do?" I felt totally helpless. I couldn't even afford to buy enough petrol to drive the long distance to Belfast, to lend a hand at the charity. I had no money either to donate towards the desperate needs. I felt frustrated and yet I couldn't forget this urgent appeal. It was in my thoughts constantly.

Then, a few weeks later, on 14th December, 1998 I was to be challenged again. This time, it was going to be a very personal, very *special* day **... a day I would never forget.**

The answer to my prayers

I didn't visit our village shop every day, but on this particular day, I did. And, as I stood beside the pay desk, I noticed the picture on the *front cover* of the News Letter newspaper. *It took my breath away ...*

It was a *colour* photograph of Pastor Bob Gass holding the *skeletal* body of fourteen-year-old Diana in his arms. She was an orphan in *Moldova*. She was near death. And she was just *one* of the two hundred orphan girls he desperately wanted to help.

I stood transfixed, looking at the picture. I couldn't move. But from my lips, came the same words over and over again, *"That's it! That's it!"* Everyone in the shop that day must have thought I'd gone a little crazy, but I knew right there and then, without the slightest doubt *... **this was the work God wanted me to do.***

This was the answer to my prayers ... to help these needy orphan children in MOLDOVA, a country I'd never ever heard of before.   But how Lord?

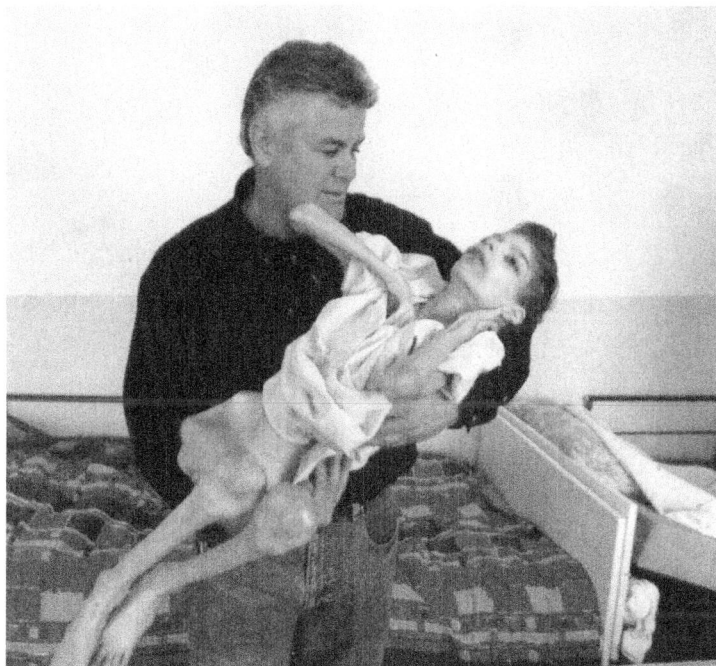

The Picture that touched so many hearts

Pastor Bob Gass holding 14 year-old Diana in his arms,
in an orphanage in Moldova

Chapter 31

A Memorable Christmas

I t was now early December 1998 and Ross was excited to put up our Christmas decorations.

"Hey Mum! Come and steady the ladder for me!"
"OK, I'm just coming."

Obediently, I stood on the bottom rung of the tall step-ladder, as Ross eagerly stretched out his arm to place a string of colourful Christmas lights around the high alcove in our living room. This was now Ross's job and he took it very seriously. He was, after all, the *man of the house* now, since his older brother Leon had left home for University in Dundee, just a few months ago.

Climbing down, Ross carefully lifted the heavy ladder to the far side of the alcove and, in his youthful enthusiasm to do a good job, instructed me, *"Steady it again Mum, so I can finish this!"* And what a splendid job he did.

A huge, natural looking Christmas tree stood majestically before our tall front window, adorned in all its glittering finery. The fireplace was garlanded in luxurious tinsel, red velvet bows and colourful candles, and on our front door hung a welcoming wreath of fir cones, holly and ribbons.

It all looked perfect and so Ross and I should have been brimming over with festive cheer. But instead, we were feeling lonely and sad. To our great disappointment, Leon had decided to stay in Scotland and not come home for Christmas. Money was scarce for all of us and the fares home were just too expensive. This was going to be our first Christmas without him and we were painfully aware that it wouldn't be the same. We were already missing him terribly.

No hot food

B ut many other families too, will remember this particular Christmas with some degree of sadness and disappointment, due to it's unexpected hardships. For it was the Christmas of *power cuts* and ruined Christmas dinners, as ferocious gales tore across much of Northern Ireland, tearing down power lines. Thousands of homes were left with no electricity, no heat, no light and no means of cooking food. And worse still, the electricity remained *off* for at least *four* days over Christmas.

Our stone built period cottage with its high ceilings and open aspect towards the Sperrin Mountains soon became incredibly cold. My thoughts began lamenting, *"What a Christmas this has turned out to be. Perishing cold, missing Leon and **no hot food** to eat."*

Then a few evenings later, Ross and many of the other children from our village went off on their Sunday School Christmas outing. This was always a special occasion and they were all very excited. But even more so this year, eager to leave their freezing cold homes behind them for a few hours of fun and laughter. To their surprise and great joy, they were taken to a café in Coleraine which had electric light and was serving *hot* meals. As you can imagine, they were delighted. And totally ravenous!

However, I stayed at home alone that evening, feeling a bit miserable and sorry for myself. It was *bitterly* cold and we had hardly any coal and only a few logs left to burn in our open fireplace. Sitting on the floor, huddled in front of a meager fire, I tried to warm myself.

By teatime, our house was in complete darkness, except for a few strategically placed candles. Outside, there were no street lights to brighten the night sky or shine a welcome ray of light through our front windows. Our Christmas tree, adorned with tinsel, bows and coloured balls stood in the shadows and the fairy lights that Ross had so carefully strung around our living room window and the large alcove beside our fireplace hung lifeless, failing to deliver their festive twinkling charm.

It was so quiet and yet so very *peaceful.* No television, no music, no children's excited banter, no boisterous laughter and no thundering footsteps racing up and down our steep twisting staircase. *Just stillness.* The flickering flames in the open fireplace created the only sound and the cheery array of Christmas candles placed around the hearth gave a calming and comforting aura.

Gradually, I began to relax, closing my eyes and enjoying the welcome heat upon my chilled face. In this soothing, restful atmosphere, I became *still before the Lord* and found myself praying. I was at peace and never once imagined there was a *big surprise* in store for me. Yes. It was going to be a *good* Christmas after all.

The *Divine* Presence

T he fire was glowing nicely now, as I sat in front of the hearth, listening to the crackling of the burning logs. Quietly, I began asking the Lord about *Moldova.* Asking Him to reveal His will to me and give me some guidance as to what He wanted me to do.

As I sat warming myself, talking softly to the Lord, I suddenly became aware of the *divine presence of the Lord all around me. His presence was so intense and it seemed to fill the whole room.* I could *tangibly feel Him close to me.*

Suddenly, I felt so small, like a little child ... *His child,* sitting at His feet, cocooned in *His love.* This was my *first experience* of being in the presence of my Lord and Saviour and it was *awesome.*

But there was another surprise in store for me. *He began speaking to me!* Speaking to me as a father would to his daughter, **"Why are you complaining?"**

Oh dear, I hadn't expected this and had forgotten that the Bible tells us that God knows our every thought. It never ever occurred to me that He would hear my grumbling and moaning about being cold and having no *hot* food to eat. But He did hear. *Every single complaining word.* Feebly, I tried making some excuses, *"But this is Christmas!"* and reasoned how I'd been looking forward to enjoying some *hot* roast turkey, *steaming* Christmas pudding and *warm* mince pies.

349

Yes, to the world, *it was Christmas* ... the traditional season of goodwill, exchanging gifts and *feasting*. And how easy it is to forget that *Jesus is the real reason for the season,* and *not* feasting.

God began speaking to me

Q uickly sensing that my Heavenly Father was not at all impressed with my moaning and disrespectful excuses, He continued speaking to me ...

"You've got plenty of food to eat. How can you complain and be so ungrateful? Look in your cupboards, they're bursting with food."

I couldn't answer. I was already feeling ashamed of myself and God knew my thoughts. *He was right of course.* Because Christmas was the only time of the year when my cupboards were full of food.

As I sat pondering His words, I felt God cleansing my selfish heart and filling it with *His thankfulness.* He took my ungrateful and disgruntled thoughts and replaced them with *His joy.* And my sadness and disappointment He exchanged for *new hope.* Then, He encouraged me to look afresh and see **how very blessed we really were.**

Waves of thankfulness were flooding over me now and I began rejoicing in my heart, at what we *DID* have. I *rejoiced* that Ross and I had plenty of cold cooked turkey, loaves of bread, some tasty cheeses, pickles and cracker biscuits. We had lots of salad, bowls of fresh fruit and nuts, plus tinned meat. We had a selection of breakfast cereals, some milk and a large pot of cream, and the Christmas cake and mince pies

350

I'd made. And if that wasn't enough, we had some sweets, a box of chocolates and a tin of assorted biscuits. Oh my goodness! Yes of course, the Lord was right. *We had an abundance of food.*

Then God began speaking to me *again ...*

"Why are you complaining about being cold? You've got plenty of warm clothes to wear, haven't you? And you've got extra bedding to put on your beds at night, if you're not warm enough."

Yes of course I did. I had lots of warm woolly jumpers, knitted hats, scarves and gloves in my wardrobe, plus socks and fleecy lined boots for my feet. Ross had plenty of warm clothes too. And if we felt cold in bed, we had an ample supply of blankets and spare duvets. There was no doubt about it, we had plenty and were *blessed indeed.*

However, it was not until God asked me His last, most poignant question, that I really understood *why* He was challenging me like this. *A question that pierced my heart. A question that I shall never forget.*

A question that was to change my self-centred outlook and indeed my whole life. God's question to me was ...

"How do you think
these orphan children in Moldova feel?"

Oh, this really went home and I felt so very humbled. These poor children had absolutely *NOTHING*. They were starving and literally freezing to death and here I was, so very blessed, and still grumbling about some minor discomforts. My selfish complaining was not only grieving my Heavenly Father, but

351

was actually *preventing my earnest prayers from being answered.*

You see, I had boldly prayed, *"I will do anything Lord, and go anywhere!"* and yet, with the smallest of tests, all I could think about was *myself.* The slightest bit of discomfort, and I was grumbling and complaining. Even with no electricity or any other means to cook by, I was still very blessed. *So how could I possibly give my heart to helping these needy children, if all I could do, was only think about myself?*

God was mercifully showing me that I needed to redirect my energy and concentrate my thoughts on *helping others* who were suffering in really harsh and extreme conditions. Others, who were *helpless* to help themselves.

Repentant and deeply humbled, I quickly prayed, *"I'm so sorry Lord. What do You want me to do?"*

Thankful and grateful

Through this timely reprimand, God was teaching me to be *thankful* and *grateful* in ALL circumstances and to always thank Him and praise Him for everything ...

*"Always giving thanks
to God the Father for everything,
in the name of our Lord Jesus Christ."*
(Ephesians 5:20)

My *Heavenly Father* had given me the *shake-up* that I desperately needed, just the way a loving *earthly father* would have done. He successfully directed my eyes *off* myself and *onto* these poor, suffering orphan children. And then, He filled my heart with *His love* and *His compassion* to begin helping them.

Through this experience, God was teaching me yet another vitally important lesson. I had to learn that *until* I could be *thankful* and *grateful* and *content* in my own personal circumstances, whatever those might be, whether in plenty or in lack ... *GOD would NOT open a new door for me.*

He could NOT use me, while I was still complaining and grumbling, and being discontent.

I had to learn to be THANKFUL and PRAISE THE LORD at ALL times and in ALL circumstances.

This was certainly a *new* lesson that I needed to learn, and learn it *quickly,* if I was truly serious about pleasing and serving my Heavenly Father.

And indeed, endeavoring to have a thankful and grateful attitude is a good lesson for all of us to adopt and put into practice, each and every day.

Chapter 32

New Year 1999

F or nearly one and a half years, I had been praying with all of my heart for the Lord to reveal His will to me, and now that He had, *I didn't know what to do.* I had no idea *how* or *where* to even start.

And yet, my spirit was full of *new hope* and *expectancy.* For at last, God had answered my prayers, and I was excited. Not just excited about entering a brand New Year, but elated knowing I was on the threshold of a *new chapter in my life.* A completely *new beginning* and I was going to grasp it with all my might.

God was graciously opening a brand new door for me, full of new opportunities and doubtless many challenges.   And, with His *Fatherly* chastisement still ringing in my ears, I was ready and willing *to step out in faith into the unknown,* knowing that I wouldn't have to do it alone. For our Heavenly Father has promised to, *"never leave us nor forsake us"* and He always keeps His promises.

This is true. But first, before racing off with great zeal to begin this new adventure, I needed to learn a few *home truths* about serving the Lord. I had to realize that ...

It is *not* what I can do for the Lord,
but rather ...
what the Lord can do *through* me,
when I do things His way
and not mine.
MORE OF HIM and less of me.

I also needed to learn the important lesson to **stop, pray and listen** for **His direction** and then **OBEY Him.**   And, *whatever* He asked me to do, learn that I could draw on *His* wisdom and guidance, and rely upon *His* strength and courage for each and every task.   And always, in every circumstance, to give GOD the glory and *all* the praise.

So, with the dawning of 1999, *I threw myself whole-heartedly into serving the Lord* as a volunteer with Romanian Connection.   This humanitarian aid charity, based in Belfast, was totally committed to helping Pastor Bob Gass put an *end* to the intolerable suffering, and *ease* the deplorable living conditions for these orphan children in little known *Moldova.*

"But where is Moldova?"

God touched my heart to begin serving Him in *Moldova,* Europe's poorest country which, at this time, was still under Communist rule.   Intense poverty was everywhere with unemployment reaching nearly *seventy* per cent.   The roads were deeply potholed and most rural homes had no bathrooms, inside toilets or running water. Even basic household items such as a cooking hob, oven or fridge were only distant dreams to them and hardly anyone owned a washing machine. Yet, this tiny underprivileged country that I'd never heard of before and didn't even know existed, was to change my life forever. And, before very long, I fell in love with Moldova's gently sweeping landscapes, vistas of grape vines on tiered hillsides and carpets of golden sunflowers under a hot summer sun, with piercing blue skies overhead. A country that endures suffocating heat in high summer and often, in deep winter, endures temperatures far below zero.

"But where is Moldova?" It is in Eastern Europe, nestled between Romania (to the west) and the Ukraine (to the north, east and south). It is land-locked, situated just above the Black Sea and *Chisinau* is its interesting, historic capital city. Moldova has a land area approximately twice the size of Northern Ireland and is home to more than 3.5 million souls.

This was the country God had chosen for me and I'm so thankful that He did, because I just adored this forgotten, impoverished land and its precious people. And knowing I was *where* God wanted me to be and *doing* what He wanted me to do, was truly all that mattered. It filled me with the greatest peace and a wonderful joy, expressed perfectly in this Bible verse ...

"May the God of hope
fill you with all joy and peace
as you trust in Him,
so that you may overflow with hope
by the power of the Holy Spirit."
(Romans 15:13)

Moldovan orphan children

T he orphan children that Pastor Bob Gass was deeply impassioned to help, back in the winter of 1998, were mentally and physically handicapped young girls and teenagers. Many of them were skeletal with twisted limbs, lying in filthy cots. In the freezing subzero temperatures that winter of 1998, the children were literally blue with cold and *all* of them were starving hungry.

The living conditions in the orphanage were unbelievably shocking and totally wretched, with many children lying on stinking, urine soaked mattresses and in their own excrement. A rat's nest was even found inside one the children's mattresses. And, to our absolute horror, we learnt that medical operations had been conducted on sick children *without any anaesthetic.* It was *gruesome.* It was *brutal* and sadly, twenty children died in these inhumane conditions while we struggled to get help and aid to them, to save their lives.

What could I do?

Q uite simply, *obey God,* for my time of waiting was over. *Obey His call* to help these poor orphan children out in Moldova. And, almost immediately, I found myself totally

357

engrossed in this new mission. Suddenly, everything began happening so quickly. Before I knew it, I was caught up in a whirlwind of collecting gigantic amounts of warm winter clothes, blankets, sheets, towels, toiletries, medical items, cleaning materials, cots, baby buggies, child seats, nappies and toys to be packed onto trucks heading out to the orphanage in Moldova.

Ross, only eleven years old, was as eager as I was to take up this challenge and wanted to assist me in any way he could. Having his enthusiastic support and encouragement meant so much, especially when almost overnight, our lives were completely changed and totally engulfed in this new venture.

Often, I would arrive home to find bags and boxes of aid piled up outside my front door, back door and even up the driveway and it all had to fit *inside* our small house. One day, someone left such a huge box right outside my back door, that I had to wait until Ross came home from school to help me lift it out of the way.

The aid kept arriving daily and before very long, our living room was filled to overflowing, our office had boxes stacked up to the ceiling, and only a narrow passageway remained through our hallway. There were even piles of aid on every tread of our staircase. It was *crazy.* But also, *incredibly good.* And totally *worthwhile.*

My phone never stopped ringing either, with offers of *more* aid and on most days, my little red Renault 5 could be seen valiantly struggling along the highways and byways carrying enormous loads. Sometimes, there was so much inside my car, that *I could barely find the handbrake.* But I loved every minute. I loved meeting so many kind and caring people who opened their hearts to help these children.

It was a joy and a lovely surprise too, when I received encouraging letters in the post, some of which contained much needed financial gifts. And, whenever I found a spare minute, I kept meticulous records of these gifts and wrote letters of grateful thanks to each supporter for their thoughtfulness and generous kindness. *Every gift, however small,* made a *BIG* difference and was so very welcome in our quest to help these orphan children.

Where did it all come from?

I was so thankful to the Headmaster of our village primary school, who not only welcomed the challenge to help me, but was a real inspiration too. He very kindly offered to design a poster that could be displayed in various shops and be distributed to *all* the local primary schools. It was a brilliant idea and just what I needed, especially as I didn't own a computer back then.

He worked tremendously hard on this project and the finished poster was stirring and really powerful. In the centre, he placed the heart-wrenching colour photo of Pastor Bob Gass holding the skeletal form of fourteen-year-old Diana in his arms, with lists of urgently needed items all around it.

Fourteen local primary schools agreed to take part in my *Moldova Orphan Appeal* and each one retained their own aid on their premises until the agreed collection date. However, no-one could have anticipated or even imagined the amazing response. It was overwhelming. It was as if every family in the neighbourhood was touched by the plight of these poor orphan children and wanted to help in some way.

When I visited these schools, both the staff and little children were so excited to show me what they had collected. And with great enthusiasm, they would lead me into their assembly hall to view their rising *mountain of aid.* These *mountains* increased daily and all the teachers could hardly believe the variety and quality of the donations and *neither could I.* It took our breath away to see such generosity and kindness.

Some of the pupils even wanted to help *personally* and, with compassion in their hearts, *insisted* on donating some of their precious Christmas toys. These dear children were learning at a very young age that *giving to help others* can bring *you* so much joy and, actually, be a pleasure and not a burden. Hopefully, this would become a lifelong habit for many of them.

Collection Day

I needed some help, *urgently.* Trucks *and* manpower. And in answer to my desperate prayers, a local haulage company owned by Christians, came to the rescue by generously donating two of their large curtain-sided trucks free of charge, for our collection day.

And *manpower?* Where would that come from? To my utter amazement, my ex-boyfriend rose to the occasion and offered to help me, while firmly stipulating, *"Just this once."* He took this huge task very seriously and capably organized the collection process from all fourteen primary schools, which were spread over quite a large area.   *His help was invaluable.*

With the collection date nearly upon us, he diligently began driving around collecting vast loads of aid from the more distant primary schools. This was an arduous and tiring job, but with our local Headmaster's permission, he successfully delivered it all to our village school. The children's cloakroom area in our school was rapidly becoming swamped to bursting point and yet, amazingly, no-one ever complained.

Although these school collections were going according to plan, there was still a mammoth task ahead of us on the main collection day. But thankfully, my friend had everything under control and, with his dedicated help, plus the assistance of his willing team of jovial local farmers, they all worked their boots off and did a splendid job.

At each collection point, they formed a human chain passing the hundreds of bags and boxes from inside the school storerooms to those outside, loading it onto the trucks. The last stop was at our house, where young Ross and Ian, a neighbour's teenage son, joined *the team.*   And quite wonderfully, my home was suddenly relieved of its huge stockpile of aid. Well, at least for a couple of weeks!

When at last we'd finished loading-up, both lorries were so full, that the cab drivers *couldn't see past the bulging curtain sides with their wing mirrors*, on their way down to Belfast.

It was time for our team to set off for Belfast too, and we happily piled into the back of a kind farmer's jeep, plus another helper's car. Our spirits were soaring and rose even more so when we stopped to meet a Christian man at a café, on our journey down to Belfast.

Without our knowledge, this kind man had planned an unexpected *surprise* for us. After warmly greeting us, he led us into the café and proceeded to buy each one of us a *hot meal,* to help us on our way. What a fantastic *surprise.* He must have anticipated that we would all be hungry and ready for something to eat. Every one of us was touched by his kindness and deeply appreciated his welcome treat. I know I shall always remember this friend's thoughtfulness and gene- rosity to us, and I'm sure the other team members will too.

Yes indeed, it was a long and tremendously exhausting day, especially by the time we'd finished unloading our trucks at Romanian Connection's warehouse in Belfast. But nothing seemed to deter our team and they remained cheerful and full of good humour all day. In fact, I could even confidently say, that they really enjoyed themselves.

Without a doubt, I couldn't have managed without their sterling help and enthusiastic support. It was definitely one of those days that I shall *never* forget. A day when everyone joyfully gave their *all,* to make a difference to the lives of so many helpless orphan children out in Moldova.

A very special message

To me, I had just experienced a *miracle.* The amazing *miracle* of seeing God's mighty hand at work. For only a few weeks earlier, I didn't know *where* to start or *what* to do. Yet through His faithful provision, I had collected two large truck loads of quality, first class aid *plus* managed to raise over £4,000 to help these orphan children.   I was ecstatic and totally in awe at what *God had just done* and unreservedly, I gave Him *all* the praise.

A few days after our memorable collection day, I was still trying to take it all in.   Everything had happened so quickly and my life had changed so radically. *Had it been a dream?* I found myself exclaiming, *"Wow Lord! That was amazing. How did it all happen? And where did it all come from?"*

At that very moment, my phone rang.   Picking up the receiver, I recognized the voice at the other end.   It was an elderly gentleman from Ballymena who had very kindly made a financial donation to my orphan appeal. But to my surprise, he had a very special message for me.

He proceeded to tell me, **"God has told me to ring you and tell you that He is very pleased with you."**

Oh my! I was totally humbled and completely over-whelmed, and couldn't hold back the tears. Tears of joy. Tears of gratitude.   Tears of awe, as I thought of God's faith-fulness and immense goodness.   And in my heart, I was rejoicing and kept *praising* Him ...

**"Great is the Lord,
and most worthy of praise!"**
(Psalm 48:1)

Chapter 33

Just the Beginning

This was just the beginning of my *Moldova Orphan Appeal* and from those exciting early days, my house remained full of aid for many years to come, which proved to be a constant challenge. Yet only *once,* did Ross make a comment while struggling to get down our stairs, *"Mum, I think this is getting a bit ridiculous!"*

Thankfully, a kind old lady in our village let me use her disused store with its own entrance, which was a great help. But the aid increased to such an extent, I needed a *big* store and I cried out to God to help me. Then one day, while out in my little car, collecting loads of aid donated by the pupils of a local primary school, a man stopped me and asked if I needed any help. *Oh yes please!* He enquired, *"Where are you taking all this aid?"* and I told him back to my house, as my new little store was overflowing. He was so friendly and willing to help me, that I dared ask him, *"I desperately need a big store. You don't know of one do you?"* To my utter amazement, he instantly replied, *"Yes, I have a farm!"* I looked at him in complete astonishment and asked him, *"Are you serious?"* Yes, he was serious and quite incredulously, I saw God answering my desperate prayers.

But there was another, very unexpected challenge that I had to overcome. One that took me by surprise. As my work with Romanian Connection progressed, I was frequently invited to give updates on our progress at various meetings and school assemblies. And, quite suddenly, I found myself doing what I'd most dreaded when at school ... *public speaking!* But now, I wasn't so fearful and even enjoyed the privilege of telling others what God was doing in my life. How He had turned my fear around for *good* and given me the courage and strength to do what had always been *totally impossible.* To me, this was definitely *another miracle!*

I put my heart and soul into helping these orphan children and, after only four months, I became one of the charity's full-time volunteers, working from my home. However, a year later, I really wanted to go out to Moldova and see for myself the orphanage, the children and the conditions they were living in. I felt *very* strongly, that *now* was the time to go.

First visit to Moldova

T hen one Wednesday morning in early February 2000, Karen, a Founding Member of Romanian Connection, telephoned me. She told me that several of them were leaving for Moldova the following Sunday. And, while she spoke to me, I felt an incredible and overpowering longing to go with them. I wanted to go too. As our phone call ended, I felt a surge of courage rise up within me and instinctively knew it was the Holy Spirit giving me the boldness to ring her back immediately, and ask her, **"Can I go with you to Moldova?"** Expectantly, I held my breath, waiting

for Karen's reply.   After a short pause, she kindly replied that she felt I'd more than proved my faithfulness to Romanian Connection over the previous year and, provided the other Board Members agreed, I could go with them.   I could hardly believe my ears. She explained to me that they were flying to Budapest and then driving in a hired car all through Romania and into Moldova. Upon hearing this, I was instantly anxious and nervously queried, *"If you are driving, will there be room for me in the car?"* To my great relief, only three other Members were booked to go, so there would be room for me too. But, as Karen pointed out, she didn't yet know whether there would be a spare seat for me on the same flight, and told me she would ring me the following morning with the news.

As I put the telephone receiver down, I began fervently praying, *"Dear Lord, if it's Your will for me to go on this trip to Moldova, please let there be a free seat for me on the plane. But, if I've got it all wrong, please don't let there be a free seat!"*

This was my prayer for God's guidance, and I was on tenterhooks waiting for the answer.   However, early the next morning, when my phone rang, I clearly heard Karen say, *"You're booked onto a flight to Budapest!"*

Wow! I was ecstatic with joy. At last, I was going out to Moldova. Thankfully, young Ross took the unexpected news exceptionally well and I was delighted when the parents of his best school friend offered to look after him while I was away. Then, a local church which had been fundraising for me quite amazingly, and very generously, offered to pay for all my travelling costs. Also, over the past few weeks, in the hope that I would soon be able to go out to Moldova, I'd already had all the necessary vaccinations and applied for a new passport, which arrived back super-quick. Suddenly, everything was ready for this trip and I was filled with an immense wonder and excitement at how God was so graciously leading me and providing for me, at the point of my need.

> ***"And my God will meet all your needs***
> ***according to His glorious riches in Christ Jesus"***
> (Philippians 4:19)

Furthermore, during the twenty-four hour long and tiring drive through the night to reach Moldova, I was filled with the most wonderful *calm* and *peace*. *A peace* that told me *I was doing what God wanted me to do,* and that *I was where God wanted me to be.* *A peace* that would be my reliable compass during the years ahead, serving and obeying my Lord ...

> ***"And the peace of God,***
> ***which transcends all understanding,***
> ***will guard your hearts and your minds***
> ***in Christ Jesus."***
> (Philippians 4:7)

At the orphanage

Although by now, I was well accustomed to seeing photos of the orphan children and their appalling living conditions, it was still a deeply shocking and heart-breaking experience to actually be there amongst them. In fact, only then, could I begin to fully understand the extent of the suffering, cruelty and hardship experienced by these poor children and the enormity of the challenge facing us. This was an experience I will never forget.

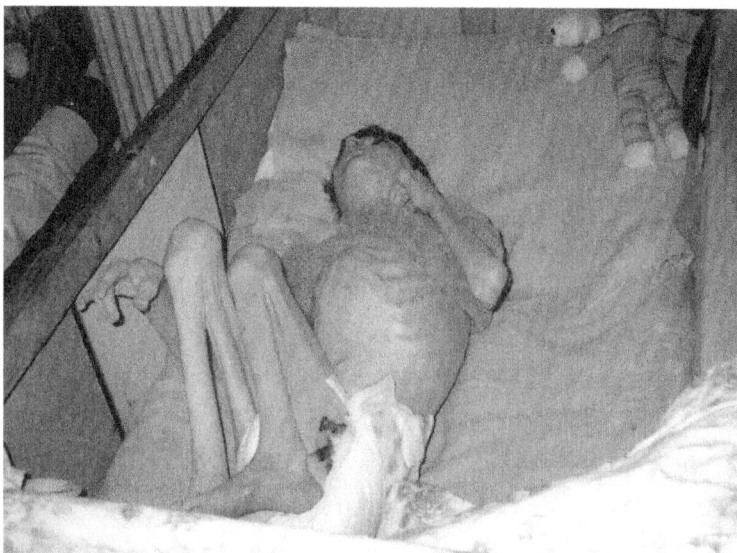

Thankfully though, I was able to see that all our deter-mined effort and hard work over the previous year to help these suffering children, had already made a significant difference. The bedridden children could now wear nappies and lie on clean mattresses in clean cots. They had new pyjamas too and lay on clean sheets, with quilts and blankets to warm them. And, for the very first time, they cuddled a soft toy all of their own. They even managed *a long-forgotten smile.*

Thankfully too, there was a plentiful supply of warm clothes and clean bedding for all the children, so generously donated by the folks back home. It was indeed wonderful to see all the aid we'd been collecting and laboriously packing and loading onto huge trucks, being so gratefully received and making such an immediate difference. Indeed, all these early improvements were thanks to the enormous response and overwhelming donations of so many kind and caring people, who were so faithfully supporting our appeal for help.

However, there was still so much more to do, especially when the orphanage building itself was in an appalling, dilapidated, run-down state. It was damp and perishing cold. The sanitary facilities were either non-existent or broken, and were unbelievably awful, filthy and stinking. There was also the constant daily and urgent need to provide enough food for all the children, and ensure that they were being fed regular meals. And yet, it was truly wonderful too, to see how these orphan children responded to our love and affection. They just wanted to be loved and cared for. Even today, I can still see their happy smiles and beaming faces, which made all our hard work worthwhile.

> **"Religion that God our Father accepts**
> **as pure and faultless is this:**
> **to look after orphans and widows**
> **in their distress"**
> (James 1:27)

Complete focus

My life was completely dedicated to helping, loving and improving the living conditions of these poor, abandoned children and after this first visit to the orphanage in Moldova, my desire to help them was even greater. The workload never ceased and there was never a dull moment, and when Pastor Bob Gass encouraged me by supporting and endorsing my work, I was really delighted.

Pastor Bob Gass and myself in Romanian Connection's Belfast store.

My energies were now directed towards helping Romanian Connection with their summer plans to take out two consecutive teams of volunteers to the orphanage. I could hardly wait to return to Moldova, especially when Karen agreed that young Ross could come too. There was so much to do to prepare for this trip and the aid kept pouring in from faithful supporters.

Amazingly too, the church that funded my first trip offered to help me again. I was so very thankful for their kindness. Then, just three weeks before Ross and I were due to leave for Moldova, a *crisis* happened.

Chapter 34

Unexpected Crisis

O ne morning at home, while I was going downstairs for breakfast, I suddenly felt something was wrong and instinctively raised my right hand up to my chest. There it was. A sizeable lump above my left breast. I tried not to become alarmed as, many years earlier, I had found some small lumps and my doctor had told me they were harmless and would just go away. And they did. Remembering this, I calmed myself by reasoning that I didn't need to be worried this time either. But, as we were due to go away in just three weeks' time, I thought it would be sensible to check it out. Fortunately, my doctor was able to see me that same day. However, I was a little surprised when she wanted me to go down to Antrim Hospital for a further check-up *straight away*. She was quite insistent about this and managed to get me an appointment in just a few days' time.

It was a lovely bright day when I drove down to Antrim Hospital by myself, having left Ross in the care of some neighbours. After all, I was expecting to get the *all clear* and be straight home.

Arriving at the hospital, I found about a dozen other women waiting and I silently joined them. One by one, they went off to have a mammogram and, afterwards, some of them waited to see a doctor. Then it was my turn. This was the first time I'd had a mammogram and didn't know what to expect. Thankfully, it wasn't too bad. More uncomfortable, than painful. Then more waiting to see a doctor. The hours ticked by and gradually, one by one, the women left to go home until there were only three of us left. Then, after a while, the other two left as well. Finally, I was the only one left, *by myself.* I couldn't believe it. What was happening? This wasn't what I'd anticipated.

A very kind nurse then informed me that the doctors wanted to do a biopsy test on me and she led me downstairs to a treatment room to await the test. When the two doctors arrived and were about to begin, this kind nurse stood behind me, gripping both my shoulders very tightly. I had no idea what to expect but remained cheerful, thinking about what Jesus went through for me. I thought, *"This is nothing compared to what Jesus went through!"*

I didn't look down to watch what the doctors were doing, but kept looking ahead, keeping as calm as I could, thinking about *Jesus.* I was determined to keep my eyes and thoughts *on Him* and, *in His great faithfulness,* He took away all my fears and filled me the courage I needed.

Every time the doctors took a tissue sample, there was a loud *bang!* It was like a gun exploding inside me and as my body lurched, the kind nurse firmly held me down. Each time, she asked me if I was alright and I cheerily replied, *"Yes, I'm fine thanks!"* This happened several times before it was over and then, at last, I looked down and saw the blood on my chest, which was a momentary shock.

As the nurse dressed my wound, she was curious to know how I'd kept so cheerful and remained so calm. This gave me a perfect opportunity to tell her about *my faith in Jesus.* She didn't seem to be in any hurry and listened eagerly. As we chatted together, feeling at ease with each other, our conversation succeeded in taking *my eyes off myself and put them back on to Jesus.* By the time I went back upstairs to see the doctors, I was feeling encouraged and much stronger. How *faithful* God is. He knew my faith needed building up, ready to hear the news the doctors were about to tell me.

Firstly, they told me they didn't like *the shadow* on my mammogram and secondly, they told me the tissue samples they'd just taken were *not normal.* Even worse, they told me I needed an operation as soon as possible. This certainly was not what I'd expected.

I explained to the doctors that I was going to Moldova in two weeks' time and that I really wanted to go. They both became very serious and firmly stressed how dangerous it could be to delay operating and advised me to have it as soon as possible. When I stubbornly objected and insisted on going to Moldova *first*, they became quite distressed.

Finally, when they realised I wasn't going to change my mind, they had a quick tete-a-tete and offered me a solution. *"As it is almost August and the surgeon in Antrim and the surgeon in Coleraine are both taking their holidays in August, you can go IF you promise to have an operation as soon as you return."* I was delighted and happily agreed. Confidently, I said *"good-bye"* to the surprised and exasperated doctors and made my way out of the hospital.

Up to this point, I'd been so brave, keeping my eyes firmly fixed on Jesus and drawing upon His strength. But as I stepped outside into the evening air, my world suddenly crashed all around me and I burst into tears. I walked to my car crying uncontrollably. The doctor's words were now sinking in and the stark realization that my lump, in their opinion, looked malignant and the horror of having an operation and its consequences, began to become a frightening reality. The burden weighed heavily on me as I sat crying in my car. *What was happening to me?* A few hours ago my world looked so bright and hopeful and now, I faced the grim possibility of breast cancer. The doctors hadn't actually used the word *cancer,* but I knew that's what they meant and why they wanted to operate so quickly.

But, I also knew that God had answered my persistent prayers and called me to work in Moldova and, more precisely, to work in this particular orphanage. I'd been working to help these orphan children for the last eighteen months and I wasn't about to lose this opportunity of going out to help them now. I knew I was going to *where* God wanted me to go, and *do* what He wanted me to do and *obeying God came first in my life.* When Leon and young Ross heard my news, they were both tearful and very frightened.

Broken inside

T hankfully, Ross and I had planned to go to *New Horizon,* which ended the day before we were leaving for Moldova. We both felt it would encourage us and build us up spiritually before our three-week-long ordeal, living in one of the worst orphanages imaginable. Each summer, Ross and I looked forward to this seven-day Christian event and always attended every day. I thoroughly enjoyed the praise and Bible teaching held in a huge tent, while Ross enjoyed meeting his friends at the youth meetings held around the campus, where his faith was challenged and stretched. It was always a *good* time for both of us.

I especially loved the evening praise time when I could *quieten and still* myself and focus completely on Jesus, leaving all my worries, cares and fears behind. For me, this was such a blessed time of refreshing, to be able to just praise and adore my Lord, surrounded by 3,000 other worshippers.

On the evening of Monday, 31st July 2000, the praise time proved to be as mighty and stirring as ever. And, as we began singing a song that was new to me, *'Jesus Christ, I think upon Your sacrifice'*, the beauty of the words saturated my spirit. They were so powerful, so meaningful, so wonderful. But, as we sung the chorus again and again, *"I'm broken inside,"* it suddenly became too personal, too painful, too real and I collapsed in a crumpled heap on my seat, weeping helplessly. *"Oh Lord, I'm broken, I'm broken inside!"* As these words tore into my heart, I cried out in desperate agony, *"Oh Lord, please help me! I'm broken. I'm broken inside."*

I might have been able to hide my fears from my two sons and those I knew, but *I couldn't hide them from God.* He looked right into my heart and knew I was hurting, knew I was frightened. He saw me *humbled at the foot of the Cross, broken, weak and helpless.* He knew I had no family to help me, He knew how I'd struggled to bring up my two sons on my own, He knew all about the burden of debts my ex-husband had left me with. *He knew all my inner fears.* He knew *everything* about me.

As I sat weeping before my Lord, I suddenly knew I wasn't alone any more. I knew He would help me and my heart cried out, *"Jesus, Jesus, I love You! You are my hope, my rock and I know You'll never let me down. You are always there when I need You. You are so faithful."*

Then, three nights later on Thursday, 3rd August during the praise time, I was mightily touched again while singing the chorus to the song, *'What Love is This?'* As I sung the words, from the very depths of my heart, *"I surrender, I surrender, I surrender all to You!"* I was completely overwhelmed. No-one else in the tent mattered at that moment. It was just God and me. I totally and utterly surrendered everything to Jesus. My life, my ambitions, my home, my hopes, my fears. Everything I had, belonged to Him. He was my life, my ALL. As I made this complete surrender and unburdened my heart to Jesus, He took away all my fear and gave me a new strength, and the courage I lacked. *How great is His faithfulness!*

At the end of that week, Ross and I left *New Horizon* feeling spiritually renewed and strengthened, and excited at the prospect of beginning our journey to Moldova the very next day. We were flying out from Dublin Airport and had arranged to stay with some friends in Dublin at boths ends of our journey. They were a lovely Christian couple who had told me they would anoint me with oil and pray for my healing when we arrived at their home. But they seemed to forget about it, and Ross and I left them for Moldova without this blessing.

Ross's first visit to Moldova

At Dublin Airport, we joined a large team of excited volunteers, all ready and willing to live and work in the orphanage for the next three weeks. Ross was only twelve years old and the only junior in our team, and yet he adjusted to the orphan children and difficult conditions wonderfully. We had no running water and what water we had, came through a hose pipe to our 'kitchen' door. We had no inside toilets or washing facilities near our dormitory quarters but, during the daytime, we were allocated a few of the orphans' toilets. Of course, there were no locks on the toilet doors, so Ross and I stood guard outside the door for each other, to avoid the intrusion of a mass of curious eyes!

However, night-time was a different matter. There was no choice but to duck behind some bushes outside and hope there were no wild or stray dogs lurking around. This was so daunting, that when one of us couldn't wait any longer and just had to go outside, it was quite humorous to see how many other women had been waiting for someone to make the first move. All of a sudden, a whole group of us rose from their beds and dashed outside!

Because Ross was still so young and the only child in our team, he was allowed to sleep in the women's dormitory beside me, which was a great comfort. During the afternoons, when the heat was well over 45°C, many of us collapsed onto our metal beds exhausted. Ross then very kindly stood at the end of each of our beds waving two large raffia fans, trying his best to cool us. He then cheerily offered to make us all a cup of tea!

However, Ross had been given a very specific job during our stay in the orphanage. He was given joint responsibility of looking after the two hundred chickens in the new chicken houses and large run that Romanian Connection had just built for the orphanage. Several times a day, Ross could be seen dutifully pushing his wheelbarrow and spade towards the chicken houses to feed them, collect the eggs and clean the hen houses. He took this task seriously and even enjoyed it. Then, in the afternoons, while many of the adults were resting, he loved taking the handicapped children for walks, pushing them along in the wheelchairs we'd brought out.

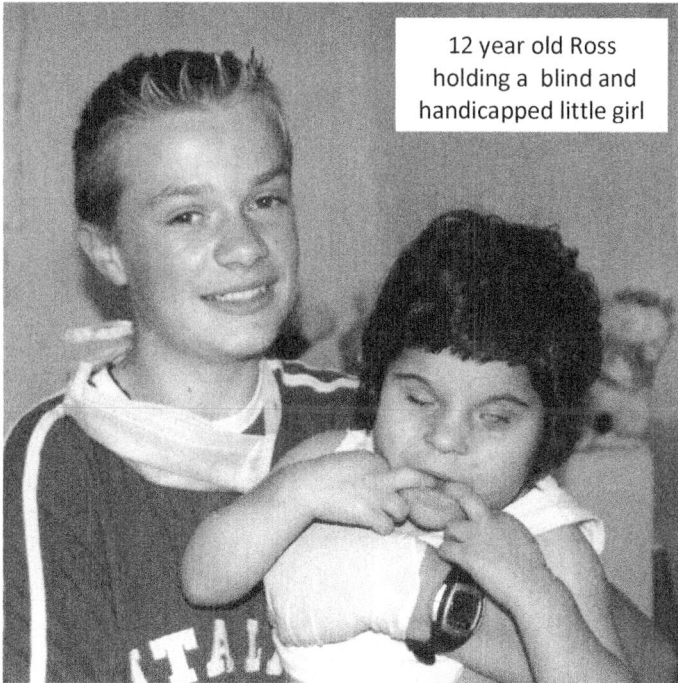

12 year old Ross holding a blind and handicapped little girl

Ross thoroughly enjoyed his first mission trip to Moldova. Although he experienced harsh, upsetting and difficult situations first hand, he never complained or flinched from anything and indeed, this trip marked the beginning of many years ahead for both of us travelling and working together as a team, to love and help the poorest people of Moldova.

Back in Dublin

W hen Ross and I arrived back in Dublin Airport from our visit to Moldova, we again stayed a night with our dear friends. We'd had such a long and tiring day, that Ross excused himself and went up to bed early. Our friends were excited to hear all about our experience at the orphanage and we chatted for hours. But just before we retired, they suddenly remembered their promise to me. Together, we knelt on the floor and, after pouring oil upon my head, they laid their hands on my head and prayed in the power of the Holy Spirit over me. It was a very emotional experience.

Time to keep my promise

I kept my promise to the doctors and, within a few days of returning home, I was booked in for my operation in Coleraine Hospital. The night before my operation, I had everything planned and ready for an early start the next morning. Ross, who was already back at school, had been invited to have breakfast at the farm opposite us and they very kindly offered to look after him until his school bus arrived. Some other good friends from our village had also offered to help by collecting me at 7 a.m., to get me to hospital by 8 a.m.

I was organised and had my clothes laid out ready for the morning, choosing something loose in case I was a bit sore after the operation. I was at peace and not at all fearful,

380

knowing that God was in control and I went to bed, falling asleep straight away. *Then around 3 a.m., GOD WOKE ME UP! Audibly, God spoke very loudly to me, **"TAKE A BAG!"***

I sat bolt upright in bed and repeated God's words to me, *"Take a bag!"* I questioned, *"What does that mean? Surely it must mean I'm NOT coming home tomorrow night as I'm expecting. Oh my goodness! What will they find when they operate?"* And I began to feel fearful and cry.

But quickly, I pulled myself together, knowing I needed to obey God and pack an overnight bag. My mind was racing now as I thought, *"Well someone will have to stay tomorrow night with Ross, if I'm not coming home."* So I made up the spare bed and continued getting things ready. At last, I went back to bed and amazingly, fell fast asleep.

Off to hospital

I decided not to tell Ross about God's message to me during the night, so as not to cause him any alarm. When our neighbours called for me at 7 a.m., I gave Ross a big hug and a kiss, and told him I loved him. As my friends and I began our journey to Coleraine Hospital, I nervously told them, *"I don't think I'm coming home tonight!"* and proceeded to relate to them how God had woken me up at 3 a.m. and told me to *"Take a bag!"*

We arrived at the hospital in plenty of time, and very soon a nurse was filling in my details on a form. As she did so, I calmly told her that I was a Christian. Smiling at me, she replied that she was too. I told her what God had said to me and that I felt *I wasn't going home tonight.* Then quite suddenly, I knew God was watching over me. I could feel the comfort of His arms all around me as I realized He had arranged for a Christian nurse to help me and that the surgeon who was about to operate on me, Mr. Mullen, was also a Christian. Yes, God was in control of *everything!*

After the operation, I woke up to find myself in a private room and feeling surprisingly OK. A nurse came in to see me and brought me some toast to eat. It tasted good! Then gradually as the anaesthetic wore off, I felt the onset of intense pain. Thankfully, I was given some pain relief medication.

However, as the pain lessened, I began to feel really *ill.* I thought perhaps the toast I'd eaten had upset me, but I began to feel increasingly worse. I tried in vain to lower my back rest and kept pressing the buzzer for the nurse to come. The back rest seemed jammed and I just couldn't get it to budge. I pressed the buzzer with more and more urgency, but no-one came.

About twenty minutes later, a nurse rushed in and I told her how terrible I felt. She promptly lowered my back rest and immediately, without any warning, I went into a seizure and became completely paralysed. I couldn't move a finger. I could barely open my eyes and could hardly muster even a whisper.

The alarmed nurse shot out of my room and seconds later, I was aware of people rushing around me. I heard a nurse say, *"I can't get a blood pressure!"* Then a doctor knelt beside me and asked, *"Are you allergic to anything?"* I sensed his intense urgency but I couldn't think of anything and yet, my whole body was being tormented with pins and needles. My mind searched, *where had I felt this before?* Then I remembered, *on my lips!* Years ago, I discovered that a certain pain killer gave me pins and needles in my lips and, consequently, I stopped using it.   As I whispered this to the doctor, he leapt up in jubilation. *This was the clue he needed.* Suddenly, the room went crazy with nurses racing about.   One was giving me injections and another was putting tubes in my arms.

That night, some close friends brought Ross in to see me. I was still so weak that when he gave me a card to open, I couldn't even move my fingers.   Quite definitely, *I wasn't going home tonight!*   And, of course, I did need *a bag* of overnight things, just as God had warned me. In fact, I was in the hospital for two nights before the doctors considered me fit enough to go home.   It took me nearly a week to fully recover and get my strength back, just in time to return to Antrim Hospital for the results.

During that week of recuperation, I prayed and prepared myself for the worst of news. Both my sons were frightened. Leon, my eldest son was still at Dundee University and Ross was only twelve years old. We had no other family to help us, and I desperately wanted to *live. I needed to live.*

I drove down to Antrim Hospital alone, to receive the results of my operation. As I sat in the waiting room, I kept praying and hoping that the doctor would say the words I longed to hear, *non-malignant.* At last, the nurse called my name and the doctor greeted me warmly.   Before I could barely respond to him, he jubilantly exclaimed, *"You are completely healed!"*   I just stood there stunned, as his words sunk in.

Tentatively, I dared to ask, *"What about the shadow?"* The doctor replied, *"You are completely healed!"*

I asked again, *"What about the bad tissue samples?"* The doctor again replied, *"You are completely healed!"*

I persisted, *"Do I need to come back for some check-ups?"* Smiling broadly, the doctor kindly reassured me, *"No! You are completely HEALED!"*

Wow! I was totally and utterly overjoyed. For the doctor didn't say *non-malignant,* but *healed! Thank You Jesus!*

Even today, whenever I take a look at the little scar on my chest, I *rejoice* and say, *"That's where God's finger touched me and healed me!"*

You may ask, "Is God really *faithful* in difficult times?" *Yes, He is.* Don't ever doubt it. Keep your eyes on *Jesus.* Never take them off Him. For He will never leave you nor forsake you. *Never.*

Over the years, I have learnt that God doesn't always prevent us from going through testing and difficult times, but *He is always with us as we go through them.* He is always ready to help us, strengthen us, protect us and give us His peace, when we call out to Him. For Jesus told us ...

"I am with you always."
(Matthew 28:20)

Chapter 35

Beyond my Expectations

For the next year, I remained a full-time volunteer with Romanian Connection, becoming a Board Member and being responsible for the *Christian-side* of this humanitarian charity. I thoroughly enjoyed this new position with its many challenges and worked three days a week from my own office within the charity's depot in Belfast. Quite wonderfully, we continued to see God's mighty hand of provision meet the vast needs.

Then one day, I had a wonderful surprise when Dr. Helen Roseveare came to visit me in my office. I was overjoyed to see her and she stayed chatting to me for quite a while. Then, before leaving, she gave me a very kind donation from her Girls' Crusader Union class, which was a lovely surprise, and it touched my heart greatly.

The lady who introduced me to Jesus!
Dr. Helen Roseveare

New challenges

O ver the next few years, the Lord continued to open unexpected and new doors for me in Moldova. The most challenging of which was His clear instruction to set up *my own registered charity.*

This was definitely a step that I didn't take lightly and an instruction which took a lot of courage to fulfil. But I knew deep down in my heart that it was God's will for me. I knew too, that if I obeyed Him and trusted Him completely, He would open new doors and enable me to achieve even *beyond my wildest expectations,* and that is exactly what happened. In fact, His *new* plans for me dovetailed and fitted in perfectly with Romanian Connection's *new* plans. Let me explain ...

Summer 2001 in Romania

T his summer, Ross and I faced another challenge together, but this time in Romania. We were to be *house parents* to a lively group of ten to thirteen-year-old orphan boys and girls, who were enjoying a welcome holiday from their orphanage in Moldova.   We all lived under the same roof in a typically rural village house. This simply meant we had no bathroom, no kitchen, no running water and just one crude *outside, freshly dug deep pit toilet* with a plank of wood with a round hole cut in it and supported on a raised platform over the hole, for all *seventeen* of us. Often, especially before meal times, there was a long queue waiting to use it. But these Moldovan orphan children didn't care about trivial things like the toilet. They just loved being on holiday and were full of fun and mischief, and it was quite a job keeping up with them.

But for Ross and me, and a brave lady volunteer who came out with us, plus the two Moldovan lady helpers and a teenage son who brought these children from Moldova, it was hectic and *very* hard work. Several times a day Ross, now thirteen years old, took on the responsibility of refilling our large water containers from the village well and I helped with cooking lunch and dinner for everyone in a makeshift *outside* kitchen area.

However, my day began early around 5 a.m. whilst everyone else was fast asleep. My first job every morning was to boil huge pots of water on the calor gas rings. I then had the unpleasant job of thoroughly clean-ing the *outside* kitchen surfaces, table, pans etc.,

Ross at the water pump

because they had all been inspected during the previous night by inquisitive *furry, four-legged visitors.* This essential ritual had to be done each morning *before* preparing breakfast for the hungry hoard, and repeated again for lunch and dinner. Whenever I had a spare minute, I donned a pair of rubber gloves and, with a stout scrubbing brush and strong bleach, cleaned the constantly used outside toilet. And in between? It was *non-stop* activity.

But it wasn't all hard work. We had great fun too with the children and took them for daily outings, including visiting the nearby *hot-springs* swimming pools where, most thank-fully, we could all wash ourselves under the excellent outside

387

showers. There were several hot-spring pools for us to enjoy and the water was wonderfully soothing and warm. To keep the children safe, they were all given buoyant arm bands to wear during their playful time in the pools. However, during our first visit, we suddenly noticed a pair of arm bands floating on the surface with *a pair of feet protruding from them.* Somehow, one of the children had placed the arm bands around their ankles instead of their upper arms. A mild panic resulted to get the child *the right way up!*

It was truly wonderful to see these orphan children laughing and enjoying themselves so much and, to our delight, the more we loved them, the more they responded and bonded to us. In fact, one of the older boys, and then another one, even got up early in the morning to help me prepare breakfast. I was really touched by this act of kindness, knowing it was their way of showing me their love and appreciation. For a precious hour or so each morning, these two orphan boys and I worked together *as a family,* preparing food for the others.

At bedtime each evening, we sat with the children and listened to Children's Bible Stories on cassettes, in their Romanian language, that I'd brought out in my suitcase. One of the Moldovan helpers kindly offered to help me by holding up large colourful flipchart pictures depicting these stories and also answered any queries from the children. This special time each evening of sitting quietly with the children, while listening to Bible stories, proved to be a wonderful way of bonding with them. Yet at first, they were a bit aloof and sat apart from us. Then suddenly, on the third evening, it was as if God touched the children's hearts and they all wanted to be cuddled and sit close to us. It was really wonderful and we all became *one big family* for the rest of the holiday.

Some unexpected news

T hen one evening during this holiday, I took a few hours off to visit Karen and some of the other leaders of Romanian Connection, who were staying in a friend's home in a different area of the village. They were all involved in another current project that we'd been working on, *to build a brand new home for orphan children* in this same village.

I knew all about this new project for, over the last few months, it had been my responsibility to source huge quantities of timber and roofing tiles, together with ridge tiles, specialist insulation and even nails for this new building. To my joy, all these invaluable materials had been donated to us *free of charge* from timber yards and building contractors throughout Ireland. It was totally admirable that so many companies were willing to help us. Now, during this summer visit to Romania, I was able to see these building materials being skilfully used and appreciated, in the construction of this new children's home.

However, unbeknown to me, Karen had been preparing to share some unexpected news with me, and I was about to hear it that evening. *The news that Romanian Connection was leaving Moldova.* Karen told me that, after much consideration, they had decided to put all their future energies and resources into completing this new children's home. Also, they felt that the time had come for them to return to their orphan work in Romania. I was stunned and had never expected this to happen. And yet, their decision clearly *opened the door* for me to go ahead and set up my own charity in Moldova, without stepping on their toes.

During that evening, in rural Romania, the leaders and I sat outside enjoying the warm night air. We relaxed together, reminiscing over all that we'd done and been able to achieve, to help so many poor orphan girls in Moldova. We'd worked tirelessly together for the last two and a half years but now, it seemed, it was time for us to go our separate ways. For the leaders knew, without even asking me, that my heart lay in Moldova and that was where I was going to stay.

Quite unexpectedly, but in God's *perfect* timing, He had opened this new door for me *more quickly* and *more easily* than I could ever have imagined.

Y ou may well be wondering, *"Whatever happened to the children in that orphanage after Romanian Connection left Moldova?"* Well never fear. Our loving Heavenly Father didn't abandon them. For He opened yet another door of opportunity. This time, for a caring and compassionate trainee doctor from Dublin to begin *her own medical outreach charity in Moldova,* to continue looking after these needy children.

Ross and I had first met this very capable trainee doctor during our stay in the orphanage the previous summer, when we were all part of a huge team of volunteers working to help these girls. This dedicated and compassionate trainee doctor literally took these orphan children, many of whom were mentally and physically handicapped, under her wings. With her medical knowledge and expertise, plus a great team of helpers, she did a truly marvellous job transforming these children's lives. *Well done Susie!*

I t was now early Autumn 2001 and I was eager to embrace the new opportunity that God was offering me, to begin my own charity. In obedience to His will and guidance, my new charity **Mission Moldova** was born with the help of three male volunteers, all of whom had approached me and asked to join me.

However, after taking these three men on a three-week visit to Moldova, when I introduced them to several pastors I knew, plus my friend and interpreter Mark in Transnistria, they informed me at a Board Meeting shortly after our return, that they wanted to go their separate ways and set up their own charity. Together, they had decided to concentrate on building a home for orphan children and, indeed, God blessed them and used them to do great work for Him in Transnistria.

Although their decision was very disappointing and deeply distressing, my good friend Rev. Howard Lewis continually encouraged me every time I spoke to him, *"Never, never, never give up!"* He too, had been working out in Moldova for several years and became my Council of Reference until his tragic death, during an operation for a brain tumour. How I missed his cheery encouragement and kind words of wisdom.

Nevertheless, I never once doubted that God had sent me to serve Him in Moldova and that He had told me to set up my own charity. In my heart, I knew that He was still in control and yet, I desperately needed help. In order for *Mission Moldova* to exist as a charity, I needed two people to help me. One to be the Treasurer and the other to be the Secretary.

But who would help me?   Who would take on this responsibility?

In the depths of my despair one evening, when I didn't know what to do, a wonderful young married couple telephoned me and stressed, *"Come round to see us this evening, right now. We'll help you!"*

God, in His unfailing faithfulness, had stirred these friends to help me at the point of my greatest need. This dear couple stood with me, encouraged me and pulled me through this very difficult patch. An accountant friend helped us too and, a few months later on 22nd April 2002, *Mission Moldova* was granted official charitable tax status by the Inland Revenue and recognised by the Charity Commission for Northern Ireland. *Hallelujah!*

For me, this was not only a new chapter in my life, but a *huge leap of faith.* A leap that would prove to be the greatest challenge of my life. It demanded my complete and utter dedication and became the focus of my whole being. From that point onwards, *I lived, breathed and ate* **Mission Moldova** *24/7 and loved every minute of it.* It was very comforting too, to be certain that I was still *where* God wanted me to be and *doing* what He wanted me to do.

I was grateful too, that young Ross was right behind me, supporting me 100%. He was a huge encouragement to me and whenever I got upset leaving him before a trip out to Moldova, he would firmly tell me, *"Mummy! You know perfectly well that when you are out in Moldova, you will be so busy that you won't have time to think about me. So stop crying!"*

T hankfully, the kind Christian couple who came to my rescue, helped me for over a year but, as the workload rapidly increased, it became too time consuming and too much of a burden for them. Of course, I was very sad and missed them greatly, especially as we'd become such close friends. And yet, I understood their situation too. In fact, I always marvelled at how they ever found the time and energy to help me at all, as they both had very responsible jobs plus two energetic young sons to look after. But I'm so thankful for the lovely and joyful memories of working with this kind and wise couple, and shall always be very grateful to them for their spontaneous help, at the time of my greatest need.

Thankfully too, my loving Heavenly Father brought along-side me a new team of faithful friends, who enthusiastically helped and supported the growing work of *Mission Moldova,* and who became my truly capable and diligent Board Members. I'm so grateful to each one of them for their years of hard work, dedication and wonderful support.

D uring the following years, as I poured myself whole-heartedly into serving the Lord in Moldova, I faced many trials and upsets. But, whenever I felt weak and help-less, tired and struggling to cope under a burden of stress and pressure, *Jesus* became my strength, *my Rock.* He was faithful in every circumstance and continually encouraged me to *never give up* and to always aim to achieve *the impossible.*

So, with my eyes fixed on Jesus, relying upon *His guidance, His strength* and *His divine favour,* that's exactly what I did. My faith grew rapidly as it was increasingly stretched and I learnt to trust God for *the impossible ...*

"Everything is possible for him (or her)
who believes."
(Mark 9:23)

However, I have learnt too, that *God's ways,* even when I don't understand them, or when they appear to cause me pain and disappointment, are always for my *good.*

For instance, back in the Autumn of 2001, when *Mission Moldova* first began, I was so excited to take the three men who approached me, out to Moldova for their very first visit and make plans for the future of the Mission. But sadly, the trip didn't go the way I'd hoped and, as we travelled around, I became acutely aware that the three men wanted to go their own way, *without me!* With my expectations dashed of strengthening and uniting our plans together, the trip ended in an uncomfortable tension between us. I was deeply disappointed and fearful for the future. And yet, amidst my anxiety, *God was still in control and even had a surprise in store for me.* For on our flight home, there was someone He wanted me to meet. Someone who would cheer and encourage me and, one day, play an important role in my life.

You see, on the last leg of our three-flight-journey home from Moldova, one of the three men had been sitting next to a Christian missionary and introduced him to me when we landed in Belfast. This stranger was tall and slim, vivacious and very interesting. Instinctively, we felt relaxed and at peace in each other's company and began walking *in-step* together, excitedly telling each other about our work for the Lord. His enthusiasm and strong faith made a great impression upon me and, before parting to go our separate ways, we exchanged phone numbers. *His name was Paul.*

394

Part Three

Mission Moldova

Mission Moldova

Ministering to the poor in body and spirit
through the grace of our
Lord Jesus Christ

Chapter 36

Mission Moldova

In the Autumn of 2001, *Mission Moldova* began its ministry, based from my home. Year by year, with the help and support of my friends, the Lord opened the door wider and wider, giving me more and more responsibility as I kept trusting in Him.   He blessed me with the support and encouragement of dedicated Mission Moldova Board Members, plus a great team of enthusiastic and hardworking volunteer supporters.

The Lord blessed me too, with a grand collection of farm outbuildings and a yard, generously donated to us by a kind family for storing and packing our massive quantity of aid. These outbuildings were truly a godsend to us, and enabled us to send out *multiple 45ft articulated lorry loads of aid each year* to help the many desperately needy orphanages, hospitals and schools in Transnistria. We also distributed large quantities of this aid to the many churches and individual poor families that we helped, plus the many centres for the blind, deaf and handicapped in both Moldova and Transnistria.

However, this was only made possible due to the compassionate and very generous help and support I received from various haulage companies in Northern Ireland. These companies kindly offered us a *free* 45ft articulated lorry to transport our aid to a depot in Cologne, Germany. Our aid, which we carefully and neatly packed on to wooden pallets, was then transferred by forklift on to a different lorry that had travelled four days from Moldova. Thankfully, we were only responsible for the haulage costs of the Moldovan vehicles. This transfer of aid in Cologne required a very strict schedule and *precise timing* was essential, as both lorries had to meet for the transfer, due to the depot having no storage facilities. Needless to say, there were some very tense moments whenever the Moldovan vehicle was even one hour late, due to an unexpected delay during the four-day journey. This whole exercise took a great deal of planning and organisation and the detailed Custom's paperwork for our aid to enter Moldova would often take me days to finalise.

Nonetheless, with Moldova being the *poorest country in Europe,* our huge truck loads of essential aid brought enormous relief and help, especially when we were able to take out vitally needed metal beds, hospital beds and waterproof mattresses for the appalling orphanages and hospitals in Transnistria. Our aim was to send out a truck three times a year to coincide with my visits. But in 2005, we excelled ourselves by sending out five trucks, which included building materials for a major project in Chisinau, the capital.

Hard work? Unbelievably so. All our volunteer helpers and active Board Members would heartily agree with me too. We worked so hard together as a team and, when finally we saw our truck loaded and ready to go, an inexpressible surge of exhilaration and joy filled our spirits as we knew we'd all done our best to serve the Lord.   We knew too, that it had been worth every minute of our back-breaking and exhausting work to bring untold relief and encouragement to so many desperately poor and needy people in Moldova and Transnistria.

Orphanages in Transnistria

During my first visits to Transnistria, my dear friend and interpreter Mark took me into many orphanages. The sights I saw were indeed pitiful and truly shocking. The

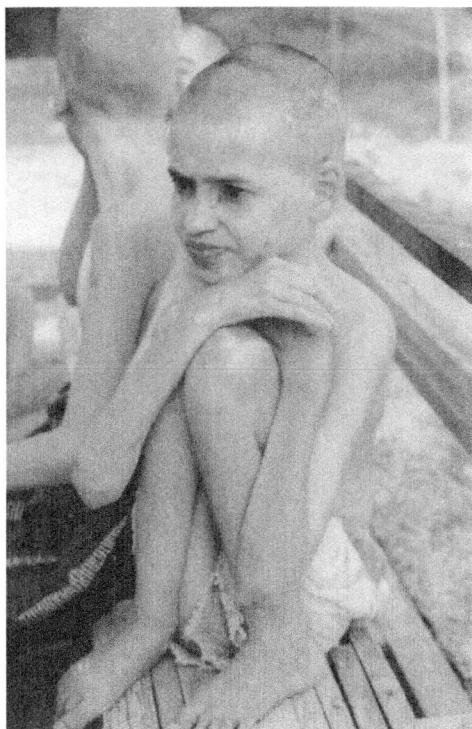

needs were horrendous and totally overwhelming, and the help that we gave, such as clothes, toiletries, food, metal beds and mattresses was always really appreciated. But one of the saddest sights I saw, which I shall never forget, was when I met some skeletal teenage girls with digestive problems. We provided this orphanage with regular supplies of vitamins, tins of food and cans of nutritious drinks.

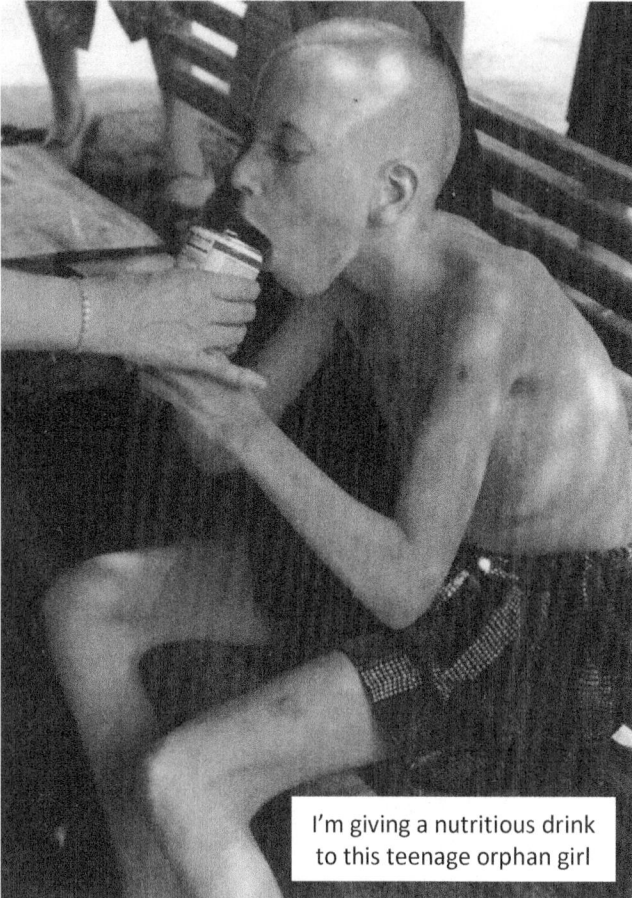

I'm giving a nutritious drink to this teenage orphan girl

When I visited a baby orphanage in Transnistria, I found it really heartbreaking to see so many lovely babies and tiny tots who had all been abandoned by their parents. Cramped, unsanitary living conditions plus extreme poverty, even today, drive parents to these lengths of despair. Sadly too, drugs and the availability of cheap alcohol often wrecks many families and, wherever I went, I met countless single mums struggling to bring up their children alone. Tragically, there are still hundreds of abandoned children growing up without the love and affection of their parents. Children who desperately need loving. Children who need to know the *love of Jesus* in their lives, and that He alone can heal them and give them *a love greater than any pain ...*

> **"Though my father and mother forsake me,**
> **the Lord** *(Jesus)* **will receive me."**
> (Psalm 27:10)

Thankfully, we were able to help this baby orphanage with lots of new cots, clean bedding, plenty of lovely baby clothes and supplies of nappies. We also gave them some beautiful hand knitted and crochet blankets for each cot, which brought a touch of warmth and colour to the rows upon rows of cots in the toddler's dormitories. Then, during one of my visits, the nurses told me about their most desperate need, and asked if we could help them. *Yes*, we could and quickly too. To the nurses' delight, we soon had *four* brand new large *washing machines* delivered to the baby orphanage, plus loads of washing powder too.

E very time I visited a women's orphanage, I always took with me carrier bags full of hundreds of small gifts, such as individually wrapped bars of soap. Whenever I gave out the first bars of soap, women of all ages would come running from every corner to eagerly receive one too.   It always touched my heart that a simple bar of soap was such a precious gift to these poor women. They would cradle it in both of their hands and look so lovingly at it. To each of them, it was their very own personal gift, which they quickly hid away from sight, in a deep and safe pocket in their clothing.

Church building projects

E ach year, we undertook a great many building projects in both Moldova and Transnistria to improve the decrepit living conditions of desperately poor families, as well as the shocking facilities in orphanages and hospitals. Our extensive building work also involved renovating several churches and, in southern Moldova, we purchased a pair of dilapidated cottages for Pastor Nicholia on a plot of land in Karaiklia Village. The smallest and most run-down cottage was completely demolished and, in its place, we built a two-storey extension. Thankfully, my good friend Pastor Alexei helped me by supervising this work and each time I visited Karaiklia, it was always so exciting to see the progress being made between my visits. After a lot of perseverance and hard work, this pair of dilapidated cottages were transformed into a practical and com-fortable church building for Pastor Nicholai and his

congregation. Prior to this, their church services were held in Pastor Nicholai's front yard outside his home. This was OK in the summer but, during the freezing winter months, they all had

to squeeze inside his small home. Pastor Nicholai and his family became dear friends of mine and we sponsored his son to attend Bible College for three years. Then, many years later, this same son sent me an email thanking me for helping him through Bible College and to tell me that he was now happily married and serving the Lord. *This was a lovely surprise and such great news, which I really appreciated.*

Camp of Joy

One of our other *first building projects* was to help Pastor Alexei with some urgent repairs at his children's Camp of Joy. This camp, in a pretty wooded area of Vidal Lui Voda, is situated only a short walking distance from the picturesque banks of the Dniester River. Each summer, hundreds of under-privileged children come to this camp for a holiday and it was important to get the facilities ready for them, so we quickly began tackling the largest and most pressing needs. This involved refitting and retiling the exterior shower block building; replacing the torn lino flooring with new wooden flooring in the large dining room and having twenty new trestle tables and forty benches made.

These benches were designed to be suspended by hidden brackets under each table when not in use, which made cleaning the dining room floor much easier. The biggest challenge, however, was to renovate the large shabby swimming pool. It had broken and chipped tiles which had become hazardous, and all of them needed to be carefully removed and replaced with good quality, frost-resistant blue ones. This took a lot of effort but was worth it, as the pool looked splendid and so inviting when it was finished. Now at last, it was safe for the hundreds of children visiting the camp to have a swim and enjoy endless hours of fun during the scorching summer months, when it often rose to over 40ºC.

A lovely refurbished clean pool

Pastor Alexei and his whole family circle run this camp, and they all became my very good friends. They worked so hard to ensure the renovations were successfully completed on time, before the arrival of the children from Chenobyl and Bellarussia. Each summer, these children come for a *health promoting holiday,* when the contamination in their young bodies can be reduced by up to 50%. This really made these renovations and everyone's efforts truly worthwhile.

O ur extensive *building projects* were varied and often very challenging. They usually involved connecting *running water* to properties, installing *new, clean and flushing toilets,* fitting showers and large cylinder hot water boilers (especially in hospitals), replacing broken wash hand basins and rotten windows, installing new plumbing and heating systems, and providing new ovens and fridges. Re-roofing and rewiring buildings was also carried out, and we even built new additional rooms for various homes and churches. Indeed, all of this was no mean feat but, as always, I trusted in the Lord for His divine help and faithful provision, to fulfil these vast needs.

A disgusting toilet in the deaf hostel

New toilets on 5 floors

However, one of our most challenging projects involved the on-going renovation work in the large, dilapidated five-storey hostel in Chisinau, the capital of Moldova. This hostel is home to *188 deaf people* and installing clean flushing toilets on all five floors, was just one of the many priorities.

The list of *urgent* needs seemed endless. But, as I once explained to Ross, these renovations, even minor ones, made such a huge difference to the livelihood of every family we helped. A difference that not only touched and comforted hurting and discouraged lives, but opened hardened hearts too, to hear the *good news* message and receive the love of Jesus Christ ... *a love greater than any pain!*

Never once, did I cease to be amazed when, during every visit to Moldova, I was able to see the vast difference each finished project had made. However, to assist me in organizing some of this extensive renovation work, we employed the full-time services of Gennady, a reliable and qualified Christian builder who was a member of the Bethel Church in Chisinau, which we also helped. He was honest and undertook each task with great dedication. I could trust him to submit detailed plans and accurate estimates, and then complete each project on time and to the highest standard. He was indeed, a real blessing.

I also worked alongside several Moldovan and Trans-nistrian pastors whom I found I could trust completely. We worked as a team, encouraging each other as a deep friend-ship and respect developed between us. Then, each summer, it was a pleasure to sponsor many of these pastors' six-day children's summer camps, when hundreds of children would enjoy themselves and have great fun together. During these camps, every child was given two meals-a-day and we also provided the necessary sports and games equipment, including gifts and prizes for the children. Then, at the end of each camp, we gave every child a beautifully illustrated Children's Bible in Russian or Romanian.

We also sponsored Easter and Christmas children's parties in these churches. And, at the end of each party, every child was overjoyed to receive a beautiful hand knitted chick and crème egg at Easter, and a fabric drawstring bag full of gifts at Christmas.   It was always our prayer that these precious young lives, through the Bible teaching they received at these camps and parties, would let them grow up in the sure knowledge that Jesus Christ loves and cares for them.

It saddened me greatly to discover that many of the churches we helped had very few *Bibles* and even less *hymn books.* I soon learnt too, that owning a Bible was a rarity and indeed, a prized possession. Consequently, whenever I visited a church, I would politely ask the pastor how many Bibles and hymn books he needed. Often, very timidly, he would dare to ask for perhaps, *ten?* I would then ask him again and say, *"How many do you **really** need?"*

This direct confrontation seemed to be the only way to learn the truth. They were just too embarrassed to ask for fifty, a hundred, two hundred or even more. They were especially bashful about asking for hymn books, which they knew cost more than Bibles.

Thankfully, to fulfil this dire need, we received a wonderful response from our supporters back home to our *Give A Bible Appeal* and were able to continually purchase large quantities of quality, hardback Bibles (with maps and a small concordance) in both Russian and Romanian for only £1.75 each, Children's Illustrated Bibles at £1.50 each and hymn books at £2 each, all from the Bible Society of Moldova.

A Pastor receiving Bibles

Over the years, the demand for Bibles remained, but due to the generous support of our *Give A Bible Appeal,* funds kept coming in to cover this great need. It was always a real joy to be able to give someone their very own personal Bible and *their thankfulness and grateful smiles said it all.*

Smuggling Bibles

Y es, *I'm guilty!* You see, between Moldova and Trans-nistria (Eastern Moldova) there is a well guarded border crossing and you are not allowed to carry quantities of Bibles across this border, or any of the other remote border crossings into Transnistria. This eastern *breakaway* region across the Dniester River, is a *self-proclaimed independent country* and has its own government, constitution, flag and coat of arms, army and currency (the Transnistrian ruble), border Custom posts and a population of approximately 500,000 people. And yet, you will not find this tiny state on most maps and not a single member of the United Nations recognizes its existence. Its ruble is only legal currency in Transnistria and all educational qualifications are only accepted and recognized in Transnistria. The whole region is like stepping back into a bygone communist socialist era and you are literally entering into *no-man's land,* with no Consulates or Embassies to call upon if needed.

As you cross through the border, after complying with all the forms and legalities, and head towards Tiraspol, the capital of Transnistria, you cannot help noticing disused army tanks under camouflage netting. These are, presumably, a permanent reminder of the bitter civil war which took place with Moldova in 1992, in order to gain their *independence.* Also, wherever you go in this bleak region, you are confronted with large statues of Lenin plus large murals on walls, together with conscripted army men walking the streets. It can be quite unsettling until you get used to it.

Yet, each visit to Moldova, I always went into Transnistria to visit the many churches, orphanages, schools, hospitals and prisons that we helped, plus the *deaf church* run by Pastor Oleg, who was always so cheerful and smiling, and whose family became very dear friends of mine.

Pastor Oleg signing for me in the deaf church in Transnistria

However, during one summer visit to Moldova, while making the necessary arrangements to visit Transnistria, young Ross was strongly resisting coming with me across the border and firmly declared, *"It's such a horrible place Mummy. It looks so terrible and I don't want to go there!"*

Understanding completely what he meant, I replied, *"But what about the people Ross? Do you like them?"* Without any hesitation he replied, *"Oh yes Mummy, I like the people!"* Gently I answered him, *"Well, it's the people we go to see, not the place."* Ross never resisted me again.

But, of course, Ross was right. For indeed, it is a dismal region of great poverty, with some of the worst orphanages I've ever seen. Also, in some areas, I saw that Christians and some churches came under government scrutiny and hence, the strong resistance to bringing Bibles into this region. All the churches I visited were desperate for Bibles and hymn books, and I was determined they should have as many as they needed. And so, by many different ways, we *succeeded* in getting them across the border and into very thankful hands.

Just a few more boxes

On one particular visit to Transnistria I was, as usual, *smuggling Bibles* across the border. If we just took a few boxes with us, containing a dozen or so Bibles, we were able to hide them and get them through. But, on this occasion, we'd decided to take just a few more boxes, which we knew could be risky.

As my driver and I approached the ominous border crossing, I sat in the front passenger seat earnestly praying, *"Please Lord,* **close the eyes** *of the guards so they won't find our precious Bibles."* Minutes later though, I suddenly heard the words *"Biblia! Biblia!"* as the guards began searching our vehicle and found our Bibles. Immediately, I was summoned to leave our car and join the group of guards standing beside my very nervous and visibly shaken driver. My heart was pounding, *"Would I be detained or fined? And my driver too? And would our precious Bibles be confiscated?"* For indeed, this was a real possibility. However, to my great surprise and utter relief, one of the guards suddenly asked me, *"Can we each have one of your Bibles? And we want you to put your charity label inside each one too!"*

Well, God taught me a very important lesson that day. For He didn't *close* the eyes of the guards as I had prayed, He **opened** them!

Chapter 37

I met Victoria

During one of my early visits to Moldova, I went to the Bible Society of Moldova and met the Director, Pastor Anton and his capable assistant Victoria, who spoke excellent English and had a great desire to serve the Lord. She was also an excellent Bible teacher and adeptly led a group of deaf people, using sign language.

On this particular visit to the Bible Society, while purchasing a quantity of Bibles, Victoria and I began chatting. Beside us, on one of the display tables, I noticed a wind-

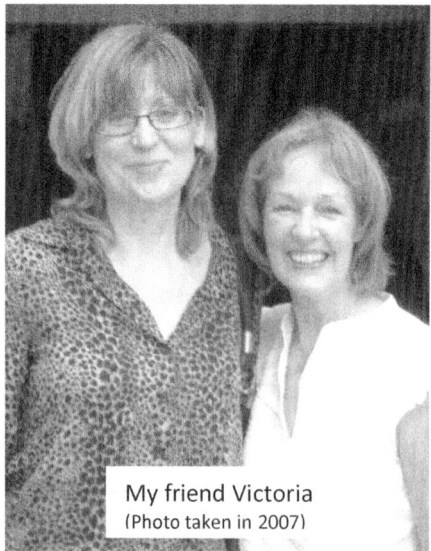

My friend Victoria
(Photo taken in 2007)

up cassette player and was instantly intrigued, because I'd brought *two* of them out with me in my suitcase. Victoria was delighted when I questioned her about this machine, which worked without any electricity or batteries. *Perfect* for poor families. And *perfect* for use in places with no electricity.

Victoria continued to explain to me that the Bible Society of Moldova had just begun two new projects. One was ministering to the blind and the other was working with deaf people. She told me that they'd found these wind-up machines to be ideal for the blind, especially blind children, who enjoyed the challenge of winding-up the handle as fast as they could. As Victoria told me more about these two new projects, she suddenly became serious and, looking me straight in the eye, openly challenged me, *"Will you help us with our two new projects with the blind and the deaf?"*

I was totally unprepared for this challenge and she took me by complete surprise. They both sounded like huge projects to me and *who was I to undertake such a great responsibility?* And besides, I was only just beginning my new mission and had no accrued funds. *So what would my answer be?* Before replying, I looked up towards Heaven and silently prayed, *"Lord, I have never even met a blind person before and I know nothing about the deaf."* And yet, I heard myself saying, *"Yes!"*

This was the beginning of a completely new, often testing but exciting ministry for me. A ministry based on trusting God to lead and guide me, and provide for our growing needs. Every day seemed to be *a mighty step of faith* and I had plenty to learn and a great deal to do. Victoria and I became good friends and close working partners and I respected her wisdom and advice. Over the next few years, we experienced many joys and sorrows together as we successfully formed a church and Bible study group for the deaf in a large annex behind the Bethel Church in Chisinau, where Paston Anton was the Senior Pastor. We appointed four of the most experienced deaf Christians to be the Senior Leaders in this church and they each had separate duties and responsibilities.

Victoria using *sign language* and teaching in the deaf church in Chisinau

Every time I visited Moldova, Victoria and I held a one-day *Leaders' Meeting* to discuss any current problems or special needs in the deaf church, or with any members of the congregation. We also discussed relevant topics such as organising deaf teachers for the Bible study sessions held on Sunday afternoons and on a midweek evening, plus any helpful equipment and teaching aids that they might need. We also planned future evangelism projects, which often included visiting a women's prison.

However, I soon learnt that these deaf Leaders' Meetings could be quite volatile, with emotions running high due to someone being offended, resulting in tears. Victoria and I then had to be peace makers and settle any disagreements. You see, deaf people chat to each other in sign language, which is visible to everyone. They cannot turn to each other or go off into a corner and speak a quiet word. No, their sign language is seen by everyone. Therefore, *no secrets!* All is revealed, with the consequence that someone often gets offended. And yet, I was always amazed at how forgiving they were and that they could be friends again in a few minutes. Thus, very often, these meetings were quite testing as we sought to gain mutual agreement upon many issues. And all the while, Victoria very kindly and patiently interpreted their lengthy sign language discussions to me. Indeed, this was a huge and very difficult commitment to fulfil, but I soon came to know their individual personalities and needs, and grew to love each one of them. Remarkably, they quickly became my *new* family and even today, they still hold a very special place in my heart.

Deaf families

S adly, most of the families who attended our deaf church were extremely poor and, whenever I visited them in their homes, I was always deeply saddened by the ex-

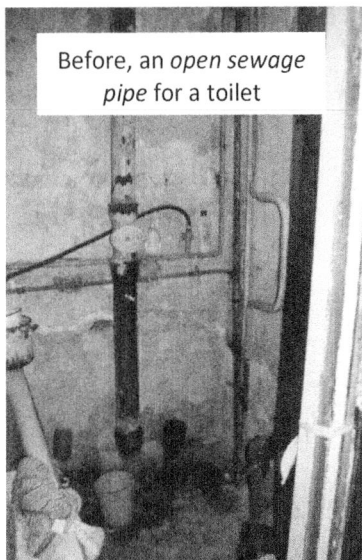

Before, an *open sewage pipe* for a toilet

After!

tent of the disrepair of their living conditions.   One deaf family's home was particularly shocking, when I found nine people living in just two squalid rooms.   Their kitchen was horrendous and unspeakably appalling with its blackened, mouldy walls and ceiling.   But, to my horror, their bathroom was even worse.   There was no toilet for this family of nine, just an *open sewage pipe.*

The father of this family was an unbeliever, but when he saw how we, as Christians, built a beautiful new bathroom and a *separate toilet* in his home for his family, he was so amazed and thankful, that he began attending our deaf church.   Everyone was delighted to see him and made him feel very welcome.   I was delighted too, to see his family looking so genuinely happy and enjoying meeting so many other deaf believers.   We all prayed that he would soon give his heart to Jesus Christ and that the angels in Heaven would be rejoicing over his name being written in the *Lamb's Book of Life* (Revelation 21:27 NKJV).

Deaf families' homes

What I saw during my visits to our deaf families' homes was so unbelievably awful, that I just had to help them.   And, with God's divine help and amazing provision, we helped *over thirty* needy deaf families who attended our deaf church in Chisinau.   One by one, they each experienced the amazing grace of God in their lives, as their homes were improved and repaired, and their most urgent needs met.   These repairs were often a tremendous testimony to members of their own family and friends too, of God's unfailing love for them.

Violetta

The *urgent* needs of the deaf also included medical care. For over a year, we looked after Violetta, one of our hard-of-hearing young ladies who lived in *one room* with three other partially deaf girls, in the five-storey deaf hostel in Chisinau.

These girls each had a single bed squeezed into this one room, without a wardrobe or even a chest of drawers between them. The first time I visited them, I couldn't help enquiring where all their belongings were kept. One of the girls went over to a table in their room and lifted a tea towel covering an oblong tray. Their belongings, including cups, plates and cutlery *all fitted on to this one tray.* I was deeply humbled by this, and have never forgotten this experience.

And yet, all these four girls kept so happy and cheerful and were always smiling. When they sang together in the deaf church, gracefully using sign language and tapping a foot to keep in rhythm, their faces literally shone with the love of Christ in their hearts. Their faith was always an inspiration and great encouragement to me ...

"Has not God chosen those
who are poor in the eyes of the world
to be rich in faith?"
(James 2:5)

Then one day, due to Violetta's deafness, she had a terrible accident. While getting off a trolley bus, she didn't hear a truck roaring along. It knocked her down and stopped on her lower right leg. When the horrified truck driver realised this and moved his truck, her foot and lower leg were mangled.

Everyone was shocked and desperately upset and we all feared she would lose part of her leg.

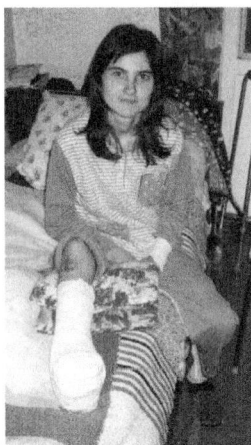

We helped Violetta in every way we could and supported her through three subsequent serious and very painful operations, including one for skin grafting. She was unable to stand or walk without great discomfort for many months.

Sadly though, when in hospital in Moldova, there is a daily charge for your bed, all medication and even medical dressings, and family or friends have to provide all the food. We made sure Violetta had everything she needed and provided daily food for her, which members of the deaf church kindly cooked for her.

During Violetta's lengthy stay in hospital, Victoria only allowed me to visit her once. This was due to the sad fact that had the doctors seen me, they would have regarded me as *a rich foreigner* and charged us even more for Violetta's treatment.   Then late one night, I crept into the ward un-noticed, to see her.

When at last Violetta was able to leave the hospital and return to the deaf hostel, she needed constant nursing. Thankfully, we were able to find a very caring woman from our deaf church to look after Violetta throughout the many months of her painful ordeal. A nurse regularly visited too, to check on her progress and change her dressings. Eventually, she did manage to walk again, although the skin grafts still caused her a lot of discomfort and pain.

I'm so very thankful that we were able to help and support Violetta in her time of great need and that she didn't lose her right foot or lower leg as once feared. Yes indeed, it was a great privilege to bless Violetta, especially when her *deaf pension was only £1.50 per month. Yes, only £1.50.*

Vasia and Nadia

I will always remember visiting Vasia and Nadia, a young deaf married couple who had a lovely little four-year-old son Vasika but, the day I arrived, he wasn't with them. When I enquired where he was, they told me the most heart-breaking news. The news that they couldn't afford to feed or look after their little boy any longer and he had gone to live in the country. This dear couple were sobbing their hearts out and I couldn't bear to see their pain.

Straight away, we began helping them with urgent household repairs and bought them items they really needed, such as a cooker. We also gave them children's items, clothes and aid from our truck. Vasia, the husband, was very skilful at carpentry but, when I learnt he had no tools of his own, we bought him what he needed, including an electric jigsaw and drill. He was so very grateful and immediately began making attractive wooden articles, which he was able to sell to help support his family.

When I next visited them, I was delighted to see their little boy back home living with them again and soon afterwards, I heard the good news that they were expecting their second child. They were at long last, *a happy family again,* full of new hope for the future and praising God for His great faithfulness and love to them.

Deaf children's camp

B oth Victoria and I wanted to reach the deaf children living *all over Moldova* and not just those living near Chisinau, the capital. We wanted to give them all the opportunity of hearing the good news of the gospel message. *But how could* we *do this?* Victoria came up with the answer, a *fun* answer. We could hold a ten-day residential camp in Pastor Alexei's Camp of Joy, near the sandy banks of the Dniester River. A camp that we'd recently renovated! *Perfect.*

This idea was jubilantly welcomed by all of our deaf church leaders in both Moldova and Transnistria and, after many months of exhaustive preparations, we were ready to hold our *first deaf children's residential camp* for 71 deaf children, plus 2 blind girls (Olga and Inna, whom we helped).

As planned, each of the 19 deaf leaders had diligently prepared their daily Bible study lessons, the crafts teachers had their materials ready, the drama teachers had their Bible stories ready for the children to enact each evening during the worship service, and the sports instructor and his helpers had a series of games and activities planned. And Ross and I took out with us two students who enthusiastically and energetically joined in with all the activities, crafts and drama.

420

Every day was fun!

It was an amazing camp and every day was filled with joy, laughter and happiness. Yet, for all the leaders it was exhausting, as each day began with prayer at 7.30 a.m. and ended in prayer at 11 p.m. after our evening worship service. The days were long but thrilling too, as we watched our deaf children having tremendous fun together playing games, swimming in the camp's lovely retiled swimming pool, eating good nourishing meals in the renovated dining room, making new friends and, every day, learning more about Jesus.

Regrettably though, many of these deaf children came from such poor homes, that all they were used to eating was a type of grainy porridge. Now at our camp, when they were given good food to eat, some of them suffered with intense stomach pains. The attendant Nurse informed me that many of these children had stomach ulcers due to their poor diet and I was really upset to learn this. Sadly, the medication she gave them didn't seem to help them and they kept on crying in pain. But thankfully, I had my own first-aid kit with me and was able to give these poor children some medicine that calmed their stomachs, stopped their crying and let them get a good night's sleep. Remembering my own crippling pain with a gastric ulcer so many years ago, gave me great compassion for these youngsters and I was pleased that I could help them.

Towards the end of the camp ...

We held a special *Salvation Message* worship service led by Pastor Anton, when all the children were reminded of Jesus' own words ...

> *"I am the way and the truth and the life.*
> *No-one comes to the Father except through Me."*
> (John 14:6)

Pastor Anton also spoke about the important eternal truth that they all needed to understand and remember, that ...

> *"Salvation is found in no-one else, (Jesus)*
> *for there is no other name under Heaven given to men*
> *by which we must be saved."*
> (Acts 4:12)

The deaf and hard-of-hearing children were all so amazingly attentive and, during this service, we gave the older youth a *modern translation* New Testament Bible each and the younger ones were given a lovely Children's Illustrated Bible (both in either Russian or Romanian). Pastor Anton ended his Salvation Message by encouraging the children to ask Jesus into their hearts. Wonderfully, *so very many did ...*

> *"For, 'everyone who calls on the name of the Lord*
> *will be saved.'"*
> (Romans 10:13)

The last evening of our ten-day camp was *party night.* We went to great lengths to provide a special celebration party for all the children with games, lots of food and many treats. And, without fail, the children always asked for *bananas* to eat. Victoria explained to me that in Moldova, *only rich people eat bananas.* So, each year, in preparation for this special party, Victoria and I went off to the markets to buy as much fruit, bananas and treats as we possibly could, and the children shrieked with delight when they saw their party tables laden with bananas, tasty meats, cheese and cakes!

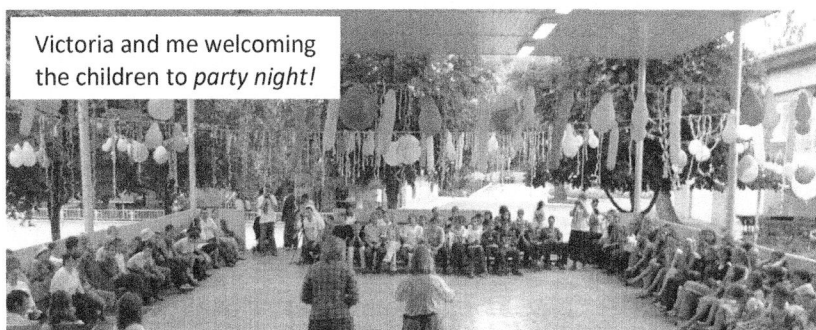

Victoria and me welcoming the children to *party night!*

All the children were so happy after their special party tea and enthusiastically welcomed spending the next few hours playing some hilarious and very energetic team games, which were always tremendous fun. But the excitement wasn't over yet, as there was still one more big surprise in store for them.

With darkness upon us and the usual bedtime long past, the children were led through the camp grounds to a safe and specially built concrete arena, with tiered seating, where a *massive bonfire* had been lit. It looked so dramatic in the darkness and the children were delighted. I gave out toy whistles, feather blowers and hooters which the younger hard-of-hearing children especially loved, as they ran around blowing their whistles directly into each other's ears. Even young *blind Inna,* who sadly couldn't see the bonfire, had a tremendous time blowing her hooter and really enjoyed

423

herself. With the evening nearly over, there was still a final surprise in store, as we gathered together around the massive bonfire, under a warm starry night ... *it was time for ice cream! Oh, what a treat.* To these children, ice cream was an exceptional treat and they were all delighted and so excited!

Highlight of the summer

These deaf camps were often the highlight of each summer and, during Pastor Anton's final Salvation Message service, it was an incredible joy for all of us to see so many children, and older youth too, raising their arms **to accept Jesus Christ as their Lord and Saviour.** Then Gena, one of our deaf leaders from Transnistria, would lead the children in a *Prayer of Salvation,* using sign language. This was indeed the pinnacle of the camp and was always a deeply meaningful and moving experience.

Gena leading the deaf children in
a *Prayer of Salvation*

Watching so many deaf children earnestly praying the Prayer of Salvation was like seeing *a miracle happen* before us, and my heart would nearly burst with happiness. Tears of joy would roll down my cheeks as I saw the children's beaming faces and outstretched hands. *Outstretched hands to Jesus.*

Suddenly, all the effort and exhaustion of running the camp just faded away as, in a few days' time, we watched the deaf children and youth boarding coaches to return back to their homes all over Moldova, with *Jesus Christ in their hearts and a Bible in their hands.* We, in turn, thanked and praised Almighty God for *saving* these precious young souls. And then one summer, we were especially overjoyed when *86 deaf children* repented and accepted Jesus Christ as their Lord and Saviour. *Slava bogo!* (Russian for *'Praise God!'*)

O ur deaf camps became so popular, that instead of our original 71 deaf children and 2 blind young girls (Olga and Inna) plus 19 deaf leaders; our numbers quickly swelled to *113 deaf children and 30 deaf leaders,* plus Olga and Inna, and one deaf youth with cerebral palsy. *Amazing.*

It was not uncommon too, for a deaf child to arrive at the gates of the Camp of Joy and beg to be allowed in. I remember one little girl, about eight years old, who arrived in this manner and was desperate to join us. All she had with her for the whole ten days were a few items in a small plastic bag. She didn't even have a change of clothing with her, a towel or a toothbrush. Thankfully, from the quantity of aid we always took with us to the camp, we were able to give her all that she needed. Many of the deaf children arrived like this and it was such a joy to be able to help them, and then give them a wonderful time.

Christmas party

With so many deaf children giving their hearts to Jesus each summer, Victoria and I wanted to encourage these children in their new faith. So again, we questioned, *"How do we do this, when they live all over Moldova?"* This time, I came up with the answer. Another *fun* answer. I suggested holding a *Christmas party* and then an *Easter party* in the Bethel Church in Chisinau, where there was plenty of room for all the children to come.

All the deaf leaders happily agreed to this idea and so began the many months of detailed preparation for 100 deaf children and 30 deaf adults to attend our *first Christmas party.* A splendid programme was carefully planned, including a nativity play on *the birth of Jesus* and beautiful costumes were expertly made by our nimble-fingered deaf ladies. Victoria and I had fun too, going around the markets choosing dress materials and trimmings for the various outfits, especially the robes for the *three wise men.* Christmas carols were chosen and the hard-of-hearing practised signing the words in perfect synchronization to music, plus lots of games and activities were organised and delicious food was prepared.

As we'd all hoped, the party was a huge success and the Christmas drama depicting the birth of baby Jesus was excellent. Then, as the party drew to a close, we gave each child a beautiful, handmade fabric *drawstring-bag* full of Christmas gifts and toys and they were absolutely thrilled. The children's excited shrieks of delight were unforgettable, as they hugged their beautiful and colourful *drawstring bags,* which had been so lovingly made and filled with children's colouring books, crayons and toys by so many caring ladies back home in Northern Ireland. We were all delighted that our Christmas party had been such a success and that everyone had enjoyed themselves so much. But our

greatest joy was when *one of the deaf girls repented and invited Jesus into her heart.* As we rejoiced over this, we knew the angels in Heaven were rejoicing too.

Easter children's party

B efore we knew it, Victoria and I were making fresh plans for the children's *Easter party.* New costumes for the drama presentation had to be designed and diligently made by the deaf ladies in Chisinau. Meanwhile, back home in Northern Ireland, I was getting our early Spring truck packed and ready to send out in time for this party. Plus, a great many ladies were busy too. *Busy knitting colourful Easter chicks*, to send out on our truck. I was really thankful to these ladies from all over Northern Ireland who knitted *thousands* of these lovely chicks and to those who donated Cadbury's crème eggs to be popped inside each one of them. We gave these beautiful knitted chicks, with a crème egg inside them to so many children ... the deaf children coming to our Easter party, the many hundreds of children in the orphanages in Transnistria, to children attending the deaf schools and special needs kindergartens that we helped, plus the many children in the churches that we supported.

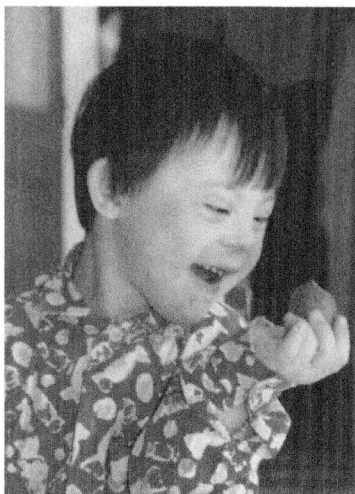
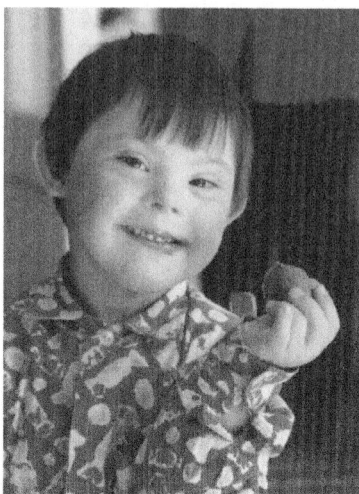

A very happy girl in a kindergarten in Transnistria

Without any doubt, every hand knitted chick and Cadbury's crème egg brought amazing joy to a child's life. And this Bible verse aptly describes their incredible joy, whenever they tasted a delicious chocolate crème egg ... *"And their joy was very great!"* *(Nehemiah 8:17)*

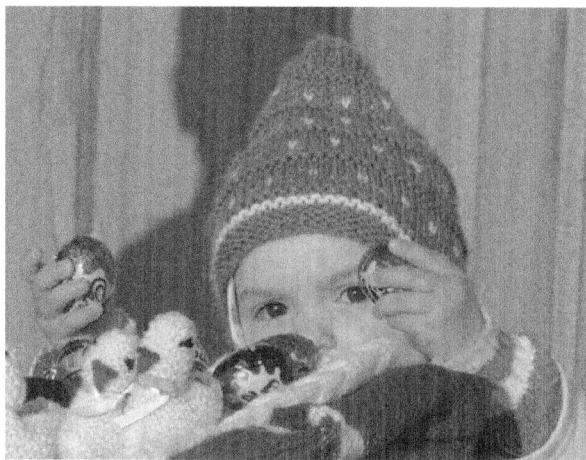

A Cadbury's creme egg inside each hand knitted chick ... Yum!

Chapter 38

Divine Thunderstorm

During the summer of 2005, we decided to give our deaf leaders a well-deserved rest and planned a big surprise for them. Pastor Anton, Victoria and I secretly planned a one-week *residential Bible teaching seminar* for them, to be held at a Christian camp set beside a beautiful lake, amidst lovely countryside. When we shared our secret with them and invited eighty deaf adults and older youth to attend, they were *ecstatic with joy,* and became as excited as little children. However, an experienced *deaf* Bible teacher was needed to conduct the daily and evening seminars, and we were delighted when a lecturer from a Deaf Bible College in Moscow agreed to come. He had a rigorous and exhausting schedule ahead of him but, each day, he was mightily encouraged by the enthusiastic response he received to his expert teaching.

Knowing our deaf friends are generally extremely poor, we had another surprise in store for them when they arrived at this camp. Wonderfully, I had both of my sons *Leon and Ross with me* and, with their help, we assembled the deaf people together on a grassy bank and gave each of them a colourful carrier bag full towels, shower gel, shampoo, soap, toothpaste, toothbrush, etc. plus the men were given shaving gel and razors, and the women were given *face cream.*

Deaf adults' camp

The previous year, at the end of our deaf children's camp, I gave *thank you* gifts to all our deaf leaders and, for the first time, I gave pots of face cream and hand cream to our female leaders. But, to my dismay, *all* the ladies wanted *face cream* and very sadly, I didn't have enough. So, when I returned home to Northern Ireland, I put out an appeal for face cream and received an amazing response. Now, at this year's camp, I had plenty with me, so no-one was going to be disappointed.

Needless to say, this adults' deaf camp was a tremendous success. And, at the end of each evening's session, they were so enthused and excited, that it was nearly impossible to get them to go to bed. However, unbeknown to me, some of the deaf ladies had a wonderful *secret surprise* for me.

A *divine* thunderstorm

I t was Sunday, 7ᵗʰ August 2005 and plans were going ahead for Ross and me to be baptised by immersion in the lake at our adults' deaf camp at 4 p.m. in the afternoon.   We'd been looking forward to *our special day* for months, especially when our good and faithful friend Pastor

Ross and me

Anton, Senior Pastor of the Bethel Church in Chisinau, offered to baptise us. Our deaf friends at the camp were very excited too and, after breakfast, I could see some of them coming out of the woods carrying armfuls of leafy branches. I couldn't help wondering, *"What are they up to?"*

But shortly afterwards, the skies rapidly darkened and then, quite suddenly, down came the rain *in torrents.* Heavier and heavier it fell. Then came enormous claps of deafening thunder (which, of course, the deaf folks couldn't hear), followed immediately by huge bolts of lightning.   I was horrified at the thought of being baptised during a torrential storm and knew the water temperature in the lake would be cooling rapidly.   And yet, the heavier the rain fell and the more dramatic the bolts of lighting, the more excited our deaf friends became and kept running up to me shouting and signing, *"You are blessed! This is a blessing from God!"* Well, I have to admit, I wasn't quite so sure, especially when the

431

sheeting rain didn't cease one bit. In fact, it just came down even heavier, the thunder became louder and the lightning more insistent. Feeling somewhat discouraged, but with the excited words of the deaf still resounding in my ears, I felt the urgent need to pray, *"Dear Lord, if this really is from You, please let the rain stop at 4 p.m. in time for our baptism!"*

A little later that morning, while the rain was still lashing down, a group of deaf ladies came up to me carrying a large square box and proudly presented it to me. *Whatever could it be?* Carefully, I opened their box and had such a surprise. For inside, wrapped in tissue paper, was a beautiful white dress, with rosebuds around the neckline. I gasped in delight. It was so lovely and such a wonderful *secret surprise for my baptism.* These dear deaf ladies, whom I loved so much, were overjoyed that they had managed to surprise me and explained that they had made my dress using *a sewing machine which I had given them* from a previous truck of aid. And, when I tried on their masterpiece of love, *it fitted me perfectly.* I was overjoyed to have such a lovely dress to wear.

A little later, the eye of the storm seemed to be moving away, and the thunder became less frequent. *Thank goodness.* But, just as I was heaving a big sigh of relief that the storm was abating, a colossal clap of thunder crashed directly overhead. *Oh no! It's come back again!* As dismay filled my thoughts, the Lord began speaking to me out of the storm ...

"I HAVE NOT GONE AWAY!
I will never go away!
Don't ever think I will leave you!"

It was Jesus, my Lord and Saviour speaking to me! And instantly, I was filled with an awesome awareness of *His*

Divine Presence. An amazing wonder filled my senses, as I attempted to grasp His immense power, majesty and Sovereignty. He alone is Supreme. His power is matchless, limitless and beyond our human understanding. Nothing is impossible for Him. And incredibly, *Jesus Christ, the Lord of Lords and Kings of Kings* was speaking to me and filling me with His glorious presence. A presence that remained with me for the next *two days,* and kept reminding me that ...

> **"Never will I leave you; never will I forsake you."**
> (Hebrews 13:5)

Jesus Christ, the One and Only *living* God, graciously revealed an amazing revelation to me. The revelation that *He was in control of the thunder storm that day,* in just the same way as He controlled the storm two thousand years ago on the Sea of Galilee (Luke 8:24-25). For, *at exactly 4 p.m. the torrential rain and thunder miraculously stopped. It was awesome!* The sky cleared and everyone cheered and praised God. In humble adoration and deep awe, I looked towards Heaven and prayed to my Lord, *"Thank you Jesus, for this wonderful miracle and for blessing us. I love You Lord and will praise You forever and ever. Amen."*

But, could there be yet another blessing in store? Yes, there was.   When the rain miraculously stopped at 4 p.m. Ross lovingly took my hand and we walked toge-ther down to the lakeside in our white baptismal

clothes. Pastor Anton, resplendent in his long turquoise robes followed us, with *my dear son Leon* and my lovely friend and interpreter *Olesya* right behind him. They were followed by Victoria and all the deaf from our camp, together with my close friend Reya, Pastor Anton's wife, plus lots of friends who had travelled from Transnistria. When we reached the lakeside, we could hardly believe our eyes. *What a fantastic surprise was waiting for us.* It was amazing! And now at last, I understood *why* the deaf had emerged from the woods very early this morning, before the storm began, carrying such large armfuls of leafy branches. They had painstakingly and creatively transformed them into a *beautiful archway at the edge of the lake and laid a chain of flowers in a circle out on to the water.* It looked incredible and took our breath away.

As our friends gathered together at the lakeside, Ross and I walked hand-in-hand into the water towards Pastor Anton, who was waiting for us. He baptised me first and then Ross, before standing together in the lake, while he prayed over us. Ross and I then walked back hand-in-hand to the laughter and

cheers of all our friends, and a few kind ladies quickly wrapped us up in large dry towels. When we had changed into dry clothes, everyone gathered together in the big dining hall to continue the baptismal service. Solemnly, Ross and I knelt before Pastor Anton and two other pastors, who laid their hands on our heads and prayed over us. After taking the bread and wine of Holy Communion, Pastor Anton then presented both Ross and me with a beautiful *Bethel Church Baptism Certificate*, as a lovely keepsake. During our celebration tea with everyone, there was yet *another surprise blessing*. Choirs from two of the churches we helped in Transnistria had made the great effort to come to be with us and it touched my heart listening to their beautiful singing. When the time came for our guests to leave, Ross and I experienced a lovely Moldovan custom. We were literally swamped with *gifts of flowers* and could barely hold the enormous armfuls of colourful gladioli and roses. This was a beautiful and loving touch at the end of a truly amazing and joyful day.

Ross and me with Leon, after our baptism service

Pastor Anton too, gave us a lovely wooden carved plaque to commemorate our baptism and, to this day, I still treasure his gift. **This was certainly a *divine* and very *special* day that Ross and I, and Leon too, will never forget.**

Chapter 39

God used my Pain

O ver the years since April 1997, I have often been surprised, and indeed delighted, to see that God's timing is always *perfect,* even if I thought otherwise. I have also learnt that *God is never too late* and *He never wastes any of our experiences,* whether they have been good, bad, downright painful or utterly shameful. God will use them *all,* if we'll let Him. And He will use them for *good* to help others.

Let me tell you a story that is very dear to my heart. A story of how I learnt this truth firsthand when, one day in Moldova, God used my painful past for *good.*

D uring one of my trips to Moldova, I was invited to visit a *women's prison* with Victoria and some of our partially deaf Moldovan girls from the deaf church.

This was to be my first-ever experience of entering a prison and what I saw in this Eastern European prison came as quite a shock. As Jesus said, *"I was in prison, and you came to Me."* (Matthew 25:36 NASB).

When the time eventually came for us to meet this sad and bedraggled group of women, my heart went out to them, even though we'd been told several of them had murdered their husbands. Many of them too, looked so young and I wondered what crime they'd committed to deserve being shut up in such an appalling place.

We were led into a large dismal room, with a few narrow benches at one end for the prisoners to sit on and some chairs for us at the other end. The atmosphere was heavy in those stark surroundings, as grim faces examined us.

Victoria, our group leader, began by speaking in Russian to the women prisoners, introducing ourselves and explaining the purpose of our visit. Their expressions remained unchanged and it wasn't until some of our partially deaf companions began singing and signing to the Christian praise music playing on our CD player, that the oppressive atmosphere lightened a little.

Meanwhile, I'd decided to join the prisoners at the far end of the room and sat tightly squeezed amongst them on the narrow benches. In fact, it was such a squash, that I even had one of them sitting on my lap. But from this unusual vantage point, I was able to capture the moment by taking some photographs of my partially deaf friends' singing, followed by their humorous drama presentation. I was fascinated, as I watched them communicate in an amusing and captivating way to the surly faced women sitting beside me.

Then, to my surprise, Victoria tiptoed down the room and whispered to me, *"Will you speak to these women when I motion to you?"*

Panic immediately filled my heart and I could feel it pounding. My thoughts began racing as I questioned, *how could I, a rich and prosperous Westerner in their eyes,* possibly reach out to these hapless souls living in these bleak, horrible conditions? This was certainly a totally new experience for me and I felt an urgency to pray for immediate help. Silently, I asked God, *"Oh Lord, what can I say to these women? How can I reach them? Please help me."*

Instantly, the Lord answered my earnest prayer with *six words,* direct from the Holy Spirit within me. *Six words* that deeply touched my own heart and, hopefully, would touch the stony hearts of these women too ... ***"You will never be abandoned again!"***

I was overwhelmed by God's goodness and love through this amazing promise. A promise that meant the world to me. *"Thank You Lord. Thank You."* That's all God said to me, just these *six words,* but that's all I needed.

You see, God *always* hears our prayers, even our silent ones, and He's *always* ready to help us when we humbly ask Him. *Only God knew what these women really needed to hear.* Only God knew how to break open their hardened hearts to receive His love. And my Heavenly Father has never let me down and He didn't this time either. He faithfully gave me His help, His words and His direction at the point of my weakness and great need. His help, as always, *wasn't too late.*

These six precious words, *"You will never be abandoned again!"* also gave me the strength and courage I lacked to face these sullen-faced women, sitting huddled together on their narrow benches in a bare, cold and dimly lit prison room.

It was only when Victoria motioned for me to stand up and speak, that I realized how significant it had been that I'd gladly chosen to sit amongst these women prisoners. I'd been sitting tightly squashed between them, with one of them on my lap, instead of distancing myself from them by sitting on a chair, at the far end of the room. It was as if this simple act of trust and friendship had helped to bridge the gap between us and silently bond us together.

As I stood in front of these women, with my dear friend Victoria at my side, interpreting in Russian for me, I began telling them about the years of my *own* suffering. The pain, the violence, the abuse, the infidelity, the uncontrollable rage and anger from an alcoholic husband. Plus my own fears, poverty, times of hunger and cold, and the struggle to bring up two children by myself with no family to help me. Yes, I was certainly *not* the rich Westerner they were expecting.

I also knew that the ravages of alcoholism was something many poor Moldovan families have to endure. With a bottle of vodka costing *less* than fifty pence, it is an easy and cheap way to numb the pain and sorrow of extreme poverty. But tragically too, every bottle of alcohol purchased means less food for a family to eat. This is still one of the reasons *why* the orphanages in Moldova and Transnistria are always full to capacity. Full of neglected and abandoned children.

As I stood before these women, speaking with compassion for them and bearing open my own heart, I saw an expression of surprise, of understanding and even tenderness enter some of their eyes. One by one, they lifted their gaze from the cold bare floor to look up at me. The barrier between us was slowly breaking down as they began to listen, to respond, and let the *healing love of Jesus* touch their own scarred and hurting hearts. It was at this crucial point of breakthrough, that I momentarily paused and looked up towards Heaven. Silently, I glorified God and prayed ...

"Oh Lord. NOW I know WHY I went through so many years of pain and fear, abuse and suffering. If I hadn't known suffering myself, how could I ever begin to understand what these poor women have gone through to end up in this terrible prison? How could I possibly hope to touch their hurting and crushed hearts, and reach deep into their lives with Your love, Your forgiveness and Your compassion?"

I was always totally amazed at how God used *my pain* to help so many people. Not only these women prisoners, but some male prisoners too, in another prison in Transnistria. Plus many, many others ... the blind, the deaf, the handicapped, countless orphans, the elderly, the destitute, the forgotten and the *abandoned.* They are *all* God's precious children who need to know the truth that, **"Jesus loves them.** *Really* loves them. *Just the way they are, and wherever they are."*

Was it worth all the years of pain?

Y ou might be surprised the way God used my pain for *good* and how He used it to open hardened hearts. You may even ask me, *"Was it worth all the years of pain?"* And I can truthfully reply, ***"Yes. It was worth every single minute."***

"But why?" you may question. I can answer that too. ***"Because God was using my pain to help others. Whenever I saw solemn faces and grim expressions soften and tears run down the cheeks of hardened men and women, I***

knew hearts were being healed.   When a prisoner steps forward and is ready to pray the Prayer of Salvation, I knew a life was being changed. Changed for the better."

To me, speaking in this women's prison, was just one of the greatest privileges that God ever gave me. The privilege to tell these women, so often considered as social outcasts, just how much *He loves them.* To tell them that they are not forgotten, nor despised or worthless, and that they, just like me, **will never be abandoned again.**

God gave me these wonderful opportunities to speak in this and other prisons, to tell so many suffering people about His amazing, healing, forgiving and unconditional love for them ... *a love greater than any pain!*

Y ou see, I've found a *priceless* love, a *precious* love that I want to share with *you,* and with others too ...

THE LOVE OF JESUS CHRIST!
A perfect love, a divine love, that turned
my pain into a blessing!
A blessing to help others and give me
a joyous victory.

Hallelujah!

Chapter 40

Opening Closed Doors

M y greatest delight, and indeed pleasure, was not only being able to ease the dire physical needs and living conditions of those I met, but seeing long-standing barriers and strongholds to the gospel of Jesus Christ being broken down. In fact, the more we helped, the more we saw closed doors *open* to us. So, in perpetual awe, I watched God's mighty hand at work as He continued to offer me windows of opportunity. Precious opportunities to reach out to so many needy people and share *the love of Jesus Christ* with them. *This was what it was all about.* This was the real prize and the real joy. Let me tell you about one particular closed door that *opened to us,* in an orphanage in Transnistria.

Orphanages in Transnistria

W hen I first visited these orphanages in 2001, I found the most appalling, unspeakable conditions imaginable and I just had to do something to help. I simply could not ignore what I'd seen. And yet, the need was so overwhelming, it made me feel that whatever we did, it would

442

seem insignificant. I remember one day, when young Ross was totally bewildered too, by the extreme enormity facing us. I explained to him that although I couldn't do it all, I could do something and help a few. And to those few, it would make a huge difference to their lives. This simple explanation settled Ross as he realised that whatever we could do, it was worth the effort.

Wherever I went, the needs were the same. Disgusting, stinking and deeply encrusted broken toilets, many of which didn't flush. Filthy and rusty wash basins, with missing taps and often no running water. Metal beds that had huge jagged holes in the bases, and mattresses that were filthy and urine stained, with many of them on the point of disintegration.

Our first job in each of these orphanages was to replace as many of the worst beds and mattresses as quickly as possible. On one visit alone, I was able to purchase *250 metal beds and order 260 new mattresses to be made,* thanks to the assistance of my dear friend and interpreter Mark. On another visit, I

Mark admiring our new metal beds and mattresses in an orphanage

was able to provide *90 new metal beds and 90 new mattresses.* To these orphan children, it made a *huge* difference.

Our second challenge seemed even greater, when we tackled the horrific, soiled toilets and washbasins. So often, it meant replacing a complete system of corroded and broken plumbing pipes running throughout a building, in order to enable a water supply to reach the washrooms we were renovating.

These were *big projects* and in 2004, we tackled the most challenging in Parkani Orphanage in Transnistria. I was so grateful to my friend Mark for offering to oversee this project for me and I knew too, that I could trust him completely to instruct honest and capable plumbers and builders. Mark had been my faithful friend for several years and now runs his own mission to help orphans in Transnistria, *Help the Children.* He speaks perfect English too, having been to Bible College in South Wales. Systematically, we worked our way through *ten* horrendous, *foul-smelling,* squalid washrooms with filthy, encrusted, broken toilets and awful, rusty, stained washbasins, *the worst I'd ever seen.*

By the time we'd finished this huge project, we'd installed new, clean, flushing toilets and new washbasins with running water, plus new pipework, in all of the *ten* washrooms. It had been an enormous feat and we were delighted. And so was the Director of the Orphanage. In fact, he was so delighted with our renovation work that he *opened the door* for us to speak to the orphan children. This was definitely an answer to prayer as, due to the former Soviet Communist regime, this Transnistrian orphanage had always been closed to the gospel message.

Julie

However, the Director kept his word to us and, on Saturday, 11th December 2004, we held our first *Christmas party* for the 270 orphan children led by Julie, our young missionary in Transnistria. We noticed that the Director himself attended our party and sat listening intently to our Christmas message. *What would his reaction be?*

To our great relief, and to Julie's credit, he was delighted with our presentation. He was moved too, at the children's obvious pleasure and enthusiasm, and even more surprised when we gave each child a bag of lovely Christmas gifts. To see these poor orphan children brimming over with such joy and excitement, was truly wonderful. Never, shall I forget their happy, smiling faces and shining eyes.

445

But this isn't the end of this story. After the party, Julie and I had a meeting with the Director and we obtained permission for Julie to visit the orphanage every Friday afternoon to teach Bible lessons to the children. This was indeed *a miracle.* Then, in the Spring of 2005, we arranged for a trained sports teacher to join Julie at Parkani Orphanage to reach out to the older children through football, volleyball and aerobics, on Monday afternoons.

We were also given permission to hold an *Easter party* for the 270 children, and we were especially delighted that the Director of the orphanage, along with all the precious children, sat listening attentively to Julie's Easter message. She told them that Jesus Christ, the Son of God, loves them all so very much and that He suffered and died on a cross at Calvary. She explained that He was *innocent* of any crime and yet, He took all our sins upon Himself and was crucified in our place, to set us free. Julie continued to tell the children that three days later, Jesus rose victorious from the grave, to live forever and ever. And the *good news* for all of us, is that when we sincerely repent of our sins and ask Jesus to be our Lord and Saviour, we too will live forever and ever with Him in Heaven when we die.

At the end of this Easter party, we had a very special surprise gift for each of the happy and excited children. We told them to *"hold out your hands!"* and then we placed a lovely knitted chick with a Cadbury's crème egg inside, into their expectant little hands. Well, their faces lit up with absolute joy! And many of the children told us that they could not forget eating their crème egg, as it was the *best and most tastiest thing they had ever had.*

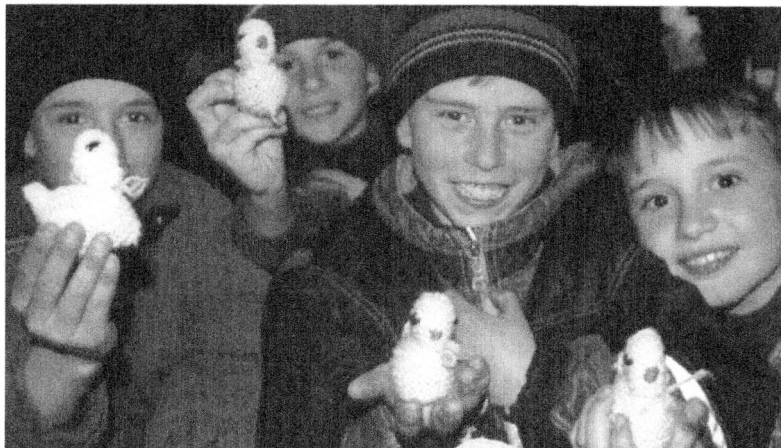

In fact, we took thousands of crème eggs out to Moldova to distribute to excited children in many orphanages, hospitals, schools and churches, and many adults enjoyed them too. These hand knitted chicks and chocolate crème eggs became so popular and in such demand that one Easter, on our early Spring truck, we took out over **4,000** hand knitted chicks and a staggering **18,000** Cadbury's crème eggs.   *It was simply amazing!*

Julie, our enthusiastic and splendid young missionary, also taught three times a week in a special needs kindergarten, and two afternoons each week in a home for children with physical and mental disabilities. She taught these children Bible stories, hymns and prayers and they really loved and looked forward to their lessons. Then one day, the children told Julie that, *"they are not afraid of the dark any more, because Jesus loves them!"* This really touched all of our hearts.

Prison ministry

I worked too, with Julie's father Valentin, who was totally committed to serving the Lord in prison ministry. We supported him in this truly worthwhile voluntary work in two men's prisons in Tiraspol, the capital of Transnistria. One was a men's pre-release prison and we were delighted when this prison granted us permission to renovate a room as a worship room, where Valentin could minister to the male prisoners. We also began a library of Christian literature for them too.

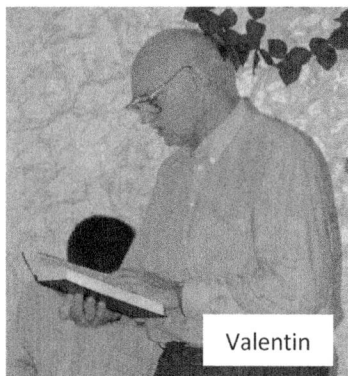

Valentin

On several occasions, I had the privilege to attend Sunday afternoon services led by Valentin, accompanied by his pastor and other church members, and my dear friend *Olesya* came too, as my interpreter. I was often invited to speak to the prisoners and, on one of these occasions, we were overjoyed when a prisoner stepped forward to repent of his sins and receive Jesus Christ as his Lord and Saviour. Wonderfully, a total of *sixteen* other prisoners had already repented under his ministry.

Valentin ministered in a *high security* prison too, and we provided Bibles and hymn books for both prisons. We often helped Valentin's group of prisoners

A prisoner praying the Prayer of Salvation

with their personal needs, such as writing paper, stamps, and clothes. To continue encouraging these men in their new faith in Jesus, Valentin had a *follow-up ministry* helping the prisoners upon their release, to find a place to live, get a job and join a church that would support them and help them spiritually to stay close to the Lord.

On several occasions, Valentin invited me to his home and I enjoyed spending time with him and his wife, who always took great trouble to give me some tasty food to eat. Occasionally, their daughter Julie would be there too and indeed, it was a great pleasure to support this family and encourage them in their difficult and challenging ministries.

Visits to Moldova

I visited Moldova three times a year. Generally two weeks in March ready for Easter, six weeks in the summer and another two weeks in late November ready for Christmas. Ross always accompanied me every summer but, as he grew older, he began coming out with me on my other visits too. Sometimes, in the summer, he chose to remain in

Moldova after I returned home, to oversee some of our many on-going renovation projects and spend some well-deserved time relaxing with his many young friends before school began again.   Finally, Ross was capable of going out by himself. He had learnt *the ropes* and was incredibly capable at organising multiple major building projects, children's out-reach camps and teams of volunteers which included his older brother *Leon,* who came out for his second summer. *Thank you and well done Leon, for returning to help us in Moldova. And well done Ross, for all your faithful hard work. I'm so proud of you both!*

However, towards the end of our Summer 2004 visit, I became very ill and had a difficult journey home. I had con-tracted gastroenteritis and was forced to rest from all my duties for several weeks. It was during this recuperation period that I received an unexpected telephone call.   The caller asked, *"Do you remember me?"* Of course I did! It was *Paul,* the man I'd met three years earlier at Belfast International Airport. He continued, *"Well, I'll be with you in twenty minutes!"* True to his word, he arrived at my front door with a bottle of Schloer and a Battenburg sponge cake, *my favourites.* We chatted for hours together and then he stayed for dinner with Ross and me. Paul visited me several times during my convalescence, before returning to Papua New Guinea to serve the Lord. Thankfully, I soon regained my health and began my work for the Lord too, with fresh gusto.

Leon's first visit

For the first time ever, in the summer of 2005, I had the joy and pleasure of having *both* my dear sons *Leon* and *Ross* with me in Moldova. As usual, we had a full schedule ahead of us, with never a spare minute to ourselves. We were constantly travelling around Moldova and Transnistria visiting orphanages, hospitals, churches, children's camps, prisons, poor families, and overseeing building projects. As always, wherever we went, we were busy distributing aid from our Summer truck, including Every Home Crusade gospel literature, in both Russian and Romanian. This hectic 2005 summer visit culminated in our deaf adults' Bible study residential camp, where Ross and I were baptised by Pastor Anton.

E very circumstance and experience was so new and very different for Leon, during his first visit to Moldova. Although he'd seen photos of our work and become accustomed to what we did, he still found himself deeply shocked and challenged by the many sights and situations he experienced. But thankfully, due to what he saw and the needy people he met, and being able to see firsthand how we helped them, plus being present to witness Ross and me being baptised *for our faith in Jesus Christ,* he returned back home to Dundee in Scotland, and gave his own heart to the Lord Jesus too. *Thank You Lord for blessing Leon, and for answering our prayers for him.*

Families we loved

R oss and I enjoyed taking Leon to meet some of the poorest families we'd been helping over the years and whom we'd grown to love. None of them, however, had a telephone, so we always arrived unexpected. This was good on two counts. Firstly, it always succeeded in giving them a huge surprise, especially when we arrived with boxes of aid for them.   Secondly, it meant we could see for ourselves exactly the way they were living every day. They didn't have time to cover anything up or hide things.   This may sound cruel, but it was often the only way to find out their real needs.   And these needs were often horrific and cried out for immediate help.

I was always filled with deep compassion and a compelling drive to help the many suffering families we met, all of whom struggled to live on literally just a few pounds a month.   And, all too often, I found them trying to look after an elderly or severely handicapped loved one with no help, not even a wheelchair.   Other times, I found them fearful of the oncoming winter, when they faced the inevitable sub-zero, freezing weather conditions, knowing that they had no heating fuel, very little food, no warm clothes or even any proper shoes.

Yes, the needs were enormous, but I firmly believed that every time God showed me a dire need, He would faithfully supply the resources.   And He always did.   So, before each challenging day of visiting these families, never knowing what new needs would confront us, we would fill our vehicle with as many boxes of essential aid, toiletries and food as possible, plus some *drawstring bags of gifts* for the children.   When we entered a home, it didn't take us very long to learn the greatest needs of each family or individual, and our aim was always the same, *to help them as much as possible.*

The Elderly Couple

How I loved this couple.   The elderly husband was blind and his wife had been paralyzed for over fifteen years, due to a severe stroke.   Whenever we arrived to visit them, the husband gave me the biggest, welcoming hugs imaginable and then, using his hands, *felt* Ross to find out how much taller he'd grown! His wife too, gave us loving smiles, as she lay quietly in bed, waiting for me to come to her. Then, as I crossed the room to her bedside, her face lit up in genuine friendship as I held her crippled hands in mine and lovingly kissed her cheek.

During each visit to them, we did our best to provide for them and to make their lives more comfortable. First of all, we accomplished the daunting task of connecting running water into their little house and then we replaced their old, broken heating boiler with a brand new one, which pleased the blind man immensely. Next, came a new, clean bath, then a desperately needed new gas cooker and a much longed for fridge. We even managed to install a washing machine for them which was a tremendous help, as it saved the dear old blind man bending down to do their washing in the bath.

The *blind* husband had to do everything in the house from nursing his wife, to doing the washing and the cooking. He explained to me one day, that

The Elderly Couple with Ross, Leon and me

when he wants to cook some potatoes, he puts them in a bowl and peels them as best he can. He then carries the bowl of potatoes over to his crippled wife, who points out to him the bits he has missed. I was deeply touched by this, and marvelled at how this lovely couple worked together as a team, helping each other to do what we would consider to be simple, everyday tasks. Then one day, I asked the elderly husband how he finds his way around the yard outside their home. He promptly took me to their doorway and showed me a series of washing lines, all of which were attached to a point above their entrance door. He then showed me that each washing line was stretched across the yard and attached to a different point on the far side. All he had to do was learn which washing line led to where and, by holding on to one of them, let it guide him to where he wanted to go. Once again, I was totally amazed at this simple answer to my question.

Then one day, while visiting this Elderly Couple, we brought them one of our much-loved *Family Boxes*. These were very large and deep oblong boxes filled to capacity with all sorts of household and toiletry items, clothing and toys that a poor family in Moldova would like. They included useful items such as a box of matches, candles, potato peeler, washing-up bowl and brush, dustpan and brush, cleaning cloths, shoe polish, sewing kit, pots and pans, warm hats, scarves and gloves for the very cold winters, nightwear, new underwear, cutlery, cutting boards, etc., plus colouring books, crayons, felt-tip pens and toys for the children. These wonderful *treasure trove Family Boxes* of mixed aid were packed and donated to us by kind and generous supporters throughout Northern Ireland. It took tremendous work to fill just one box, and I was always amazed at the quantity of *Family Boxes* we kept receiving to send out on our lorries. However, although we gladly issued a *Suggestion List* of suitable items to pack inside these boxes, it could still be like a lucky dip, as every box was individually packed by a different person, family or group, and I never knew exactly what was inside any one of them.

One particular day, when we were planning to visit the Elderly Couple, we chose *at random* a Family Box for them from our store of aid in Transnistria, hoping it would be a nice surprise for them. However, when we arrived at their home with our special gift, I was slightly alarmed when the blind husband made a very specific request, *"I need a new frying pan. My old one is worn out. I hope there's one inside this box!"* Well, to be honest, during each trip, I had given away huge quantities of Family Boxes and watched them being opened by delighted families, but I'd *never* seen a frying pan inside one of them. Immediately, I began silently praying, *"Oh Lord, please let there be a frying pan inside this box!"*

As we helped the eager and very hopeful elderly husband pull off the brown parcel tape and open the large box, I kept on praying. He lifted out each item, one by one, which had so lovingly been packed by supporters back home. He and his wife were pleased and very grateful for each item, but I could clearly see that he was firmly focused on receiving just one specific item, and he wasn't about to give up. And then, as he felt down further into the box, he suddenly let out a shriek of delight and *held up a frying pan!* I could hardly believe me eyes and breathed a big sigh of relief. The tense atmosphere was immediately broken and we all burst out laughing. The old man was so thrilled with his new frying pan and kept waving it around to show us. I was thrilled for him too, as it was such a joy to see him and his wife so happy. But I knew too, that God had guided us to choose this particular box for them, and quietly thanked Him for this *miracle.*

This dear old blind man knew what he wanted, and refused to give up hope. He had the faith to believe that God would provide what he desperately needed, and that it would be inside this box. *"Thank you Jesus, for Your love and faithfulness to this dear blind husband and for rewarding his faith."* When it was time for us to leave this dear Elderly Couple, we gave them both loving and affectionate good-bye hugs, and Ross whispered to me, *"Don't cry Mum!"*

From tears of sorrow, to tears of *joy!*

We never ever knew when a really *urgent* call for help would come, but I always believed that if God showed us a desperate need, then He would faithfully provide the means to answer the call and He always did, without fail.

One of those sudden urgent calls came one bitterly cold and snowy day in March 2005, when a pastor in Transnistria asked me if I could possibly help a family in his congregation who was in *utter despair.*   When I went to visit this desperately poor family and their two small children, I learnt that their chimney had caught fire and *burnt the whole roof off* their single storey home. Only a few charred rafters remained and the whole interior of their home was blackened and completely sodden. It was a real mess and all their belongings had been ruined too. It was indeed a heartbreaking disaster and the poor family were truly desperate and so very fearful. They needed help straight away and yet, *how on earth could they repair such extensive damage?* But God made a way for them and led us to help them, by funding all the repairs. One kind neighbour helped too, by donating some large timber poles and others shared their homes with them. Before too long, *their home was completely rebuilt* and the interior was clean and habitable again. We gave them lots of essential aid from our trucks, including some beautiful hand knitted warm blankets and Family Boxes, plus some toys for their two small children. We continued to help this family until they had fully recovered from their frightening ordeal and, when I visited them in their refurbished home, I was greeted with grateful hugs and *tears of joy* which, thankfully, had replaced their *tears of sorrow*. Once again, we thanked God for His mercy and wonderful provision, and for the opportunity to show His love to this dear family in a very real way.

Burnt house and roof

All restored!

Chocolate!

There were so very many poor families that we helped and loved, and each one of them has a touching story to tell.   But this particular story is about nine-year-old Christina, who has cerebral palsy. She could not stand or walk, or chew her food, but she simply loved the Weetabix we brought her from our aid. We also discovered that she really loves chocolate, and I always made sure I had some for her. Then, when one of our kind supporters back home heard me speaking about her at a meeting, they raised enough money to buy her *two* special incontinence underblankets, which was a truly wonderful gift for her. Another kind supporter bought her large supplies of nappies, which was a tremendous blessing. Both of these generous donations to Christina were a most welcome help for her Mum, as they had no running water in their home. Although we made every effort to rectify this, it sadly proved to be impossible as, apparently, the water pipes would have had to pass right under their house. But thankfully, we were able to help them in many other ways, including giving them a new portable 2-ring electric hob and oven for their kitchen. Ross and I took Leon to visit her during the summer of 2005 and we were all delighted when Christina sat quietly on her Mum's lap and happily held Leon's hand. It was a precious moment for all of us.

Leon with Christina

Happy Birthday Alexei!

We also took Leon to visit our dear friend Alexei, whom we'd been visiting since he was eighteen years old. He was a pitiful sight when I first saw him in 2002 and I knew I had to help him. He was lying with a broken back and huge raw bedsores on both hips, in appalling conditions in an orphanage for mentally and physically handicapped men in Transnistria. It was the most depressing place and it broke my heart to see Alexei confined there.

However, I soon found out that he had sustained his broken back from a diving accident and was now, tragically, paralyzed from the waist down. Consequently, his parents abandoned him and placed him in this terrible place. Very sadly too, his mother refused to ever contact him again. Needless to say, when I first saw Alexei, he was in a desperate state both physically and emotionally, but I knew God had led me to meet him and I just couldn't forget about him.

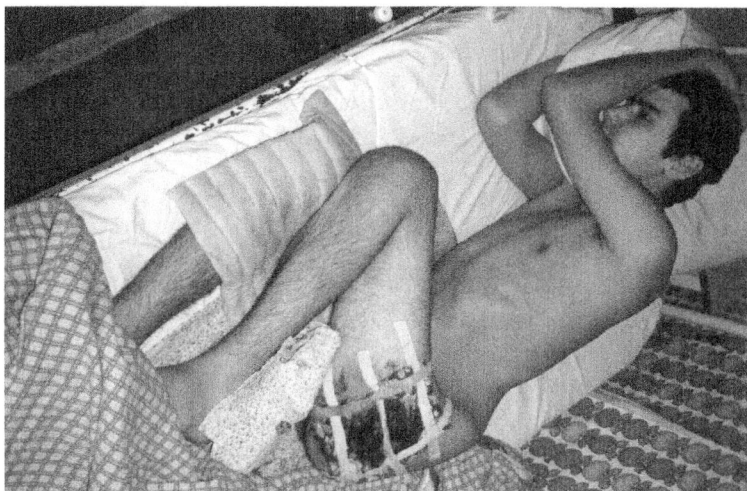

So, from that point on, we began helping him in earnest and my first desire was to get him into a room of his own and away from the alarming outbursts, taunting and bullying of the other male patients. But this was not an easy option, and was far more difficult to achieve than I first imagined. In fact, it was only after a great deal of determined negotiation with the Director of this institution, that we were granted permission to completely renovate a disused, derelict, corner room. But it was *a room with a view,* due to its double aspect windows overlooking trees and the surrounding grounds. *It was perfect* and just what we wanted for Alexei.

Clearly, from the outset, this was going to be another *challenging project* and I was so grateful yet again, that my dear friend and interpreter Mark agreed to oversee the

459

lengthy renovation work for me. He was very pleased too, to be able to help Alexei and soon instructed builders to begin the task of completely rebuilding this decrepit room. We knew these renovations were going to be considerable, including a complete new concrete floor, and they were! The crumbling walls and ceiling had to be repaired and re-plastered, the ancient windows needed replacing, heating radiators had to be installed, and running water brought into his room so he could have his own wash basin.

Alexei in a new room of his own. Clean and light!

However, this project turned out to be even bigger than we first anticipated, especially when we kept encountering unexpected problems. But in the end, it was worth all the effort because *Alexei now has a splendid room all of his own.* He was overjoyed and so were we. *"Thank You Mark, for all your invaluable help."* And a sincere *thank you* too, to all our supporters back home in Northern Ireland, for helping Alexei get his lovely new room.

Next, we needed a good bed for Alexei and we brought him a special hospital bed with a waterproof mattress on one of our trucks. We also brought him an overhanging pulley, which was especially donated for him, so he could pull himself up from a lying position more easily. Someone else donated a special massage mattress for him too. So many of our kind supporters back home cared about him and donated lots of gifts, including a new TV, video player, Playstation, and lots of games that children eagerly gave us when they'd finished playing with them. So, every time I visited Alexei, I had new computer games to give him. His ambition now, was to practice playing them between my visits, so that when Ross was with me, the two of them could battle it out together. As you can imagine, *Alexei usually won!* And then, when we took Leon to meet him, Alexei and Leon talked non-stop about *computers.*   Alexei was thrilled to meet Leon and have this stimulating conversation.

We continued to visit Alexei as often as we could, but every summer we made every effort to visit him on his birthday and, the day we took Leon to see him, it was his twenty-first birthday. As in previous years, we took him gifts and treats and, of course, a birthday cake. *Happy Birthday Alexei!*

Yes, we love Alexei and we always will.   But what is even more important, is that *he knows we love him and pray for him.* He knows too, that *Jesus loves him and always will.*

Dreams can come true

During one summer in Transnistria, Ross and I first visited Ludmilla and Alla, her thirty-two-year-old daughter, and I learnt that Alla had been paralyzed for the last thirty years. She was lying on a filthy collapsing bed, and she and her mum lived together in just one room, with no bathroom, kitchen, toilet or running

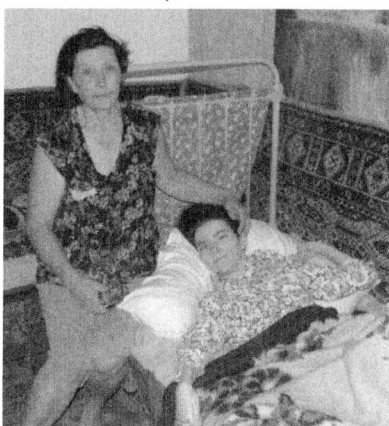

water. They were indeed desperately poor and were living on barely £15 per month. Their clothes were torn, Alla's bed sheets were terrible and they had very little food. However, the day of our first visit, we had three large boxes of ladies' clothes with us and, to our amazement, it was Ludmilla's birthday! Yes, God is so good and His timing is always perfect. Ludmilla squealed with delight as she tried on lots of new clothes and winter coats.   It was so wonderful to see her happy, especially on her birthday.

We had some special gifts for Alla too, all donated to us by generous supporters back home. We gave her a new support pillow and *two* special incontinence underblankets that hold two litres of fluid, plus some incontinence pads. We had some beautiful hand knitted warm blankets for them too. *Thank You Lord, for letting us help these two women and bring joy into their impoverished lives.*

A few months later, I visited them again but this time, instead of seeing hopeless, despairing faces, I was greeted

Ludmilla's awful old cooking contraption

with happy, cheerful smiles. Ludmilla too, was looking lovely in her new clothes and she proudly showed me the brand new gas cooker that we'd just had installed for her.   Her old, miniscule cooking *contraption* was unspeakably awful, and I don't know how she managed to cook anything on it. In fact, I'm not sure it was ever supposed to be used for cooking, as it looked more like a tiny room heater. But now, *her dream of having a new oven* had come true and she was thrilled.

But during our first visit to them, I learnt that *Alla also had a dream.* She dreamt of having a TV to watch while she lay in bed all day. And *her dream finally came true* when we gave her a brand new TV and she was totally overjoyed. We also brought them a new bed each and some new bed linen from our truck of aid.

But we had yet another *big surprise* in store for them when, the following year, we made another dream come true. We built them a new extension to their home, providing a proper kitchen and a brand new bathroom *with running water.* Ludmilla told us that she kept waking up in the middle of the night, to go into her new kitchen and bathroom to make sure she wasn't dreaming, and that they were still there!

Ludmilla in her new clothes, standing
beside her new gas oven

Yes, with God, dreams can come true!

Chapter 41

The Real Joy

Needless to say, the constant appeals for *urgent* help were simply **enormous.** And yet, the bigger the need, the more thrilling and amazing it was to see how God would always *faithfully* and wonderfully provide for us, and at just the right time ...

> *"And my God will meet all your needs*
> *according to His glorious riches*
> *in Christ Jesus."*
> (Philippians 4:19)

Continually, year after year, I never stopped thanking and praising the Lord for His awesome provision of our ever increasing needs, and that we were able to give **100% of every single financial donation that we received** towards our projects in Moldova.

Thankfully, our two **Mission Moldova Sunflower charity shops**, staffed by a faithful team of great volunteers, provided sufficient funds to adequately cover all the charity's growing expenses and operating costs. This meant that *100%* of every gift that we received, was used *100%* for our Mission Moldova projects. This was such a wonderful blessing.

One of our charity shops

An Urgent appeal for help

In early January 2003, we received an urgent email concerning the plight of thirty-two children in a TB Hospital situated in Benderi, Transnistria. The youngest child was only fourteen months old and the oldest was seventeen years old.

This TB hospital had no funds to buy the vital medication needed to treat the children and, when it did, they could only afford medication that treated the TB, but destroyed the liver. This hospital also had no hot water nor even any light bulbs, and the children were sleeping on filthy, urine stained mattresses with torn blankets. Their desperate heart cry in their email read, *"Can you please help us?"* And our reply? ....*"Yes we can!"*

Immediately, we arranged for sufficient funds to be released to buy everything they needed. Within days, their *cry for help* was answered and the aid was delivered to them by one of the pastors we worked with. We also arranged for a quantity of Children's Illustrated Russian Bibles to be taken into the hospital and we prayed that these children would soon learn that Jesus loved them and wanted to be their personal Saviour and best Friend.

Over the following months, we continued helping this TB Hospital by ripping out all their old, broken toilets and wash-basins, and replacing them with new ones. We installed new,

Some new mattresses with waterproof covers, plus aid

wall-mounted hot water boilers in the bathrooms and, on our next truck, we brought out two large portable water boilers that had been donated specifically for this hospital. We also provided them with *thirty* new metal beds and *ninety-five* new mattresses with detachable waterproof covers, plus lots of tins of paint to refresh the walls and, of course, plenty of light bulbs. We also gave them supplies of sheets, towels, new pyjamas and toys for the children and made sure that the doctors had the essential TB medication they really needed.

Then, we had the pleasure of fulfilling the hope of a local pastor, who'd been praying for a TV and video recorder in the wards, so that he could teach the children Bible stories. Unbeknown to him, we went to a local electrical store near to the TB hospital and bought him just what he wanted.   He was really delighted with this surprise gift.

I visited this children's TB hospital on several occasions and took them lots of aid from our trucks, including lovely soft toys for the little ones. It was always a treat to see these children looking so happy in their new clean beds, cuddling their new toys. The doctors and nurses were very happy too and extremely thankful that we'd responded so quickly to their urgent appeal for help and for everything we'd done for them.

But I too, was so grateful and thankful. Thankful to the Lord for giving us so many generous and kind supporters back home, who enabled us to respond immediately to this hospital's urgent call for help.

A New oven

During one of my early visits to Moldova, I was taken to see a woman who was struggling to bring up her six children by herself. It was summertime, and we found her cooking outside in her yard. She looked tired and the children seemed listless. Then I noticed her *cooker.* It was just one very small blackened and corroded electric ring with an even unhealthier looking frying pan upon it. This was her sole means of cooking meals for all seven of them.

Although we were able to cheer her young children with some new knitted teddies and toys, I held a lingering sadness in my heart for this family. I wanted to help them and I wanted to see these children happy.

Back home in Northern Ireland, when telling of her plight at a church meeting, a gentleman came up to me and told me that he had an electrical shop in town and that he wanted to donate a brand new electric cooker, just for this lady. I was absolutely delighted at his generous and kind offer and, on our next truck, we took out this new oven.

At last, the day arrived to deliver our precious cargo to this family and we took a qualified electrician with us to carry out the necessary installation. As usual, our arrival was a surprise and when we told them the purpose of our visit, their excitement reached fever level. It was just like Christmas for them, as the children's little hands worked overtime tearing off the plastic and cardboard protective wrappings to reveal their brand new oven. Suddenly, there was a hushed silence, as everyone gasped at the sight of this *splendid new cooker.* I was impressed too and so happy for them ...

> *" So in everything, do to others*
> *what you would have them do to you."*
> (Matthew 7:12)

With great enthusiasm, we were shown where they wanted their prized new possession to be placed and our electrician set to work. Then alas, we heard the worst of news. The electricity supply in this home was incapable of empowering even *one single ring* of this cooker, let alone a whole oven. Instantly, despair and huge disappointment filled everyone's hearts and all the children were nearly in tears.

So what was the answer? Surely we couldn't disappoint them now? There was only one answer. And that was to *completely rewire* their entire home. And that's exactly what we did.

When I next visited this family, I arrived on the perfect day, *baking day.* The mother proudly carried out to me a tray of the most delicious looking bread buns that she'd just baked in her new oven, and she even insisted on giving me a bagful. This splendid new cooker changed their lives enormously. Instead of being greeted with sadness, the children's faces now beamed with happiness and real *joy.*

Slobodzea Hospital

This was another desperately needy hospital in Transnistria that we helped considerably. On my first visit, I was taken to the two children's wards, the infectious diseases ward, the operating theatre and the maternity ward. I was totally appalled at what I saw and could hardly believe the antiquated equipment being used, the filthy mattresses that patients had to lie on, the broken toilets, wash basins with no taps, and *no hot water at all* in the hospital.

But what appalled me most, was what I saw in the maternity ward. The nurses held up for me pieces of discoloured and foul-smelling cotton sheeting material, approximately 3ft x 4ft, that were placed

Getting ready to visit the infectious diseases ward

under women when giving birth and also used for wrapping newborn babies in. A piece of this stained, horrible material

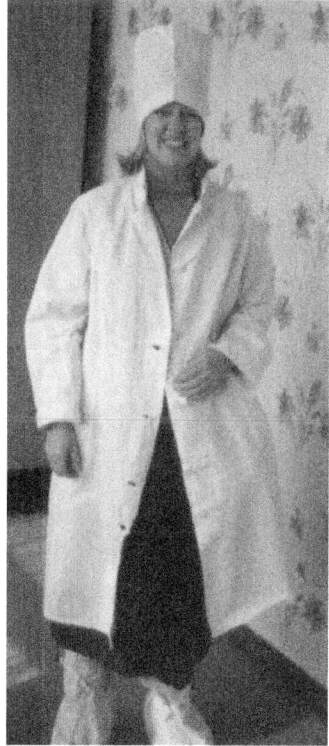

469

was a baby's nappy and clothes *all in one*. With no hot water in the maternity ward to wash either the women after giving birth or their newborn babies, and no hot water to wash these soiled birthing cloths, I was determined that large, wall-mounted water boilers had to be installed as quickly as possible. To me, this was a real priority.

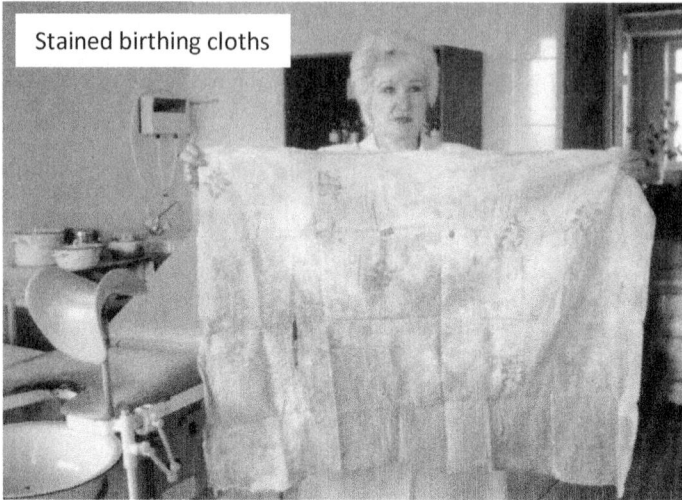

Stained birthing cloths

The doctors and nurses were desperate for our help and without delay, we responded to their great need by providing new hospital beds, 150 new clean mattresses with detachable waterproof covers, new large wall-mounted water boilers, baby hospital beds, medication, tins of paint and, of course, this hospital needed lots of light bulbs too! We then began working our way through the hospital, ward by ward, replacing and repairing the broken toilets and washbasins. But I was particularly pleased when the new water boilers were installed in the maternity ward so that mothers could, at long last, wash themselves and their newborn babies properly in *hot* water. Several more additional free-standing water boilers were donated from churches back home for this ward and now, quite wonderfully, from having no hot water

470

at all, they suddenly had plenty! I was very thankful too, that ladies back home quickly responded to another great need in this maternity ward, by making lots of new *birthing cloths* out of strong, clean 100% cotton material.

All the doctors and nurses, especially those in the maternity ward, were so very grateful for our help and our genuine concern for them and told me that they had not received any help for the last *twenty-six years.* I visited this hospital as often as I could and I too was very thankful, as our much needed aid and improvements *opened the door* for Pastor Victor and members of his local church to visit and befriend the many hapless patients. Their regular visits brought welcome cheer, encouragement and *fresh hope* to the staff and patients alike.

Young brothers

S lobodzea Hospital often became a temporary orphanage, as well as a hospital. Children, and even babies, were regularly abandoned by their parents and the hospital staff were left to look after them. This was an incredibly distressing experience for the children and their behaviour often became extremely difficult to handle. On one of

Two sad brothers

my visits, I was taken to see a pair of young brothers who had been abandoned. At first, they were angry and wild, and very destructive. They would tear their clothes and even tried to shred their mattresses. They were a real problem to the hospital staff until, finally, they were taken to an orphanage.

471

Several years later, when I was visiting one of the three orphanages we were helping in Transnistria, I was taken to see a group of young children. To my great surprise, I recognised the older one of these two brothers and he remembered me too. He had calmed down by now and become a lovely child. To my delight, he came forward to greet me and even gave me a big hug, which really tugged at my heart. I then enquired about his younger brother and was so pleased to learn that he too, was in the same orphanage. To my great joy, I was taken to see a group of younger children and was able to meet this little one as well.

A brave little boy

On a later visit to Slobodzea Hospital, the nurses took me to see a sad little boy, who was about three years old, lying in a cot. They told me that he'd been found on a rubbish tip and that he'd been lying there, during the freezing cold weather, for three whole days. His little body was so frozen, that he couldn't walk and the doctors feared that he never would be able to again. My heart broke when I heard this story.

Then, nearly a year later, on another visit to this hospital, *word went around* that I'd arrived.   Hurriedly, some flowers growing outside the hospital were picked and guess who brought them to me? Walking up the corridor towards me, carrying a bunch of lovely flowers, was the little boy from the rubbish tip. *He was healed and walking! It was a miracle* and I was absolutely thrilled to greet this brave little boy and receive his kind gift. *Thank You Lord* for healing this dear child and for answering our prayers to heal him.

Pastor Victor and his church

When I first met Pastor Victor, he took me to see his little church in Slobodzea, not too far from the hospital.   The single storey building I saw that day, very obviously needed an enormous amount of *tender loving care.* But, first of all, I made sure his congregation had all the Bibles and hymn books they needed, before starting on the building work, which was *extensive.*   Yet Pastor Victor and his gathering of believers were grateful for any kind of building and overjoyed to have a place of their own in which to worship the Lord Jesus. But, to be truthful, the building needed *everything* from exterior plastering, guttering, windows, gas central heating, a kitchen, dining room with tables and chairs, lighting, outside toilet house, exterior paved area, plus new seating for the congregation. *A substantial list.*

Praise God! A lovely little church when we finished

It took a great deal of work to transform this meagre building into a lovely place of worship, but eventually it was finished and everyone was delighted. The newly paved exterior areas were perfect for children's summer camps, which we gladly supported. It was always wonderful to see so many children having fun and enjoying themselves, while hearing the gospel message too. At the end of each camp, we gave every child a lovely Children's Illustrated Bible.

Pastor Victor and his whole family soon became very dear friends of mine and his wife was a super cook. Whenever I visited their home, she made some delicious *borscht soup* especially for me and, without fail, it was the best I'd ever tasted. She always

Lovely church interior too!

gave me another treat too, one of her large jars of *blackcurrant preserve,* which I absolutely adored!

Feeding the Poor

Our *Feeding the Poor* programme provided good healthy meals to those in need and it began in Pastor Vitali's church in Speir, Transnistria. Having recently extensively renovated his church too, including central heating, a kitchen and dining room, we began feeding poor children and the elderly six days a week with a bowl of hot soup and bread, followed by a main course. This new project not only fed these people physically, but spiritually too, as many of them came to his church for the very first time and experienced the loving care of Jesus in their lives.

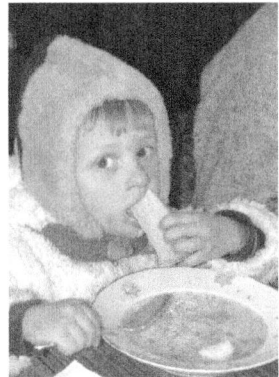

Pastor Vitali and his whole family also became very dear friends of mine and it was always a pleasure to see them. In fact, every time I met Pastor Vitali, he would smile warmly and say to me, *"Don't forget Philippians 1:6".* This was always a great encourage to me ...

"Being confident of this,
that He who began a good work in you
will carry it on to completion
until the day of Christ Jesus"
(Philippians 1:6)

Our *Feeding the Poor* project was so successful in Pastor Vitali's church, that we extended it to Pastor Victor's church in Slobodzea too.   Thus, their newly equipped kitchen and dining room was quickly put to good use by providing wholesome meals for poor children and the elderly, four days a week.

"Now, is there anything you need?"

I was busy working one day in one of our two *Mission Moldova Sunflower charity shops*, when a customer began chatting to me about our projects in Moldova.   Then, quite unexpectedly, she asked me a direct question, *"Is there anything you **really** need now in Moldova?   Anything in particular?"*

This was an easy question to answer, *"Floor tiles!"*   I told her that we'd recently begun helping the Agape Church in Chisinau with their immense four-storey church building programme and they needed floor tiles ... *masses of them.* She stood pondering this for a moment before replying, *"I think I know someone who might help you."*

God's hand of blessing was most certainly working in an amazing way as, just a few days later, I received a phone call inviting me to visit a large tile company, not too far away from my home. When I arrived at their impressive showroom, I was met by one of the Christian owners who said, *"Yes, we can help you. We can supply all the tiles you need for the church you are helping!"* Whaoo, this was absolutely amazing!

And better still, this kind man insisted on donating the very best porcelain floor tiles *and* wall tiles for the Agape Church. He then asked me about our other projects in Moldova and I told him we were planning to renovate the terrible men's and women's cloakrooms in the Bethel Church in Chisinau, by installing ten new toilets and washbasins. To my complete amazement, he offered to provide the same beautiful floor and wall tiles for the Bethel Church too!

All in all, we needed a staggering *33 tons of tiles* from the

manufacturers in Italy. This *lion-hearted man* agreed to donate ALL of them to us. What an incredible *miracle!* And what a huge *blessing* and great *kindness* too.

Thankfully, Ross offered to help me by arranging for *two* Moldovan trucks to travel all the way to Italy to collect this massive quantity of tiles and, as soon as they arrived back in Chisinau, work began in both churches immediately. Pastor Anton and everyone in the

476

Bethel Church were all delighted with their newly renovated and beautifully tiled cloakrooms.   And indeed, they looked *splendid.*   It was so exciting too, to see the first of these beautiful porcelain floor tiles being laid in the Agape Church. They looked really *fantastic.*

But it was even more exciting for me personally when, just two years later, Ross married his beautiful sweetheart *Olesya,* my dear friend and interpreter, in the newly completed and splendidly tiled Agape Church, which made a perfect setting for their wedding.

"Thank You Lord, for these wonderful and divine blessings!"

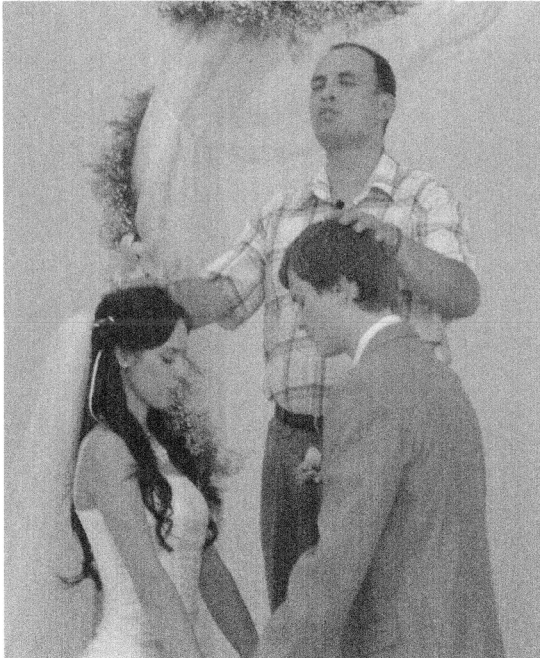

Ross and Olesya at their wedding

Chapter 42

Give God the Glory!

Victoria, my good friend, was not about to let me forget *my promise.* My promise to help The Bible Society of Moldova, by sponsoring their new *True Light project* to share the good news of the gospel of Jesus Christ with *blind and partially sighted people.* I soon realised that this was going to be a huge undertaking, as approximately *forty* centres for the blind operate throughout Moldova. But wonderfully, we succeeded in sponsoring all but a few of them.

Having never personally met a blind person before, I simply had no idea of the impact that this ministry would have upon me. Seeing so many blind and partially sighted people living in extreme poverty, struggling to cope with their daily difficulties and hardships, was very disturbing and tore at my heartstrings.

However, one of my first experiences happened to be both happy and very encouraging, when Victoria took me to the home of a young blind girl. During our visit, I had the joy of giving this little girl one of my *wind-up cassette players,* together with a full set of Children's Bible Stories, on cassettes

478

in her own Russian language. As I guided her hand to the handle and encouraged her to turn it round and round, she soon grasped how to do it. It became a new challenge to her, to *wind-up* the machine as fast as she could. This was something she could do all by herself, and happily listen to her Bible stories as often

Blind girl using a *wind-up* cassette player

as she liked. Several months later, Victoria told me that this little girl loved her machine so much and had learnt all the Bible stories by heart. I was so pleased that my gift had brought her so much joy and lots of fun too.

During every visit to Moldova, I attended one or two of the *True Light* evangelism meetings that we held at blind centres. Pastor Anton, being the Director of The Bible Society of Moldova, welcomed everyone and then told them about the love of Jesus Christ. I then followed, with Victoria interpreting for me. Sometimes, we took with us some blind Christian men who played their piano accordion and sang from Braille hymn sheets. Then, twenty-year-old blind *Olga*, whose family we helped and who came to our deaf children's summer camps, read some poems to everyone, using Braille.

These marvellous opportunities of witnessing to blind people were often very powerful, with many women in tears. Hardened hearts were visibly touched, as they began to understand that they are *special* and very *precious* to Jesus, and not social outcasts, and that the Lord loves them dearly. Towards the end of each meeting, we always gave every blind person the *Bible on cassette* (in Russian or Romanian). The partially sighted were each given *two* large hardback books, one containing the Psalms and the other the Four Gospels, both in *very large, clear black print* (in Russian, Romanian or Cyrillic script). We also presented each Blind Unit with new, easy-to-use cassette players, to be used by those who didn't possess one of their own at home.

We then provided a light meal, consisting of bread, buns, cold meats and cheese, plus soft drinks for the people to eat before their journey home. But it always saddened me when I saw a blind person hiding this food in a bag, to take home and eat later. Consequently, especially in the cold winter months, Victoria and I prepared carrier bags full of essential food items to give to each blind person as they left, and these were always very gratefully received. I also gave out quantities of old, but perfectly good spectacles, that opticians back home had collected for me. A partially sighted man at one of our meetings was particularly pleased to receive a pair of these glasses. All he had up till then, was a *single glass lens* which he held up to one of his eyes.

Ross often came with me to these blind evangelizations and we both developed a love and deep compassion for these people and it was always such a joy to be able to help them, even if only in the smallest of ways.

No wood!

During one bitterly cold winter, after a *True Light* evangelisation at a blind centre, Pastor Anton took Victoria and me to visit a poor elderly couple, who couldn't make it to our meeting. It was absolutely *freezing cold* and all the trees were white and glistening from the heavy frost. As we entered their tiny home, the elderly couple sat huddled together trying to keep warm, and tears ran down the cheeks of this blind and handicapped old man. They were both in a deeply distressed state and kept repeating, *"No wood! We have no wood!"*

It was so very upsetting to witness their intense anxiety and fear caused by their dire poverty, and we simply couldn't leave them like this. Thanks to Pastor Anton's help, we managed to make arrangements with a kind neighbour to get them enough wood for the whole winter. *What a blessing to be able to do this.*

Winter fuel fund

After this upsetting experience, I became acutely aware of the desperate need to provide winter fuel help and I set up a *Winter fuel fund.* Henceforth, during my winter visits, I made it a priority to help our very poor *deaf and blind families,* plus the poorest and most vulnerable families in many of the churches that we helped. In the winter of 2004, we were delighted to be able to help over *90 needy families plus 120 blind people.*

Our *Winter fuel fund* proved to be a great blessing to many people during spells of severe cold, and it particularly helped Valya, a single parent with two very young children. She cried out for our help, as her little ones were literally freezing. Very quickly, we were able to provide her with a large quantity of wood. This help not only warmed them physically but also warmed the heart of Valya's landlady, who was *totally against Christians and all their beliefs.* But, when she saw the way Christians cared about each other, she changed her mind and decided to go to Valya's church to get to know Christians better. *Hallelujah!*

Vera and Vanya with the new boots

Then one winter, I received an urgent appeal to help many of the people in our *deaf church in Transnistria* and the poorest families in another church too. *They all desperately needed new winter shoes.* After getting their individual shoe sizes, we bought them all sturdy *black leather, warm fleecy lined, ankle boots* from a local factory. And only just in time, because that winter in Transnistria, the temperatures plummeted to -25ºC with deep snow. My dear friends Vera and Vanya, very kindly organised this project for me.

Blind Inna

I n March 2003, thirteen-year-old blind Inna underwent a serious operation for a brain tumour. It so happened that my flight into Moldova arrived on the evening of her operation and Victoria met me at Chisinau Airport to tell me the awful news. Inna, along with her younger brother, had both repented and accepted Jesus into their hearts at our previous year's deaf children's summer camp and now, very sadly, she was in desperate need of help.

Victoria quickly explained to me that primarily, and most urgently, Inna needed *medication* that the hospital either didn't have or would not supply. Victoria showed me a list that ran into two pages of everything Inna needed, even down to bandages and tape. I was horrified that *nothing* was supplied by the hospital. We spent the next few hours that evening frantically visiting every pharmacy we could find that was still open, trying to fulfil the extensive list of medical needs.

Having successfully bought most of the items and ordered the rest, we then delivered them to Inna's distraught mother, who was sitting at her daughter's bedside. By now, it was getting late in the evening, with no doctors around and no nurses in sight, so Victoria allowed me to sneak in with her, for a quick visit. And what a very sad sight met me, as Inna lay unconscious after her operation, with one side of her face swollen and bandages around her head. The depressing, unkempt ward was crowded, with barely any space between the beds. Nothing looked clean and no-one wore bedclothes. Everyone appeared to be wearing their daytime clothes in bed.   There were certainly no crisp clean sheets or neat bedside lockers in *here*. It was so very different to the clean conditions that, regrettably, I just took for granted in our hospitals back home. But I was really glad that I'd arrived into Moldova just in time to buy Inna's medication, and meet all her hospital needs. Thankfully, she was soon home again, where she lived with her mother and younger brother.

When Victoria and I visited Inna, we found her well and not in any pain after her operation, which was wonderful news. But their flat was absolutely *freezing*. They kept their oven door open with the gas on very low to try to get some heat, but the fumes gave Inna bad headaches. Again, I was horrified and promptly bought them a heater, some food and paid their utility bills.

Blind Olga teaching blind Inna Braille

Young Inna had never been to school and could not read Braille or do even basic maths. However, blind Olga was delighted when we asked her if she would be willing to teach Inna and, every Saturday morning, we arranged for a reliable taxi to bring her to Inna's home and begin teaching her Braille.

We were all really thankful that Inna recovered so well after her operation and that she was able to attend our next children's deaf summer camp with her younger brother. This was indeed, *brilliant news.*

Holly bags

E ver since I first took chocolate bars into an orphanage in Transnistria at Christmastime and saw the sheer delight on the children's faces as they tasted chocolate, possibly for the very first time, I was saddened that the children could enjoy this delicious treat only *once a year*. Being a chocolate lover myself, I knew this was definitely *not enough.* So I decided that the children should have *two* bars each, to extend their joy!

When I shared this idea with some supporters back home and mentioned that it would be nice to give each child a little drawstring bag containing two large choc bars, a kind lady suggesting *knitting* a cheerful little red drawstring bag. Then another lady suggested knitting some green holly leaves and red berries to decorate the bags. And hence, the popular *Mission Moldova Holly Bag* was born!

Two very happy boys with their Holly Bags

Thereafter, every meeting I spoke at in Northern Ireland about Mission Moldova's work, I encouraged ladies to knit these little bags and, to my great surprise, the response was *tremendous.* Parcels of Holly Bags began arriving in the post to my home or were left at one of our Mission Moldova Sunflower charity shops.

By the time I left for Moldova that winter, in late November, I had *1,000 beautiful hand knitted red Holly Bags* packed into my two suitcases, to give to orphan children in Transnistria. And, quite wonderfully, I got my two over-weight suitcases through *free of charge* on the two-flight journey from Dublin Airport out to Moldova. And then, while taking my two large suitcases past the guards at the border crossing into Transnistria, I had no problems either. I thanked God for this blessing, and reckoned that He must have *shut* the eyes of the guards this time!

When I arrived at Vera and Vanya's home, our missionaries in Transnistria, they had already made the necessary arrangements for me to be able to purchase 1,000 *jumbo* size bars of both Mars and Snickers. I then had the enjoyable task of putting one bar of each inside the 1,000 Holly Bags and safely enclosing them, by pulling the crochet cords carefully threaded through the top of each bag.

A few days later, we visited the orphanages with our gifts. When the children realised that they were each receiving a lovely hand knitted Holly Bag containing *two huge choc bars,* their excitement was simply *unbelievable!* It was so amazing and such a wonderful blessing *to see the joy on their faces.*

However, on my flight out to Moldova with these lovely knitted gifts, I'd prayed that God would give me a simple gospel message to give to the orphan children, when I gave them their Holly Bags. And He did. He showed me that ...

- **The holly leaf** is evergreen and does not die ... *the Lord Jesus rose from the grave and lives forever! And so will we too, when we trust in Jesus and live forever with Him in Heaven.*
- **The prickles** around the holly leaf protect the leaf and the holly tree ... *the loving arms of Jesus and the blessed Holy Spirit surround and protect us when we love and trust in Him.*
- The **round holly berries** *remind us of the nail holes in Jesus' hands and feet, when He sacrificially died for us on the cross.*
- The **red holly berries** *remind us of the precious blood of Jesus Christ shed on the cross at Calvary, to cleanse us from our sins, when we repent to Him.*
- The **joy and excitement** of receiving the choc bars *'inside'* the holly bag, *reminds us of the joy and excitement 'inside' our hearts when we receive Jesus as our Lord and Saviour!*

"Oh, give thanks to the Lord, for He is good!
For His mercy endures forever."
(Psalm 107:1 NKJV)

Surprise, surprise

In the winter of 2003, I had an extended stay of one month in Moldova and, as usual, I visited many of our *deaf* friends who lived in the 5-storey deaf hostel in Chisinau, the capital. This crumbling, dilapidated building was unbelievably awful and yet, it was home to 188 deaf men, women and children.

A long dark corridor ran down the centre of each of the upper four floors, with rooms off on either side. Each room housed a family, or up to four individual people (like Violetta and her friends). Everyone had to use the communal cooking area on each floor, which had no storage cupboards and often only two working ovens, shared by countless families. Two separate small areas housed the horrendous, noxious toilet cubicles, four each for men and women. Then, instead of communal wash basins on each floor, there was just *one long trough* covered in broken and chipped tiles, where men and women washed themselves and their clothes. There was no privacy at all. Working light bulbs along the dark corridors and up the dingy stairways was rare, and windows in the building were rotten and did not close properly. It's an horrendous place. But what broke my heart, was that so many of the deaf people we loved so dearly, *lived there.*

At the beginning of my winter 2003 visit, Pastor Anton took me to see the terrible conditions on the fifth floor. I hadn't been up to this top floor before and was shocked at what I saw. The ceilings and walls were black with mould, doors and windows didn't shut, and there was no heating. The people were becoming ill, due to the penetrating damp and unhealthy conditions. I knew in my heart that something just had to be done about this appalling situation, *before* the oncoming winter really set in and snow began falling. *But what?* I had no idea. However, I was completely stunned when Pastor Anton told me the answer to my question, "*A new roof!*" Wow, I hadn't expected this. *A new roof! How much was that going to cost?*

Surprise, surprise, Pastor Anton knew the answer to this question too. But what surprised me even more, was that I discovered, after a careful count of my remaining funds, that *I had just enough money left to pay for this new roof!* And, incredibly, this was *after* meeting all our planned commitments in both Moldova and Transnistria.

As usual, I never knew in advance how much money I would take out with me on each trip, as the amount always varied according to the donations Mission Moldova received. But God knew how much I needed to meet this urgent need, and He sent me out with just the right amount of money. *Praise You Lord!*

However, before any work could begin, Pastor Anton, Victoria and I first had to receive permission from the Director of the Deaf Association and the Director of the hostel. Without any hesitation, they both gave us their agreement to build a new roof and so we began the work *immediately.* A team of local Christian builders came to help us and instead of the normal freezing cold weather at that time of year, the Lord blessed us with fine, dry weather. The

A New Roof being installed!

builders worked tirelessly and just two days before I returned home on 6th December, the new roof was completed. And only just in time, as *snow* was forecast the following day. Even in this finite detail, God was in full control of the weather conditions, holding back the snow until the very last nail was hammered in. He didn't let anything hamper the building of this new roof, not even the weather, until it was all finished. God alone knew the powerful impact that this new roof would have upon the deaf people living in this hostel and upon the heart of the atheist Director of the Deaf Association.   This new roof, built by Christians, was an act of love and kindness that they'd never known before. It touched many hardened hearts with the Lord's love and suddenly, they were all more *open and willing* to listen to the message of salvation from the Christians living amongst them.

> *"We give thanks to You, O God,*
> *we give thanks!"*
> (Psalm 75:1 NKJV)

We kept going..

With the new roof completed and the deaf people rejoicing, we began further urgent renovations without delay. Out came the foul toilets and in went clean new ones. To my surprise, the washing troughs were more popular than individual hand basins on all but the ground floor, especially for washing their clothes. So each trough was meticulously rebuilt and retiled, and the walls around them were retiled too.

Some of our deaf Christian ladies even offered to replaster crumbling areas of the ceilings and walls in the communal areas and then tackled some painting too. They did a splendid job. *Well done ladies!* Everyone was feeling encouraged by now and many offered to help us whenever they could.

However, in the late autumn of 2004, repairs to the *exterior* of the hostel yet again, became very urgent. This time, we planned to tackle the huge job of replacing the rotten windows in the communal areas with new pvc ones, plus replace the missing and disintegrated guttering and drain-pipes. To make this job a little easier, the communal areas on each floor were, thankfully, all positioned above each other at the same end of the building. As our builders set to work, pulling out over twenty old rotten windows, a cry of dismay was heard. The exterior stonework around the windows was crumbling so badly, that fitting new ones was totally impossible. *Oh no! What to do now?*

There appeared to be only one, satisfactory remedy. The *whole gable end and return section* of the hostel, reaching back to about one-third of the length of the building, had to be completely reinforced and replastered. This extensive area stretched from under the new roof on the fifth floor, down to ground level. Horrors! Another *enormous* expense that I hadn't expected. In dismay, I cried out, "*Oh Lord, I need Your help again!*"

But I shouldn't have feared, for yet again, I experienced God's wonderful faithfulness and His hand of divine blessing and provision, as He *knowingly* sent me out to Moldova with

sufficient funds to cover this un-expected and urgent need. Before returning back home, I was able to see the completion of this work and everyone was so delighted at the *miraculous transformation* of this end of the hostel. The once crumbling and deeply pitted stone walls had been expertly reinforced and newly rendered. The workmanship looked splendid with gleaming white, new pvc windows safely installed and brand new guttering and drainpipes fitted. The improvements were so dramatic and so amazing, that *everyone* was happy and praising the Lord. But this is not the end of the story, for God had even more challenging plans waiting for us to fulfil, and a few more miracles in store too!

> *"Commit to the Lord whatever you do,*
> *and your plans will succeed."*
> (Proverbs 16:3)

With a little help from my new friends

I was always truly thankful for the help and encourage-ment that my faithful friends Pastor Anton and his wife Reya, and Victoria gave me during each visit to Moldova and for welcoming me so warmly into their homes. Then in Transnistria, my kind elderly friends Gregory and Sveta, and our dear missionary couple Vera and Vanya, kindly invited Ross and me to stay with them and, of course, my good friend Mark was a tremendous help to us. Olesya's parents, Vova and Nadya, who live in Chisinau, also became my very close

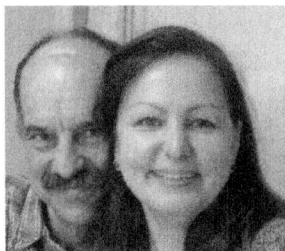
Vova and Nadya

friends and invaluable helpers. Vova organised the Moldovan 45ft lorries to collect our aid from Cologne, and Nadya began helping needy new mums, by giving them baby items and equipment from our aid. *Thank you my precious friends,* for your wonder-ful help and the fun we had working together.

Chapter 43

Step of Faith Project

During the summer of 2005, we boldly began our *Step of faith project* to install *twenty-two solar panels* upon the new roof of the deaf hostel. The aim of this project was to provide *hot* water in all the communal rooms, plus build the first-ever tiled shower enclosure on each floor. This was, without any doubt, an ambitious project and a brave team of three male Christian volunteers from Northern Ireland offered to go out for three weeks to undertake this huge challenge. A further two male volunteers planned to go out for the last three days to help with the *final fix*. Our reliable builder, Gennady, plus a few keen volunteers from the deaf hostel joined our team and Ross helped too, by becoming the team co-ordinator. We were all set and ready to begin, but little did any of us realise what a huge challenge this *Step of faith project* was really going to be and how *our faith* was going to be tested!

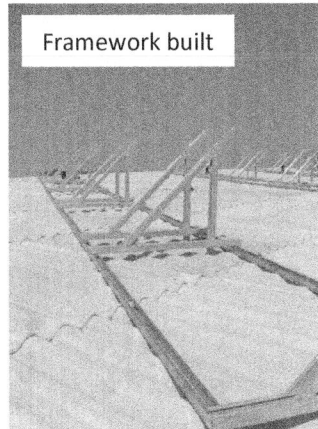

Framework built

The first three volunteers, none of whom had been in Moldova before, were full of optimism and keen to begin this project. Enthusiastically, they began the exacting task of fitting all the steel girders and frames for the solar panels *on top* of the new roof. This was incredibly hot work, as the scorching Moldovan summer sun beat down on them mercilessly as they worked atop the *metal* roof, which intensified the glare and heat. It was indeed, gruelling work. They suffered too, in overpowering heat *under* the metal roof as they used blow torches to solder the enormous quantity of copper pipes that passed down through five floors beneath them.

Needless to say, our tight daily schedule didn't always go to plan, and this happened when Gennady came to fit the enormous, tall stainless steel water tanks on each floor. Alas, he discovered that the flooring beneath each tank was not strong enough to carry the weight of a full tank of water. This not only presented an unexpected delay, but a major problem too. But Gennady solved it by building a wide concrete platform on each floor for the tanks to sit upon. Then, when one of our team members found he had to work in the gloomy, dirty basement area for several days making some urgently needed new metal fittings, his courage was tested to the limit when he was confronted with *rats the size of cats.* But he was determined that these *monsters* would not deter him from his work, and he valiantly succeeded in making all the essential fittings they needed. Our volunteers were indeed *brave souls and became heros* in everyone's eyes.

However, we hadn't anticipated another major delay. This time, it was our Moldovan truck carrying the solar panels from the depot in Cologne to Moldova. First of all, it was held up for several days at the German border and then for *several more days* at the Moldovan border. This was really scary, as solar panels at that time in Moldova were very rare, and so very valuable and desirable. Everyone, including our deaf Christians, were praying for a miracle, as there was a very real possibility that our precious solar panels would be confiscated by the border guards and never be seen again.

Eventually, Ross and our dear Moldovan friend Vova and his son Sasha (Olesya's father and brother), were instructed by the border guards to unload our truck at the Moldovan border. This was really *bad news.* But, after hours of *very tense* waiting and frantic phone calls to friends who knew people in high places, permission was given (from the Prime Minister) to *reload* our truck. This was really *great news!* And yet, we had to wait a further two days before the truck was released to us. This was potentially disastrous, as our team had a very tight three-week schedule in which to complete the whole project and time was rapidly running out. But surely, wasn't this our *Step of faith project?* Didn't we truly believe that *God was in complete control* and wasn't about to let us fail? We kept praying for a *miracle* to happen.

With our strict deadline now in serious jeopardy, we realised that we didn't have the time we'd anticipated to hoist the solar panels one-by-one up on to the roof by using the small winch we'd brought with us. There simply were not enough days left to do this. Our dilemma called for serious prayer and yet again, I cried out to the Lord ...

"How on earth, are we going to get twenty-two fragile and very heavy glass solar panels lifted up on to the fifth floor roof in time? Please Lord, we need Your help!"

We all prayed, seeking the Lord's help and yet, there didn't seem to be an answer. Our spirits were being sorely tested, as it appeared our *Step of faith project* was about to fail and not be completed. To us, the situation seemed all but hopeless, but to Almighty God, there is no failure, *only victory.*

With time rapidly running out and our solar panels only released to us by the Customs the previous evening, *we needed a miracle.* Early the next morning, while it was still relatively cool, our three brave volunteers and Gennady, plus some more helpers, along with Vova, Sasha, Ross and myself, all met at the deaf hostel to begin unloading the solar panels from the truck, together with a large quantity of extremely heavy containers of anti-freeze. Even this task was hard work, as it took four men to carefully lift each heavy and fragile solar panel out of the truck and stack them on to pallets.

All the while, no-one dared ask the question that was burning in each of our hearts, *"How can we possibly lift all these heavy solar panels up on to the roof with our tiny winch? A winch that looks like a matchstick projecting out from the fifth floor roof?"*

But we had failed to notice something. Something very important. Only when the delivery truck pulled away, did we see *the miracle* that God had in store for us. **A miracle that none of us will ever forget.**

There, just a few yards from us, sat *the biggest, most beautiful, incredible crane!* And the driver of the crane was just sitting there doing nothing. When we asked him if he could help us, he replied, *"OK"* and then only asked us for *$10!*

Within two hours, all of our fragile and weighty solar panels were lifted swiftly, safely and *effortlessly* up on to the fifth floor roof of the hostel, together with all the heavy containers of anti-freeze. *It was totally and utterly awesome!* **And an incredible miracle!**

Our faithful and loving Heavenly Father did hear our prayers and wonderfully answered them in a way far beyond our expectations.   He is a mighty God, who fulfilled His word in the Bible to us ...

> *"Before they call I will answer;*
> *while they are still speaking I will hear."*
> (Isaiah 65:24)

The *miracle* crane!

So at last ...

O ur three volunteers were able to install the twenty-two solar panels on to the deaf hostel roof. A back-breaking, arduous task, that they barely finished by the time the two remaining members of the team arrived in Moldova, for the *final fix.* Due to all the previous unforeseen delays, there was not a moment to lose and the pressure was on.

Their days began early and ended late, as the team worked frantically to finalise the installation technicalities and complete the trial tests to check that everything was working properly. Hot and totally exhausted, they succeeded in completing our *Step of faith project* and literally finished minutes before the deadline of the official Opening Ceremony at 5 p.m.

Finished!

Opening Ceremony

T here was a tremendous air of excitement and anticipation amongst the deaf inhabitants of the hostel, including all our deaf friends, as they gathered together near the main entrance. A row of chairs had been arranged in a semi-circle for our special guests and, to our

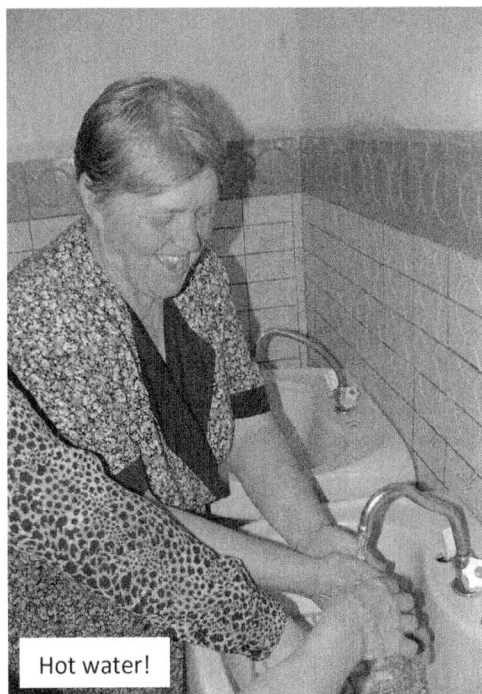

Hot water!

delight, the atheist Director of the Deaf Association and his assistant were already seated.

However, before the proceedings began, the Director of the hostel wanted to make sure that everything was working properly. Leaving the gathering outside for a few minutes, she found a washbasin on the ground floor and turned on a tap. *The joy on her face said it all!* It simply lit up with delight as *hot water came out!* This was the first *hot water* to ever flow in this deaf hostel. It was truly wonderful! Happy and fully satisfied, she rejoined everyone waiting outside and Pastor Anton duly opened the Ceremony. Then, standing on a raised area, so all the deaf could see her sign language, she began speaking to everyone. Our team, who hadn't even had time to wash their faces or change into clean clothes, were introduced to everyone and were heartily congratulated on their amazing achievement.

Our special guests were then given a new Bible each, but Pastor Anton had chosen a particularly beautiful one to give to the atheist Director. To be honest, we all held our breath when Pastor Anton presented this Bible to him, as we didn't know if he would accept it. But to our surprise, he was delighted with his gift *and asked if it had an Old Testament, because he wanted to read it!*

The atheist Director then stood to speak to everyone, with the Director of the hostel interpreting for him in sign language. He began by sincerely thanking our team for their great work and for installing the solar panels on to the roof of the deaf hostel. He continued to say that having *free hot water* would be a tremendous blessing for the 188 deaf people living in the hostel and that he was so thankful for all that we'd done to help so many people. In fact, he was so overwhelmed at the magnitude of what we'd done and, speaking genuinely from his heart, he boldly declared, *"This could only have been done by GOD!"*

The Director speaking and signing to the deaf

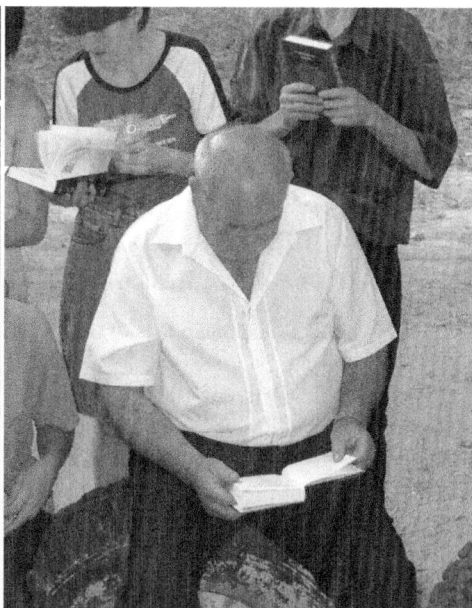

The atheist Director reading his Bible

We could hardly believe our ears when we heard this *atheist man openly acknowledging God. It was incredible!* And wonderfully too, he had readily accepted our gift of a holy Bible. This was indeed, another mighty *miracle* that none of us had expected, or will ever forget.

T he celebration spirit continued and our valiant team were each given a surprise gift to thank them for their hard work to bless so many poor, deaf people in Moldova. It was a lovely memento for them to take back home with them, early the next morning.

I too, should like to add my sincere thanks and congratulations to every team member for their sacrificial hard work in diligently completing this really gruelling and extremely difficult project. A project that we aptly named, *"Step of faith!"* For, although we were hampered by so many unexpected delays and obstacles, *God came through for us with a mighty miracle* and honoured all our hard work to bring blessings to His deaf children in Moldova. *Thank you team and thank You Lord!*

> **"Now to the King eternal,**
> **immortal, invisible, the only God,**
> **be honour and glory for ever and ever.**
> **Amen."**
> (1 Timothy 1:17)

Surprise gifts

T he celebration Ceremony was nearly over and I had a surprise gift too, for the deaf living in the hostel. Victoria and Ross kindly helped me give out the colourful plastic *bags for life* filled with bath and hand towels, face cloths, shower gel and sponges, shampoo and soap, toothpaste and toothbrushes, ready for them to enjoy using the *hot water* in their clean and fresh washrooms and newly built showers.

To end this splendid and most joyful Ceremony, three of our partially deaf girls (Violetta's room mates), formed a small choir and enthusiastically sang songs to music, while signing the words too. With their feet tapping in unison to keep a rhythm, and their hands signing in perfect syn-chronization, *they lifted up their beaming faces towards Heaven,* as they sang praises and thanks to Jesus, our Sovereign Lord ...

> *"Great is the Lord and most worthy of praise;*
> *His greatness no-one can fathom."*
> (Psalm 145:3)

My happy deaf friends receiving their *bags for life*

Chapter 44

My new life with Jesus

I can honestly say that my life has never been the same since that night back in April 1997. In fact, my life was only just *beginning ... my new life with Jesus.* I took my first step onto the *ladder of faith* that leads to Heaven and I have never regretted it. I was on the very first rung, with a lot to learn and a long way to go, but it was the beginning of my new life, the *best* life.

Jesus didn't choose me back in April 1997 because I'd led a good, clean and perfect life. Far from it. But He didn't come to chastise me either over my past mistakes or scold me about my failures and weaknesses. In fact, He did quite the opposite. He wasn't looking *backwards* over my sinful life, but *forwards* to the future He had planned for me. The future when, at last, I learnt to trust and obey Him and know deep in my heart that His ways were, are and always will be, far better than mine own.

Indeed, as I learnt to surrender my life to Jesus, I watched in awe, as He gently and very lovingly picked up the broken and torn pieces of my battered and bruised life and slowly, carefully and patiently molded me together again. He treated me with the tenderest of love, casting out my fear and shame, healing my deepest hurts and helping me to forgive those who had caused me pain. *Pain that Jesus healed and replaced with His wonderful joy.* He then poured fresh new hope and courage into me. Hope for a *bright new future,* as He opened new doors for me.

The *richer* my life became

As I recall all of these blessings, I could never have imagined how God would answer my earnest prayers in the way He did. The more He led me to work amongst the desperately poor and needy people in Moldova, the more *I loved them.* Every single day was so full and meaningful, and the *richer* my life became.

Another special delight and joy for me, was to have my young son Ross by my side during every summer visit and, from the age of just twelve years old, he was my constant companion.   He adapted effortlessly to the different culture and challenges that faced us and made new friends easily. He quickly became my able and accomplished photographer, capturing our countless treasured memories and endearing moments, as he enthusiastically and expertly clicked away. *Well done Ross!*

And then, the *icing on the cake* was when my eldest son *Leon* came out for two summers to help us. He joined a team of volunteers who bravely undertook a major building project for a large family in southern Moldova, which was enormously hard work. *Well done Leon! And thank you guys for completing this difficult project!*

A big *"Thank you!"*

H owever, none of our work could have happened without the incredible help and support from *so many* people back home in Northern Ireland. I want to end this chapter of *My Story* by saying a big *"Thank you!"* to everyone who supported Mission Moldova in so many different ways. Whether you were a volunteer coming out to Moldova with us, whether you donated funds to support our many projects or gave valuable aid to distribute to countless poor people. I want to say a further big *"Thank you!"* to all the volunteers who worked many long, back-breaking hours in our two huge stores packing boxes for our trucks. Plus, a heartfelt *"Thank you!"* to everyone who gave their time and energy to work in our two *Mission Moldova Sunflower Shops* to raise the invaluable funds to cover all our charity's overhead expenses and operating costs.

Everyone's efforts, commitment and hard work enabled us to give the love, encouragement and hope that so many suffering and desperate lives needed out in Moldova. Lives that were touched and enriched by the love and grace of our Lord Jesus Christ.

> **"He who is kind to the poor lends to the Lord,**
> **and He will reward him** (and her) **for what he has done."**
> (Proverbs 19:17)

Hidden talents

T hankfully and most wonderfully, Jesus knows every single one of us far better than we know ourselves. He knows our weaknesses and our failures. But He also knows our capabilities and hidden talents too. He can see the great potential and creativity *inside each one of us* and, with His help and divine favour, we can ALL achieve *exceedingly abundantly above our greatest expectations ...*

> *"Now to Him (Jesus) who is able to do*
> *exceedingly abundantly above all that we ask or think,*
> *according to the power (of the Holy Spirit) that works in us."*
> (Ephesians 3:20 NKJV)

It was Almighty God alone, who opened this new and unexpected door for both me and young Ross. ***And He can open new doors for you too. Doors that you can never open by yourself.*** God can also *create fresh opportunities* for you that would never naturally come your way. He can encourage you and strengthen you to step out in faith to receive your new future. And, before you know it, you'll find yourself rejoicing and shouting, *"Hosanna! I'm on the Way."*

"HOSANNA!"

Every day is a joy, and a gift from His Hand,
Of mercy and forgiveness you understand.
With salvation He blessed me, along with His love,
And His grace overflows, from Heaven above.

So I look to my Saviour from morn till night,
Who gives me the strength, to fight the good fight.
My heart keeps rejoicing, as I praise His Name,
Oh I'm so glad, to me He came!

So onwards and upwards until life's end,
I'll walk hand in hand with my new Friend.
For He's promised to love me and beside me
He'll stay,
And I'll shout "Hosanna!" for I'm on The Way.

(Poem by Esther Barbara Dennison)

"How could I ever forget it?"

T oday, over twenty-five years later, I can fondly look back to that warm Sunday afternoon in the Autumn of 1991, when I was happily digging over our new front garden. I can laugh too, as I remember my confused and exasperated response to the two pleasant young men, who paused for a friendly chat.

In fact, *"How could I ever forget it?"*   All those *peculiar* questions they asked me. *"Are you saved? And for how long?"* But now, all these years later, those *peculiar* questions don't seem so peculiar any more. In fact, **I'm asking YOU those same questions now!**

So, when I ask you, *"Are you saved?"*   What will your answer be? I sincerely pray that you have already made this decision and invited Jesus Christ to be your Lord and Saviour. I know, without a shadow of doubt, that I made the right choice back in April 1997 and so today, I can confidently reply to these two young men's questions ....

"YES, I AM SAVED!
And more than that ...
I am cleansed, healed, restored and forgiven!
Mightily blessed and divinely favoured!

So dear Reader, the *miracle* that Jesus has done in my life, He can do in your life too ... *"For nothing is impossible for God."* (Luke 1:37)

And, without a shred of a lie, I want to tell you that, *"having the love of Jesus Christ in your heart* is **priceless."**   It's worth *more* than any money, *more* than any gold or silver, *more* than any diamonds or precious jewels. It's worth *more* than any fame or power this world can ever offer you.

> ***Jesus was ... and is today ... and always will be,
> the miracle in my life!***

Jesus loves you too, more than you can possibly imagine and He is patiently waiting. Waiting for you to ask Him to be your Lord and Saviour and be the *miracle in your life too.*

And, when you do take this step of faith to *ask* Jesus into your heart, I'm trusting that *your life story* will also tell of the healing, forgiving, restoring, undeserved, unconditional and amazing love of Jesus ... ***a love greater than any pain!***

A LOVE GREATER THAN ANY PAIN!

**Jesus, Jesus! Forever I'll love Him!
As I humbly repent, washed clean by His blood.
I'll shout, "Hallelujah! My sins are forgiven!"
For He set me free ... by His grace, mercy and love.**

**My heart now is His, when I gave Him my life,
For He rescued and saved me, from every strife.
Though nothing I've done, could warrant His grace,
I'll thank Him forever, for He died in my place.**

**To my knees do I fall and my head do I bow,
My pain is a memory, far from me now.
For I've found a new love, *Jesus* is His Name,
*A love greater than any pain!***

Poem by Esther Barbara Dennison

Epilogue

I t has truly been a pleasure to share *"My Story"* with you dear Reader, and to tell you that my bright new future is still continuing today, as I walk hand-in-hand rejoicing with my Lord and Saviour and with my husband Paul beside me. Together, we look to the Lord every day, trusting in His love and perfect guidance.

A nd Ross? *He's doing just great!* He did really well in his A'Levels and has been happily living out in Moldova since the winter of 2006. He now speaks fluent Russian too! And, when visiting our dear friends in Transnistria, it always amazes me to hear him chatting away to them in Russian. He has learnt many new skills too and, through his natural talent, hard work, and God blessing him, he has built up a very successful business with a large team of employees, based from spacious modern offices in Chisinau's city centre. Indeed, the Lord has blessed him mightily.

Looking back to the summer of 2007, Ross married his sweetheart Olesya and they now have a lovely home in Chisinau, near a picturesque park and lake.   Then, in the Spring of 2017, just a few months before their tenth wedding anniversary, Olesya gave birth to a precious little baby boy. Everyone was overjoyed and I became a *Babushka!*

I'm very thankful that my dear son *Leon* has done exceptionally well too.   And, in early 2014, I first became a *grandmother*, when he and his lovely wife had a beautiful baby boy, whom we simply adore. *Thank You Lord for these wonderful blessings!*

Although this is now the end of this book and the end of this particular chapter about *my new life with Jesus,* there is so much more I could tell. So many more wonderful stories and adventures and, better still, **the best is yet to come!** But for now, I would like to give you and your loved ones this blessing from our Heavenly Father ...

A Blessing for You

"The LORD
bless you and keep you;

The LORD
make His face shine upon you
and be gracious to you;

The LORD
turn His face towards you
and give you peace."

(Numbers 6:24-26)

Amen

Helpful notes for you

Which Bible?

The Bible is our *Guide Book for Life.* It doesn't matter which version you read, just so long as you read it! Spend some time and care choosing a version that you feel comfortable with. The **New International Version** is popular, as it uses modern-day language and is still an accurate translation. I also find a Bible Concordance really handy, as it helps to locate Bible verses quickly and easily.

Daily Helps?

Is your life really busy and time at a premium? Do you find it hard to take a break to read your Bible? Well, a *daily reading booklet* can help you. It will give you a short daily Bible reading, together with an interesting and thought-provoking story to help you start your day off on the right foot. It's just perfect for a busy person.

There are many daily reading booklets available, but there are two that I've found really helpful. Often they have not only helped me, but given me the answer to a pressing prayer. These *free* booklets are printed quarterly and you can request a copy from:

- **Our Daily Bread** RBC Ministries.
  www.rbc.org

- **The Word for Today** United Christian Broadcasters
  (UCB) www.ucb.co.uk

My Contact Details

Dear Reader,

I sincerely hope that you have been blessed through reading *"My Story"* and if you would like to contact me, please use the following email address:

Email: mystoryestherdennison@protonmail.com

My Story

a love greater than any pain!

is available from **AMAZON** web-sites worldwide.

Or, for more details, please go to my short web-site:

www.mystoryestherdennison.eu

Your friend in Christ,

Esther

Printed by Amazon Italia Logistica S.r.l.
Torrazza Piemonte (TO), Italy